Additional Praise for
A-HA! Performance

"What a fabulous book! Congratulations! It offers such excellent advice for business and for life, and it is a pleasure to read. *A-HA! Performance* is a book of gems—sound and immediately actionable advice that goes to the core of what it takes to be a successful manager. Just by recognizing a person's intrinsic motivations, Doug Walker shows how simple it is to move from objectives to exceptional achievement. I so look forward to discussing this book with you further and exploring ways we can work together. Congratulations, again!"

> Peyton Daniel
> Senior Managing Director, Coaching Practice Leader
> North America, DBM

"*A-HA! Performance* should be within reach on every manager's (or aspiring manager's) desk because it's too full of a-ha insights to collect dust on a bookshelf. Amazingly, A-HA! is equally useful for employees who want to effectively manage their managers, because the central premise of A-HA! is that managerial effectiveness—like mutually-beneficial relationships of all types, and communication in general—is inherently a two-way, not a one way street. Perhaps *A-HA! How Employees Manage Managers* or *A-HA! How to Manage Relationships* will be the sequel to this imminently readable book."

> Wilton Thomas Anderson
> Retired Professor of Marketing and Entrepreneurship
> University of Texas, California State University

"If every employee was 'given' a copy of *A-HA! Performance* without any conditions attached, watch and see what viral marketing can do. They will love it! The return on investment from them applying only a fraction of the principles would pay for the book a thousand times over!"

> Joe Andrew
> CEO, Quantum2

"If you have ever thought you needed a degree in Counseling to motivate your staff you now have all that you need in *A-HA! Performance: Building and Managing a Self-Motivated Workforce*. I was so sold on the A-HA Performance Model and its usability that we have incorporated it into our 'Coaching for Development' training for all supervisors and managers. The Model is *C*lear, *A*ttainable and will result in major *P*ayoffs in improved relationships and motivated staff."

> Susan Curtin
> Training and Development Manager, Department of Health
> and Human Services, County of San Diego

"*A-HA! Performance* is a rare gift to managers at every level. After more than 40 years in top management positions in both the government and private sectors, I truthfully say I have never read a better hands-on, practical, step-by-step guide for managers to maximize productivity, performance, and employee moral. *A-HA! Performance* is a must read for managers or wanna'be managers who want to do it right. This is the only book you need in your management library."

> Retired Rear Admiral W. E. Terry
> U.S. Navy

"As a business owner and consultant for 20 years, I have worked with amazing teams that were driven; people that worked with purpose. To my chagrin, replicating that kind of synergy was haphazard and seemed a bit magical. After reading *A-HA!* I now understand the process that motivates behavior. Now, I perceive interactions differently. My questions lead to *A-HA! Performance* moments that turn into solutions of *their* creation; strategies that they are self-motivated to implement. Thank you for creating the work I was searching for! I will recommend this book to every leader I know."

> Carla Adwell Webb
> Performance Specialist, Administaff, Inc.

"I thought the book was great!! Very Insightful and the dialogues were so real world. Great content. The best managing, coaching, and sales require employee engagement. Doug Walker clarifies the real factors that block success for managers, coaches, and salespeople and offers simple and effective methods for making managing, coaching, and sales a valuable win for everyone."

> Jim Trunick
> Senior Director, Corporate Sales Training, Allergan

"Doug Walker has been teaching his A-HA Performance Intrinsic Motivation Points model and coaching processes to managers, business owners, human resources, training, organization development and sales professionals in the San Diego State University, Professional Certificate Program in Coaching for Organizational Excellence for over four years. He easily conveys how the brain receives input and produces behavior in a way that allows business professionals to quickly grasp and effectively use it as internal and external coaches, managers, and consultants. Our students take his information and make big changes in their organizations and careers. Doug is a master coach and teacher."

> Jordan Goldrich, LCSW, CEAP
> Executive and Management Coach, Faculty Advisor, San Diego State University, Certificate Program in Coaching for Organizational Excellence

"This book characterizes through a powerful framework, real life stories and thoughtful metaphors, how managers can rely on the vested interests of others to build and manage great performance with consistent and lasting results. This is a must read for those managers who want to be extraordinary at cultivating intrinsically driven motivation in their employees to perform and with their customers to buy."

> Lisa Vander, M.Ed.
> CEO, Pacific Blue Investments
> Author of *The Real Guide to Making Millions Through Real Estate: Start Your Portfolio with as Little as $3,000*

"*A-HA! Performance* is a map to an extraordinary sustainable corporate life; in fact it is a map to an extraordinary life. The A-HA! Applications (tools) used in conjunction with the basic understanding of human nature and needs, explained herein, are the 'recipe' for excellence in human performance! The competition will want to get their hands on this."

> Marilyn M. Weakly
> Strategic Sourcing Consultant, M Squared Enterprises, LLC

"Results require execution and action and closing the gap between knowing what needs to be done and getting it done is critical to individual, team and organizational success. Using Intrinsic Motivation Points the A-HA! Performance Edge provides a proven model that empowers managers and their employees to communicate, execute, and deliver results."

> Jon Gordon
> Author of *Energy Bus: 10 Rules to Fuel Your Life, Work, and Team with Positive Energy*

"The single most important factor in building a booked solid business is the keen ability to understand the correlation between a manager's input and an employee's output so that we (and our employees) achieve our desired, ideal results. That secret formula is detailed in the pages of this book."

Michael Port
Author of *Book Yourself Solid*

"The book uses realistic examples, graphic illustrations, and focused how-to steps *that* leave the reader better equipped and more empowered to effectively manage a self-motivating workforce. Every manager and coach should read this! I can't imagine a better deal at any price, but for the cost of this book . . . it's a no brainer. Best investment you can make in maximizing your human capital."

Wendy Evers
Senior Director for Program Development, SDSU

"Understanding and managing that self-motivated workforce was as complex a puzzle as a Rubix Cube . . . until this book."

Vince Poscente
CEO, Be Invinceable Group
Author of *The Age of Speed*

"Walker's model is the heart secret of business. This formula transforms resistance into motivation. It easily engages partners and accelerates results."

Jeanete Biasotti, PhD
CEO, Quantum Leap

"So much stress arises out of frustration to meet one's deepest needs. By helping identify and bridge the 'got-want gap,' *A-HA! Performance* may well be more than a book on motivation, but also a prescription for good health!"

Daniel Friedland, MD
American Board of Internal Medicine, American Board of Holistic Medicine
President of SuperSmartHealth.com
Author of *Evidence-Based Medicine: A Framework for Clinical Practice*

"Improved performance, relationships, and conversations are at the root of this highly impactful book. *A-HA! Performance*'s innovative models will give leaders a laserlike focus on how to close the gap between current and desired behavior. An inspiring read, I recommend it to anyone who wants to move themselves and others to greater focus and action."

Vicki Halsey, PhD
Author of *The Hamster Revolution*
Vice President of Applied Learning, Ken Blanchard Companies

"When we at DCM consider investing to build the next great start-up, we look first and foremost at teams and ask, 'Is there a team of experienced and driven people coming together to achieve the nearly impossible?' Doug peels back to the kernel the motivating force behind all great entrepreneurs and does so in a way that lets entrepreneurs share this passion throughout their company. By focusing on a few simple techniques like 'creating vested interests' and artfully 'managing the gaps,' Doug lights the path for one entrepreneur's passion to spread throughout a team, a team that can break new ground and accomplish the nearly impossible. This will be required reading for the great entrepreneurs we back in the years to come."

Peter W. Moran
General Partner, DCM

"Being a leader and manager in an arena with no margin for error requires the ability to understand and exploit the maximum in creative thinking, capability, and energy from every employee. *A-HA! Performance* provides a comprehensive tool to achieve that in the workplace and to create opportunities for better understanding at home. It was a great read and will be a tremendous resource."

Don Flynn
Vice President of Security Strategies
Former Senior Executive in charge of Presidential Protection with the U.S. Secret Service

"In *A-HA! Performance*, Douglas Walker captures our essential humanity and shows us how to work and engage with each other in ways that respect and benefit from that essence by honoring the infinitely varied manners in which each of us chooses to express it. Grounded in a sophisticated and nuanced understanding of the psychology of motivation, *A-HA! Performance* is a step-by-step manual for achieving collective goals while fostering self-determination. I will be recommending this book to any manager whom I coach or advise and who wants to be more effective, and I will be reading and rereading it to learn more about how to improve my own relationships while getting more of what I want at work and at home."

Bernardo M. Ferdman, PhD
Professor, Marshall Goldsmith School of Management
Alliant International University

A-ha!
PERFORMANCE

A-ha!
PERFORMANCE

Building *and* Managing *a* Self-Motivated Workforce

DOUGLAS WALKER
with STEPHEN SORKIN

John Wiley & Sons, Inc.

Published by John Wiley & Sons, Inc., Hoboken, New Jersey.
Published simultaneously in Canada.

Wiley Bicentennial Logo: Richard J. Pacifico

For general information on our other products and services or for technical
support, please contact our Customer Care Department within the United States at
(800) 762-2974, outside the United States at (317) 572-3993 or fax (317) 572-4002.

Wiley also publishes its books in a variety of electronic formats. Some content that
appears in print may not be available in electronic books. For more information about
Wiley products, visit our web site at www.wiley.com.

Library of Congress Cataloging-in-Publication Data:

Walker, Douglas, 1946–
   A-HA! performance : building and managing a self-motivated workforce /
Douglas Walker with Stephen Sorkin.
      p.   cm.
   ISBN 978-0-470-11634-0 (cloth)
   1. Employee motivation.   2. Supervision of employees.   3. Organizational
behavior.   4. Interpersonal relations.   I. Sorkin, Stephen, 1967–   II. Title.
   HF5549.5.M63W346   2007
   658.3′14—dc22

                                                            2007002356

Printed in the United States of America.

10   9   8   7   6   5   4   3   2   1

For
My Family
and Friends in
Recognition of, and
Appreciation for,
All of the Ways
My Needs Are
Met Through
You

Douglas Walker

For Linda, Skylar, and Nathan
Who Give My Life It's Deepest Purpose

Stephen Sorkin

Contents

Foreword   xv

Acknowledgments   xix

Introduction   xxiii

1 Receptionist Goes Nuts . . . and Goes   1

2 Needs: The Hidden Fundamentals of
Motivation and Behavior   15

3 Wants: The Not-at-All Hidden
Fundamentals of Motivation and Behavior   37

4 CAP: Aligning, Setting, and Managing
Self-Motivation   49

5 Got: Our Baseline for Knowing Where
We Are Relative to Any Given Want   73

6 The Gap and the GapZap: Underwhelmed,
Overwhelmed, Whelmed Just Right   87

7 Options: The ABCs of Choices—Choosing
Our Own Behavior Means a Whole Lot
More than We May Think   107

8 Output: Chosen Behavior—Doing,
Thinking, Emoting, Physiology 133

9 Filters: Coloring What's Coming In and
Limiting What's Going Out 147

10 Addressing and Improving Inadequate
Performance Behavior 159

11 Address and Improve: Excelling a Top
Performer and Retaining Talent 187

12 Rapid Conflict Resolution and Rapid
Team Tune-Up: Dealing with Conflicted
Employees or Building Teams 207

13 Making the Shift 233

Epilogue 255

Appendix 261

Glossary 265

Index 271

Foreword

When we are personally motivated, we perform better. That truth is not a surprise to any of us. Great sports stories, courageous acts of love, even traumatic self-sacrificing heroism are all borne out of intense personal motivation. Great results require great motivation. Yet, puzzlingly, in a typical business environment, we command employees from an almost mechanical task manager mindset instead of leveraging key insights around managing motivation. The difference in results between the two approaches, managing tasks or managing motivation, is striking.

The *A-HA! Performance* book you have in your hands is a clear and unique look at that internal motivation process, allowing us at last to understand it. *A-HA! Performance* also provides a practical, proven strategy and series of ready-to-implement-today techniques for making the shift from task management to motivation management. Not only does it work for leaders, managers, and organizations as a more effective and healthy managerial approach for orchestrating work effort, it is also a great way to reinvigorate—even reengage—ourselves with our own personal drive for accomplishment, happiness, and well-being.

A-HA! Performance does this very simply by highlighting what we already know: when we become aware of the difference between what we are currently experiencing and what we truly want in our lives, the resulting gap creates a zap of energy . . . what Doug calls the GapZap. That GapZap is the motivational force that energizes us into action toward achieving our desires, dreams, and goals, including team and company goals.

Vague desires and unfocused wants alone will not be sufficient to energize us to make changes in the way we think or behave.

Wisdom through the ages has taught that to be motivated enough to truly achieve greatness while maintaining a healthy equanimity we need to fully clarify what we want in life, actively visualize that it is attainable, and ascertain that the payoff is worth the effort. *A-HA! Performance* is an immensely down-to-earth, practical tool for doing exactly this process.

As a manager of a very large number of software engineers, designers, testers, project managers, and others, once I understood the A-HA! Performance Model and started putting it into practice, both work productivity and employee motivation greatly improved. As I shifted from being a task manager with a factory pipe-line or assembly-line mentality of tasks to be accomplished in a particular order into a manager who, while still needing to get the same tasks done, became an employee motivation manager, my daily experience became more effective and enjoyable for me and I'm sure for my employees as well.

In the A-HA! Performance Model, Intrinsic Motivation Points are revealed that are the keys for making this shift.

This understanding or assumption shift has to happen first in those of us who lead, manage, or supervise others. So often, for a variety of reasons, we simply tell or command—even in a nice way—someone to do a particular task for us. We do that without considering what that person's motivation might be for doing the task. It is easy to think he should do the task merely because we told or asked him to do it. "I'm the boss, that's why!" But most of us who have tried that approach or who have held that mindset know that it only gets a marginally satisfactory result and therefore may require us to review and change the work that employee has done, thus causing resource wasting rework, in order to get the final result we need.

If, instead, we understand a few of the other person's Intrinsic Motivation Points, we can reframe our request in such a way that the work effort is performed as a motivational and motivating exercise. When people feel good about, are engaged in, and energized by their work, they do it better.

The best ideas, the most innovative concepts come from cultures where managers have created vested interest motivation from which innovative ideas and superior performance emerge. Too often motivation efforts include threats or sticks, the kinds of motivation that result in fear or anger at being coerced into performing some task perceived as meaningless or at least as unnecessary. From this level of motivation, the idea generation is generally one of pain removal and does not necessarily add value to the final result. It merely gets the task done at the lowest acceptable level.

Alternatively, when we create the kind of motivation where innovation and creativity emerge, new concepts and ways of doing work become energy-gaining activities for the individuals and improved innovative processes and products for the organization. That leads to greater delight from and increased business with, customers.

So how do we make this change from task management to motivational management? By using the A-IIA! Performance Map, as explained in this book. It will help us quickly become aware (even in our own self-talk) of the eight key Intrinsic Motivation Points that focus us on how to conduct our conversations in ways that achieve emotional commitment to producing high-performance results.

Once this process is fully understood, even those quick, on-the-run conversations can still be short efficient requests for getting work done, but now they will be seen as trusted motivational requests instead of curt demands, ensuring a better result.

Do the people you work with leave work at the end of the day with at least as much energy as they brought into the workplace at the beginning of the day?

So many workplaces literally drain the energy and vitality from their employees. These drained individuals cannot go home and respond energetically to the daily demands of their household. If they repeat this energy-draining process over time, then there is very limited opportunity for them to provide the necessary creativity and innovation that sustains high or even acceptable performance levels at work.

Continue those energy-draining practices longer, and burn-out occurs, turnover happens, or worse, people become disengaged but remain present in your workforce, unable to improve, unable to change, unable to respond to new demands.

This book is not only a call to action, but also, a call for reflection. Knowing your own Intrinsic Motivation Points will help you recognize quickly what is being called for in the day-to-day conversations you are having with others. This new awareness will guide you to higher performance for yourself while also improving your ability to manage the performance of those around you.

The final result is you will look forward to change and to new challenges in your life, both as a manager and a human being. You will create new and innovative approaches that energize and excite both you and others. The whole A-HA! Performance process ignites new fires of passion, creativity, and commitment. I have found this to be a great book, and hopefully, it will be a great guide for you, too.

SKIP ANDREWS
Chief Information Officer, SharePoint360, LLC
Former Senior Manager, Nokia Mobile Phones Inc.

Acknowledgments

No one synergizes alone, unless maybe . . . Robin Williams. I am not he. *A-HA! Performance*, and the quality of its contents, exists because of significant contributions from a number of people, including:

Daniel Walker: my father. You first taught me these ideas by example and the way you and mom raised us . . . how does a son say thank you for that? And if there is any style to my writing, it's because I grew up on, and always was moved by . . . yours. *Take a truth: Make it plain so the head understands it, moving so the heart does, and practical so that people want to do the work it takes to understand its application for their lives.* Principles that guided your writing . . . guide mine, too.

William Glasser: My original mentor in, articulate spokesperson for, creative enhancer, and unfailing champion of these ideas . . . thank you for the consistent brilliance with which you share and demonstrate both the principles and the practice. Your influence and ideas permeate this book.

William T. Powers: For pioneering this explanation of human behavior and sharing the genesis of it with a small group of us at Dr. Glasser's home years ago . . . thank you. What began as a personal a-ha has become an a-ha to share—*A-HA! Performance*. Understanding and being able to explain human behavior in these terms has made all the difference in my effectiveness as manager, coach, teacher, and parent.

Steve Sorkin: For years, people who heard the A-HA! Performance Model told me, "You're sitting on a million-dollar product. The model is great, but your marketing sucks!" Well your marketing doesn't. For more than nine years I had been "gonna write that book!" Less than nine months after partnering with you, the book is a reality. For the way you A-HA! manage your intrinsically motivated partner, for your skills in pulling from me a more practical and accessible product, for your unfailing positive attitude and "it's all good" approach. I am more grateful than I can say. Not only that, but you're a fellow graduate of Samohi (Santa Monica High School) . . . no wonder the partnership works.

Dan Tegel: For helping me understand through your Breakthrough Process Redesign work that the psychology and performance of an organization works exactly like the psychology and performance of an individual, thank you. Your work expanded my awareness of how the A-HA! Principles apply not just to individuals, but to organizations as well.

Bill Gladstone: Literary agent extraordinaire. Thanks to your expertise and Steve's suggestion that we follow it without question, we have experienced none of the struggles or frustrations in getting published that is so often reported by first-time authors. You are such a gifted professional; your expertise is matched by your care, enthusiasm, and style and our gratitude is enormous.

Joanna Swartwood: You learned a new set of ideas, brought your masterful understanding of the book-writing process and your unfailingly positive and professional approach to this project, helping produce a proposal and product that passed the publishing criteria with flying colors. When I learned you were a Samohi grad, too, I knew Bill Gladstone was right; you were the right one to help with this project. For your skills, style, patience, perseverance, and teamwork I am deeply grateful.

Jordan Goldrich: For being among the first to recognize the power of the A-HA! Performance Model for coaches and managers, for your role in getting it adopted as the meta-model of San Diego State University's Coaching for Organizational Excellence Certificate program and for encouraging and challenging me to improve the graphics that took if from what early students called the "What-Was-He-Smoking Chart" to the

A-HA! Performance Map of Intrinsic Motivation Points included in this book . . . thank you.

Mike Kennedy: For showing me just how big a CEO's heart can be and being an early supporter of these ideas.

My extraordinary colleagues over the years: For being constant examples of competence, credibility, and care. The list would be too long for this space and to name some would be to leave others out, but you know who you are . . . please know also my deep respect and appreciation.

Larry Nuffer: For your continuing support, unfailing friendship, learned expertise in writing/editing, and always cheerful willingness to serve as a sounding board . . . thank you.

Barbara Walker: The right partner in creating a loving atmosphere in the home and in raising a family is even more important than the right partner in growing a business. For being the superior practitioner of these ideas and constantly providing examples of how best to utilize them, especially with our kids, for turning the model on me gently in getting me self-motivated to do those household chores, and for cheerfully covering bases that freed me up to write . . . thank you isn't enough. Your fun, friendly, fashionable ways create a warm and welcoming environment in our home where needs are easily met not only by family, but by all who visit. What a gift you've given; what a gift you give!

Darcy, Chelsea, Courtney, and Todd—my four great kids: The best proving ground for any set of ideas such as these is always the home. Had any of you turned out badly, others would have reason to question this model. The superb ways you live your lives, the tremendous persons you each are, and the contributions you each make to the lives of those around you are perhaps the highest testimonials of all to the efficacy of this approach with people in any environment. No doubt you each are who you are because of a combination of things; your genetics, your own daily choices—and to at least some extent, being raised by parents who tried to practice these principles. Thank you for being so super. I could neither be prouder nor love you more.

Drew McLaren and Jim Kirtley: No father could want better husbands for his daughters nor fathers for his grandchildren than you each are. For the ways you help create the need satisfying environment that is each of your homes, I am deeply grateful.

Rylie and Camryn McLaren, and Gavin Kirtley: Perhaps nowhere is the truth of these ideas and the efficacy of these practices more transparent then in the lives of children. And nowhere is it more fun to watch them play out for me, than in your lives. Grandchildren. What a concept!

D. W.

I am grateful for being part of something with such deeply beneficial meaning. This book is now available to benefit others because of you special people:

Doug Walker: Working with you and bringing the A-HA Performance Model to market is an intrinsically rewarding experience through helping others live more fully. You are a true master of vested interest motivation and a gift to anyone wanting to better their relationships with self and others—including me! Your inspirational, wise, and humorous style not only provides for a dynamically meaningful partnership but also a timeless book with your personality shining through. It is an honor to work and co-author with you.

Bill Gladstone: It is an honor and privilege working with you. Thank you for all you do, which is a great deal more than being a remarkable agent! You are so appreciated.

Joanna Swartwood: You are truly talented and greatly appreciated for your central role in helping take this book from dozens of documents and audio recordings into a fine-tuned and polished final product. You're a gem. Thank you!

Linda, Skylar, and Nathan, thank you for being who you are—and for empowering me to focus on this important work. I love you.

S. S.

Introduction

It's not just about results. Everything we do produces results. It's about achieving better results or maintaining desired results in an ever-changing environment.

Getting other people to do the right thing, in the right time frame, with the right attitude is what makes success so challenging in businesses, as well as in schools and homes around the world. In fact, getting ourselves to do the *right* thing, in the *right* time frame, with the *right* attitude is not as simple as *Just DO it*.

What every manager, parent, teacher, spouse, advertiser, disgruntled customer, coach, politician, businessperson . . . actually what all of us want is direct access to, and control over, the behaviors of others. But direct access to other people's behaviors continues to prove illusive because, without the use of overpowering physical force, it's impossible. It's not the way things work. Between our input, "Would you . . . ?" and their output . . . something that can range from enthusiastic compliance through benign or hostile indifference to violent defiance . . . is a process, a series of steps, that the brain goes through before deciding and doing; before choosing and implementing a behavior.

Imagine how convenient it would be, not to mention how much less stressful it would be, if we could bypass the process part, if we could turn on desired behaviors and attitudes in others as simply as we turn on a light switch. If we want the light on, we flip the switch and the light comes on. It doesn't fight us and it doesn't try to avoid us. It just does what we want it to do. The input (what we do to control the light) is flipping the switch, while the output (the result of our input) is light.

But people are not light switches. People have cares, preferences, and beliefs about the way they think things should be. So
when we try to flip their switches—approaching them in some way
that constitutes input—they process that input in the context of
their cares. These internal cares or preferences—what I refer to as
Intrinsic Motivation Points (IMPs)—ultimately determine what
the individual decides to do; what their output is going to be. Unlike light switches, employees have options and unique preferences
as to how they're going to perform. And their decisions are more
about satisfying their IMPs than about complying with a manager's request.

Because the approach (input) of the manager is so important in
eliciting superior performance (output) from employees, not to mention maximizing strong retention, learning what the Intrinsic Motivation Points are that determine employee behaviors and attitudes is
critical. Managers who know what these Intrinsic Motivation Points
are, and how to utilize them as they manage their employees, have an
edge, the *A-HA! Performance Manager's Edge.*

In addition to revealing these IMPs, *A-HA! Performance* will
also show how the IMPs are optimized or leveraged for managing
others in ways that produce desired results in sustainable ways.

Simply put, there is a process that goes on in the brain between input and output (Input > Process > Output). Understanding this human performance process will give us more of the results
we want because our employees want to give them to us. We will
also get the results we want from ourselves on a more consistent
basis, with less effort. Using the insights and applications of *A-HA!
Performance*, we will be building and managing a self-motivated
workforce. (Quick confession here: This book's subtitle is a little
bit of a trick title because, as the book explains, human beings are
already self-motivated. We can't *build* a self-motivated workforce,
we already have one. This book is really about understanding and
managing that self-motivated workforce.)

The foundational tool is the A-HA! Performance Model (a
foundational framework for understanding why people behave) that
is graphically illustrated in the A-HA! Performance Map (showing
the sequence of events inside the mind that explain the intrinsic

motivation process). The map reveals the eight IMPs that make up this sequence of events. We can think of the map as a template we can use to focus our conversations in ways that get vested interest performance rather than balking or pushing back.

When we understand this model, we can focus quickly on the best place to start a conversation that will get buy-in to productive changes with the least amount of resistance. When our employees are producing less than stellar results or we want our top performers to develop to new levels—we can use this model to determine where the missing link is in the performance sequence, and quickly leverage that into a productive performance turnaround, or enhancement. This book teaches us how to understand and manage a self-motivated workforce in ways that money cannot buy and threats cannot force.

I learned the basics of A-HA! Performance and the Intrinsic Motivation Points it reveals while serving as a senior faculty member at the William Glasser Institute. While I had seen their power at work in the lives of psychology professionals who I taught around the world, my challenge was to take these great and practical ideas designed for counselors, therapists, corrections officers, and teachers, and present them in ways that business professionals would want to learn and utilize. *A-HA! Performance: Building and Managing a Self-Motivated Workforce* and The A-HA! Performance Map of Intrinsic Motivation Points are the result of that work.

What goes on between a manager's input and an employee's output? What are those Intrinsic Motivation Points and how do we consistently get employees (and others) to want to do what we want them to do? That knowledge is what this book is about and what gives managers the A-HA! Performance Edge.

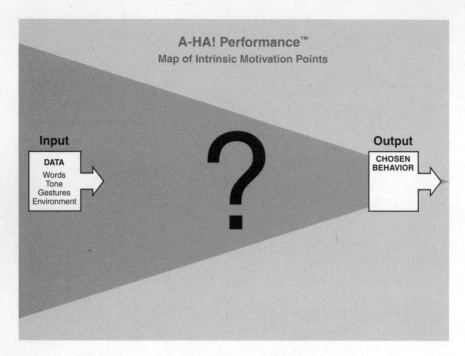

Between Input and Output

Receptionist Goes Nuts . . . and Goes

Poorly managed people have options. They can somehow rise above the way they're being managed and perform well anyway, they can withdraw and diminish their performance, or they can fight back. When a manager confronted Susan Moore, a receptionist for Office Connection, LLC, an office equipment broker, she chose the latter.

At Office Connection, Susan wore many hats—she answered the phone, gathered samples for the salespeople, filed, and did whatever she needed to do to support the company and its sales team. Hers was the voice of the company that customers heard when they called in to inquire about products, pricing, or delivery status on an order. She was supposed to be the friendly voice of support for customers, as well as help salespeople when they called in from the field and needed her to look up a product, check on availability, or confirm an appointment. The job of any sales support person, and certainly the job of 27-year-old Susan, was to put a smile on her face and cheerfully support the customer, vendor, and salesperson alike.

Unfortunately, Susan didn't do this part of her job well. She seemed chronically grumpy and consistently annoyed when anyone called in. Her curt greeting and hurried tone combined to make people feel uncomfortable when they called. Susan did have one thing going for her, however: her organizational skills. She was pretty good at filing and keeping the office organized.

When David McKennley, the fifth salesperson to join Office Connection's San Diego sales office, came on board, he quickly learned what the other four already knew: This surly receptionist was going to be an issue. When he called into the office, he found himself hoping someone else would answer the phone. Solitary tasks like filing or word processing were okay, but people skills? Not a chance. Have you ever gone into a business or agency and before you could even say anything, the person at the counter was already glaring at you? Some people just seem to arrive at work grumpy. That was Susan. And this made it hard for the salespeople because it was in their best interest to have the voice of the company be as welcoming and affable as possible.

For salespeople, great customer service starts with connecting with buyers and forming a positive relationship with them, where they know the seller cares about them and their needs. Seller credibility—which means seller competence and integrity—needs to be high, too. If salespeople achieve a relationship with their customers where they've established care and credibility, people will feel comfortable buying from them. If not, customers won't want to have anything to do with those salespeople and will instead seek out a different supplier.

Relationships that work are always about perceived care and credibility.

Actually, that same truth applies to managers. People will work well for us and stay with us longer when they believe we care and are credible.

If "location, location, location" are the three basic rules of real estate, "relationship, relationship, relationship" are the three basic rules of successful managing.

It's true for other relationships within the office, too. Care and credibility are at the core of all meaningful relationships, and meaningful relationships are the key to business success.

There's a reason why the term *team player* comes up in most job descriptions or interviews. Companies know that great working relationships are the key to business success and they want to hire employees who care and are credible, people who can form positive relationships and who work well with others. Companies where people figure out how to collaborate internally compete more effectively externally. Companies where employees don't like each other, or don't trust each other, don't do as well.

Outperforming the competition boils down to turbo-charging existing human capital. That's accomplished through *synergy*, the highest form of power there is. And synergy requires two or more people working effectively with each other. Whenever two or more people come together to achieve something, there are only three possible outcomes: synergy, samergy, or lessergy. For example, when two people come together and support each other in complimentary ways, one plus one can produce as three; synergy. Throughout high school and college, I played guitar and sang with my great friend of more than 45 years, Bill Silva. One of the highest compliments we received, which is a great summary of synergy, was, "You are two guys who sing as one and sound like three." Synergy is not the absence of tension, it's the harmonizing of tension. When two perform as one and produce as three, synergy has been achieved.

But when two or more come together and each does her own thing, one plus one only equals two, or *samergy*. People in call-center operations are an example of this. While Kim is in her cubicle making calls, Michael is in his doing the same and they have a combined productivity of hers plus his. Nothing more. Nothing less. Not as good as synergy, but not as bad as the third possible outcome of people coming together, which is *lessergy*. When one plus Susan Moore came together and got into an argument—each becoming upset— one plus one equaled minus two, or lessergy; neither as good as either would have been alone. That's why the salespeople began to believe they were better off not involving her.

When the San Diego Office Connection sales office only had four salespeople, they all seemed to be able to work around Susan's attitude and accommodate her lack of support. Office Connection's headquarters were in Los Angeles and whatever management was needed came from the Los Angeles office.

But once the San Diego office added new salesperson David McKennley, the owners decided they needed a local on-site sales manager. The likely candidate? The senior salesperson, a nice enough guy, Richard Harper, who had been there a long time and had the biggest accounts—only two customers, but they brought in a solid revenue stream. So the owners promoted him to sales manager of the San Diego sales office.

This is not an uncommon practice. Good scientists are often promoted to positions where they are managing people instead of test tubes. And productive engineers are often rewarded with promotions to managing peers rather than technology, applications, software, and data. But here's the catch: Managing employees is a different skill than managing sales, test tubes, or technology. Not everyone promoted to a managerial position is good at it or knows what to do. Not everyone knows the A-HA! Performance Map or the Intrinsic Motivation Points (IMPs) it reveals.

Like many managers, Richard had the idea that managing people meant that it was his job to control those people. It seemed to him that he was now responsible for making Susan behave in certain ways, that it was his job to make her act in a friendlier, more supportive manner. But the heart of this book and the crux of what gives managers the A-HA! Performance Edge is an understanding that what really controls people is something inside—a series of IMPs—not the orders or edicts, and not the carrots or sticks of anyone externally.

A-HA! Performance-trained managers learn to focus their conversations on the Intrinsic Motivation Points that are the Drivers of desired behavior, as well as on the Options that are viable for the particular employee they are addressing.

Subsequent chapters show how a manager never controls anyone else's behavior anyway. Behavior is the product of a process that involves Intrinsic Motivation Points coming together in particular ways. Managers may be held responsible by the organization for the success of their employees' performance, but managers can't control another person's behavior. They may learn or already have tremendous insights and skills at influencing employee behaviors for the better by leveraging these IMPs, but that's different than controlling another person's behavior. All of us make our own decisions and are ultimately responsible for our own actions. Other people don't control us. The A-HA! Performance Edge is not about control. It's about having those insights and skills that work, almost like magic, at influencing behavior that leads to desired performance.

Handicapped by the faulty belief that his new position as manager meant that he now had to change or control Susan, Richard began to realize that he was going to have to confront her about her performance. He had been one of the original four salespeople who had worked with her so he knew firsthand how she was.

He had also received numerous complaints about her from customers, vendors, and the other salespeople. Customers were telling Richard, "I hate to call unless I know you're there. If I get her on the phone instead of you, I just want to hang up."

People were asking, "Does she not like me? What did I do?" Worse yet, the salespeople didn't want to call into the office—even though that was part of their job. They didn't like calling because Susan would degrade them for leaving catalogues out on the table, act incredulous that they hadn't memorized all of their pricing, or put them on hold for way too long.

Increasingly, Richard was becoming aware that something had to be done. He had a significant and growing problem; there was a major difference between the performance he wanted from Susan and the performance he was getting.

This point may be obvious to some, but to others, it's an a-ha:

Problems have two ends to them, a want and a got. A problem is always a gap between the way we want something to be and the way we've currently got it. If there's no gap, then we're getting what we want and there isn't a problem.

Whenever we have a problem, it will always have two ends to it: the way we want it and the way we've currently got it. The same of course is true of other people. Anytime they come to us with a problem, there will be two ends to their problem as well. They may only present us with one end—what they've got that they don't like, for example. But if it's a problem, there will be another end to it, too—the way they would like it to be or the way they want it.

There are no exceptions to this. If we've got what we want, then it's not a problem. Whether it's a little problem, like my back itches, or a big problem, like the mortgage being due and I don't get paid for two more weeks, it's always a gap between what we want—our back not to itch or the check to come today so we can pay the bill—and what we've got—an itchy back and no check.

All problems are gaps between a want and a got.

Richard certainly had a problem—a gap between what he wanted Susan to be doing and what Susan was actually doing. What we'll see throughout this book, particularly in Chapter 6, is that our motivation to act is always about these gaps. There are a number of Intrinsic Motivation Points (IMPs) that go into making up the gap, but gap management itself is certainly one of the key IMPs that the A-HA! Performance manager learns to leverage. With a gap, there is always an urgency to do something, to act. I can't make you buy my product, but if I can get you to want my product when you don't have it yet, you'll be internally motivated to buy it.

We are driven to behave in order to close gaps between what we've got and what we want—and so are our employees.

If we get a notice in the mail that our car insurance has been canceled, for example, and we didn't want it to be canceled, we have a gap between wanting car insurance and suddenly not having it. What do we do? We have choices about what to do, but we don't really have the choice to ignore it. Gaps get and hold our attention until we figure out a way to close them. We could stop driving and therefore not want or need car insurance any more. And if we stopped wanting insurance, we'd be closing the gap by accepting what we've got. No gap. No problem.

Or we could pick up the phone, call our car insurance company, rectify the problem and get our insurance reinstated—which is what we wanted in the first place. Once we do that and have insurance again, the gap is closed. We've got what we want and thus stop behaving to get car insurance. As we see throughout the book:

Behavior happens in an effort to close gaps. No gap, no behavior. Gaps close in two ways. We can get what we want, or accept what we've got.

Either way, getting what we want or accepting what we've got, once the gap closes, we'll stop the related behaviors.

Have you ever looked for something in your house that you couldn't find? We'll give up the behavior of looking if we either find it, or accept that it's lost and it won't ever be found. Anytime we accept the situation as it is and stop wanting it to be different, we're closing the gap not by getting what we want, but by accepting what we've got. So, back to that lost treasure, let's say we're about to give up looking for it when suddenly we find it. Remember that trick question, "Why is it that we always find something in the last place we look?" Well, the reason we always find something in the last place is because once we find it, thereby closing the gap, we stop looking. No gap, no behavior.

So all problems, frustrations, and challenges are simply a difference between what we want and what we've got—the want/got gap—and can only be solved in one of two ways: get what we want, or accept what we've got.

Richard couldn't accept the situation as it stood because Susan was harming the company's reputation. Phones weren't ringing as much as they used to and when they did, it was from someone who wasn't happy.

The gap in Richard's mind got bigger and bigger with every complaint, until finally an important customer called and said, "She's unbearable." That was it. Richard's gap opened to the point where he could no longer ignore it. He knew he had to do something. But the events leading up to this point didn't make him act. It was the events relative to the way he wanted them to be—what he got as opposed to what he wanted from his receptionist that drove him to do something. The gap was significant; that's why he had to act. Gaps drive all behavior.

So he got up from his desk and with boss-like resolve walked into the reception area and asked Susan to join him in the conference room . . . now.

Richard started by laying down the law: "Your negative behavior has to stop and you have to start being more cheerful on the phone and giving better service, or else." The stick approach, or threat, is a favorite of impatient or fed-up managers. Many managers believe in the motto, "Where there's a whip, there's a way." When a manager threatens an employee with some negative sanction—the loss of her job, for example—it's the manager's attempt to control the employee through coercion. The basic message, and the core message of all performance improvement plans, is: "Do it, or we'll hurt you in some way."

How did the threat approach work on Susan?

While Richard's plan was to "fix" the situation, in less than four minutes his approach resulted in Susan going into a creative combination of *fight and flight* (a psychological term), where she stormed out of the room yelling what observers of the scene said loosely translated into, "Take your job and shove it." Stopping long enough at her desk to cram a few personal items into her purse and arms, she left.

What did those four minutes cost Richard? In addition to his wounded pride, he had after all failed to get Susan to change the way he wanted her to, he now had to answer phones for the rest of the day; had to craft and place a help-wanted ad in the paper; and had to explain to corporate leadership and the other salespeople what happened. This was going to be tough because, truthfully, it played out so quickly he didn't really know what happened. He did know, though, that he had to get the phones answered, as well as the filing and word processing covered by someone else until a new person could be hired. He had to screen applicant phone calls and resumes, conduct initial interviews, schedule additional interviews for top candidates, offer the job, and then train the new person.

This was not exactly the result Richard was looking for when he went into the conference room. The cost of turnover varies somewhat, depending on the level of the position, but hard costs alone are usually in the thousands of dollars by the time lost productivity, staff time, interviewing, and training are factored in. Most research finds that the cost of replacing employees is two to three times their annual salary.

When the door slammed and Susan was gone, the salespeople who were in the office stood stunned, staring at the closed door, wondering how that conversation could've turned so ugly so fast.

This talk didn't exactly go as planned. Richard had thought he'd simply tell her what to do and she'd comply because he was the boss and she the employee. His job was to give orders; hers was to obey them. But that wasn't the way it worked this time, and it's never the way it works.

No one was going to miss Susan's attitude and behavior, but if that couldn't be turned around, an orderly transition would have been way better than this, where Susan could not only help screen the applicants but help train her replacement as well. Those four minutes cost a great deal—in loss of productivity, staff time for covering bases, interviewing candidates, and training the new hire. Worse yet, when people called the office and asked for Susan and she wasn't there anymore, the callers would wonder what happened. Change is sometimes disconcerting to customers and vendors alike. Competitors too love to take advantage of this kind of change.

But had Richard had the A-HA! Performance Edge—building and managing a self-motivated workforce and getting desired performance without using sticks or carrots—he could've avoided the cost and trauma that followed his stick approach.

With the A-HA! Performance Edge, we can address and improve situations as tough as or worse than Susan's. Had she been approached in ways we'll talk about in this book, she might have been willing to make some changes in how she answered the phone and how she treated people. Or she may still have left but at least she would've done so without exploding out of the building. Either of those two outcomes would've been better for Richard, for the company, and for Susan as well. Unfortunately, whatever Richard said in the conference room that day, it's safe to assume it wasn't something that changed Susan's performance in the ways Richard wanted.

I said earlier that relationships are key to managing others. And in the workplace context, a solid relationship is about perceived care and credibility.

If the people we manage experience us as trying to solve problems in ways that not only serve the company and the manager, but the employee as well, then they begin to believe we care about and are looking out for their interests, too. It's reasonably simple; just think win, win, win. Three wins: the company, the employee, and the manager.

Had Richard been managing Susan all along in ways that consistently took her needs into consideration (care), she might have had a keen interest in working out a transition plan that allowed her to look for other work while continuing to do her work for Office Connection, maybe even a little better because she now saw a way out. Or she might have been willing to work with him in finding the right solution to this issue for everyone.

Credibility is about integrity and competence. Are we credible in our knowledge and are we trustworthy in our word? When we are approached by someone who we believe cares about us, and is trustworthy, we're much more likely to work with that person toward finding equitable solutions to problems. That's why I stress in the A-HA! Performance model the strength of the relationship.

If Richard and Susan had a better relationship, where Susan trusted Richard and knew he cared about her in an "I know he's looking out for me in my career" type of way, the conversation could've gone a lot smoother. But, more important, if Richard had known what pushes people into an adversarial or defensive mode, he could've avoided some pitfalls and been a lot more effective when he approached Susan that day.

I like to use the analogy of a magician putting a pin through a balloon without popping it. When most of us put a pin into a balloon, it blows up. And when some managers try to get a point across to employees, the relationship blows up. But there is a way to stick a pin into a balloon without blowing it up, just as there is a way for a manager to get a point across without blowing up relationships.

To avoid the kind of result that Richard got, it may be useful to understand part of the reason these blowups occur. There is a tiny almond-shaped group of neurons located deep within the medial temporal lobes of the brain (*Wikipedia*), called the amygdala. Its purpose is to detect threat. When our basic needs (which we'll delve into in the next chapter) are threatened, we are designed to act to counter that threat. The amygdala is like a sentinel, standing guard over these needs. When it detects a threat, it secretes a chemical that shuts down the frontal lobe and sends us into fight or flight mode—a term used in psychology that describes a person's quick adjustment to a threat, and the inability to think through any options. We are designed to act quickly to neutralize a threat. Kill it or get away from it.

If a rattlesnake suddenly dropped from a rock we were walking by, our amygdala would be triggered and we'd go instantly into fight or flight—either moving away as fast as we could or picking up a rock or stick and attacking the snake. When something comes at us that is a threat to our well-being, like a snake, we don't have time to think about our best options because we'd be injured or dead by the time we figured out what to do. When the amygdala senses a threat, it shuts down the rest of the brain and leaves two choices: Attack the threat or get away from the threat—don't think about it, just keep the system safe.

If we as managers come off as abrasive or threatening to employees and trigger their amygdala, they won't be able to come up with any creative or thoughtful solutions to a problem we're trying to address with them because they won't have full access to their frontal lobe and will instead be physiologically limited to fight or flight behaviors. These may include quitting and storming out the door, withdrawing, attacking, pushing back, or "going postal."

Without getting too technical, we simply need to know that when a conversation turns adversarial in any way, the individual we're trying to work toward a solution with may not have access to different ideas or behaviors besides the fight or flight ones. And if that person only has access to fight or flight options, it's going to reduce the chances of her using her whole brain to come up with a good solution.

So before we act impulsively out of frustration, as Richard did, we'll want to make sure our approach is one that doesn't trigger the amygdala. Furthermore, we'll want to make sure it is an approach that takes into account all of the IMPs revealed in A-HA! Performance. After all, employee turnover is expensive and having an opportunity to resolve something productively—rather than blowing up the situation because we didn't understand the power of employees' needs and the brain's role in protecting them—is much more cost effective. The A-HA! Performance Edge provides the insights and practices to avoid paying the cost, while progressively building a foundation of care and credibility.

It demonstrates how Richard could've approached this situation in order to achieve not only a less costly outcome, but a beneficial one for the company, Susan, and for him. A-HA! Performance provides the insights as to why Richard's approach will always lead to people quitting and leaving, or worse, quitting and staying. The model provides managers with an understanding, a foundational framework, and, an "a-ha so that's why that happened and this is what to do to avoid getting the costly outcome Richard got." That's an a-ha most managers, especially new ones, can use. Once we understand why that happened to Richard, we won't have to pay the price that often accompanies being unaware. Our dealing with these types of performance issues with vested interest will often make the difference between coming up with a creative solution and getting the door slammed in our face as an employee storms out.

Needs: The Hidden Fundamentals of Motivation and Behavior

etween Richard's input and Susan's output, what happened? (See Figure 2.1.) Why did Susan yell at her boss and storm out the door? While the amygdala activated and limited her options, leading her into flight and fight, that's only part of it. The other reasons for her behavior are deeper. So what else could've been at work? Was it something in her genes? Did her parents teach her to behave like that? Can we blame her behavior on Richard? Was it the weather? Or does Susan have choices about how to handle situations and is she therefore responsible for what she does, regardless of how she's treated? Who was responsible for what she did?

That's the fundamental question because the answer helps us understand how to address our behavior-changing conversations. If it's just genes, there's nothing we can do. If it's training; the way she was brought up by her parents, we're stuck again. But if there's a process, if there's something that goes on between Richard's input and

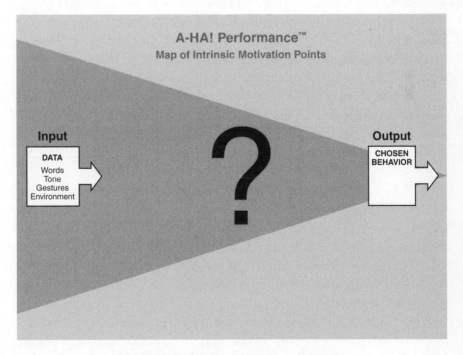

Figure 2.1   Between Input and Output

Susan's output where pieces line up a certain way before a decision is made, then we have a chance of impacting that process in a way that produces a different output.

And who was responsible for the way Richard approached the issue? Did Susan make him so mad he had to talk to her like that? Are bosses responsible for the way they address performance issues, regardless of how frustrated they are by them? Are we as human beings externally motivated (controlled) by others, or are we internally motivated and therefore choose our own behavior in an effort to satisfy those internal motivators? What is the reason for and primary motivator of behavior? Is it external forces? Or is it internal forces?

The answer is tricky and one that has a couple of layers to it. As we see throughout this book, we are each responsible for what we do. Second, what we do is not about being controlled by others (such as managers, parents, or teachers); rather, it's all about satisfying or protecting powerful forces within; needs that must be tended to and satisfied because they have to do with life and death itself. So while we don't have a choice about whether or not we do something to protect or satisfy a need, we do have a choice about what to do in that pursuit.

"Doing" happens on three levels: The observable chosen behavior, the intended result of that behavior, and the hidden reason for it. As William Powers, author of *Behavior: The Control of Perception*, and one of the pioneers in these ideas, once said, "You can't always tell what a person is doing by looking at what she's doing." As succinctly as I can put it, when we behave on the outside, it's all about satisfying something on the inside.

When we understand those powerful hidden reasons for our behavior, we'll understand how to focus our conversations around need satisfaction or protection in order to get the observable behavior and performance levels we seek. People won't do anything that doesn't satisfy or protect one or more of those hidden forces; everything we do is done in an effort to protect or satisfy one or more of our basic needs. Ask someone to do something that frustrates his needs, and he will not do it. Ask someone to do something that we want him to do, and that satisfies his needs at the same time, and he is much more likely to do it.

That may seem obvious enough reading it here, but when I ask the question, "Are we internally motivated or externally motivated?" in workshops on A-HA! Performance, many groups struggle with answering it conclusively either way. They come up with the answer that it may be some of each. That sometimes we behave because we want something and other times because someone is making us. But how can we be both? Are there times when we control ourselves and other times when others control us? Excluding situations where one person is physically overpowering another person, are there some moments where we're responsible for what we do, and others where someone else is responsible for what we do? Imagine how convenient that would be. When we do good things, we could say we were internally motivated to do them and therefore deserve the credit, but when we do bad things, we could blame it on someone or something else.

A-HA! Performance explains and illustrates how before behavior, before output, we want something, a certain outcome (see Figure 2.2).

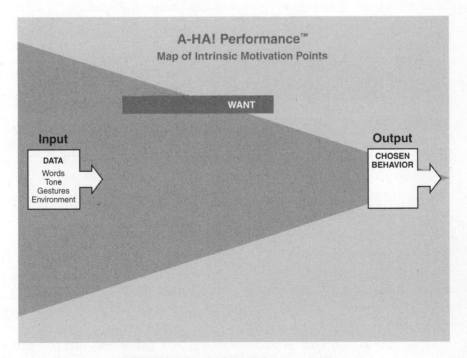

FIGURE 2.2   Before Behavior; A Want

And before the want, there are powerful needs those wants are tied to that one way or another must be satisfied. The key phrase is "one way or another."

> While we have choices about what to want and what to do, we don't have choices as to whether or not to satisfy or protect a need.

I can choose any entrée I want from the menu, but I can't choose not to eat. The need for food must be satisfied, or I'll die. My food preferences can vary from day to day, even minute to minute, but I don't have the option to not eat. And food isn't our only need.

Human beings are internally motivated by, not just one, but five powerful forces, or hungers, that must be fed, or else we suffer to the point where life itself is at risk. And these powerful forces do not turn off when we walk through the doors of our workplaces.

> We are, in effect, slaves to these hidden fundamental motivators and are constantly driven to behave in ways that keep them protected and satisfied.

So why did Susan yell at her boss and deliver such an abrupt resignation? It had to do with her needs. At the heart of it, it's the same reason we get out of bed in the morning, spend special time with those we care about, go to yoga classes, prepare and eat meals, phone a friend, go to work, spend money on cruises and ski vacations, or take a day to just sit. It's the reason we struggle to get back to the ocean's surface after being knocked over by a wave or buy flowers for someone we love. It's the reason we apply for promotions, go the extra mile for customers, and seek companionship or solitude.

The reason Susan exploded out of that room and out of that company was to protect or satisfy one or more of the five hidden fundamental motivators of all human behavior, what psychologists call our basic needs. The needs I've come to believe in are those identified by noted psychiatrist and author, William Glasser, MD, although readers who are familiar with Abraham Maslow's hierarchy of needs will find them to be essentially the same ones:

1. Survival
2. Belonging (Love)
3. Power (Achievement)
4. Fun
5. Freedom

These five needs (Figure 2.3), collectively the first of the A-HA! Performance Intrinsic Motivation Points (IMPs) are the foundational drivers of all behavior. Learning what they are will serve any manager well because once she understands just how powerful

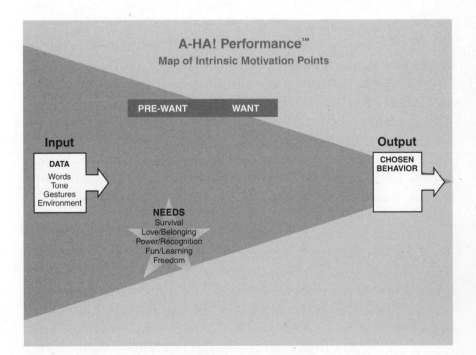

FIGURE 2.3 IMP 1—Needs

they are, she'll learn to make requests with the needs in mind and treat them with the respect they demand. Knowing that needs have to be satisfied, she'll always approach behavior-changing conversations with need-satisfying wins in mind, not only for herself, the customers, and the company, but for the employees as well. She'll begin each performance-changing conversation thinking, "For this to work, I've got to find the need-satisfying wins for this person if she is going to be willing to make the change." Any desired change in employee behavior that frustrates the employee's needs more than it satisfies them will not happen, as we saw in the Susan and Richard showdown. In that moment, Susan saw quitting as losing less than she had to gain in the job.

These needs are the source of both motivation and action.

> Buy-in to a performance change will not happen unless the request satisfies (or protects) needs more than it frustrates them.

It's that simple. Payoff versus cost. Return on investment. Here's the easy-to-remember formula: Payoff ≥ Cost.

Payoff (need satisfaction) must be greater than or equal to the cost (of need frustration). The payoff to Susan's needs for complying with Richard's edicts was less than the cost of giving in to him and changing her habits. Because her power needs were threatened so much and because she wasn't meeting many belonging needs there anyway (most of her happy conversations were on the phone with friends outside of work), she could not possibly back down and do what he wanted her to do.

Richard Harper didn't know about the first IMP—the five needs. He was completely unaware, or at least underestimated the potency, of these performance drivers and was stunned when Susan erupted in such an emotional display as she creatively compressed the usual two-week notice down to a blinding flash, and in a matter of seconds, was gone. When needs are threatened enough, we short circuit into fight or flight, sometimes fight and flight, in an effort to protect them.

The challenge many managers face today isn't lack of motivation or abundance of malice. It's a paradigm, assumption, or understanding deficiency.

When managers need motivators for getting employees to change, most only know about carrots and sticks. They simply aren't aware of any other option. They have never been taught about the basic needs and that all employees have a powerful vested interest in keeping them satisfied. When I ask managers about what they use to motivate employees to improve a performance issue, I'll hear how they use a creative variety of carrots and sticks, or bribes and threats.

I'll hear about performance improvement plans, which are really sticks or threats that organizations use because they don't know about the dramatically superior vested interest option (direct need satisfaction). Performance improvement plans all boil down to some variation of "Do it, or we'll hurt you." But that practice almost never produces the desired change. It mostly leads to a costly termination. It will sometimes lead to barely acceptable levels of performance, enough to avoid the stick, but never to the level of great quality. Threats are based on fear. When workers are afraid, they're not concerned with the organization at all, they're only concerned with protecting a threatened need. Threats create wariness in the workplace, not enthusiastic performance.

Also widely used by managers, as alternatives to threats, are employee incentive or recognition programs, which are really carrots or bribes offered to sweeten an otherwise bitter deal. The belief with this approach is that there aren't intrinsically satisfying reasons for people to do the right thing, to perform at the level that is being requested. And even these seemingly powerful motivation tools are flawed in a variety of ways.

Employee incentive programs rarely offer the right prize and often just the announcement of some new "contest" sets off a wave of complaints and dissatisfaction, ultimately lowering morale. The same people always win these contests anyway, and on closer inspection, they are the people who would be the best performers whether or not there were contests. It isn't the prize that motivates top performers. It's the personal satisfaction, which translates to need satisfaction. Second, not everybody wants another trip to Las Vegas. Third, these contests end up producing few winners, and a lot more losers. Why would we want to create a team that is mostly filled with people who come to know themselves as losers? How can losers take us to first in our industry?

I'm not saying people will turn down the trips and gold watches if offered, just that those are not the drivers of superior performance. What drives top performers are internal forces. They want to be the best in order to satisfy their power or self-esteem needs. The best definition I've ever heard for power came from Dr. Martin Luther King Jr. when he said, "Power is the ability to achieve purpose." We feel good when we are achieving purpose because our power needs are being met. Top performers like to achieve, they like the feeling it produces.

Donald Trump once said, "It's never about the money. It's about the win." Top performers want to do their jobs well so that they win or so that they don't let their manager or team members down, thereby satisfying not just their power needs, but their belonging needs, too. They want to produce great results because it's more fun. They excel because excellent performance produces excellent results and that satisfies needs.

That's why A-HA! Performance managers are always thinking: What are the need-satisfying wins for my employee, my customer, my company, and myself? (See Figure 2.4.)

As mentioned earlier, world-renowned psychiatrist, William Glasser, MD, noted author of *Reality Therapy*, *Choice Theory* and numerous other books on psychology and education, as well as Abraham Maslow, PhD, creator of the hierarchy of needs, are prominent among those experts who teach that we all have these powerful, built-in hungers that must be satisfied. Satisfy these and

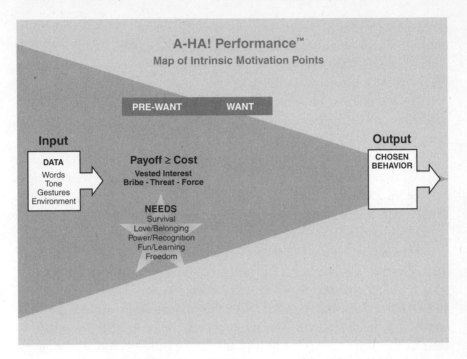

FIGURE 2.4 Possible Pathways to Need Payoff

life is good. Neglect or frustrate them and life can get bad and ten-
uous, sometimes in a hurry. People will do surprising, sometimes
desperate things to protect and satisfy their needs. It's folly to un-
derestimate the power of these needs and potentially costly to be
unaware of them.

A woman made headlines not too long ago when she put her two
young children in the back of her car and drove the car into a lake.
"How could she do that?" people asked. The answer is the same as
the answer to why Susan abruptly quit her job. She was trying to satisfy needs. The woman drowned her children in an attempt to satisfy
her love and belonging need. She was in love with a guy who said he
liked her okay, but not the kids. She had a need for love and wanted to
meet that need through this guy. The only obstacle to that love
seemed to be her kids. So she removed the obstacle. Was she thinking clearly? Probably not. But driven by the power of the needs, all of
us have done things we wish we could take back or do over (hopefully

not to the extent of what this woman did). And the reason for the choices we made? There was a need that was crying out for satisfaction or protection. And the intensity of that desire to meet the needs sometimes results in bad choices.

In the chapter on filters, we'll see how we can calibrate our output filters to limit the (negative) kinds of behavior that we have the potential to engage in. These output filters are our values. In the case I just mentioned, the woman's values filter did not kick in and the consequences were tragic. Disgruntled (need frustrated) people can be dangerous, especially if their values are not firmly in place. That's why the wise manager works at keeping her people gruntled; contented, pleased, or happy.

The shootings in the postal service—the ones that launched the term *gone postal*—were traced back to flawed management practices, which boiled down to the overuse of coercion and threats; stick practices that frustrated needs. Whether disgruntled employees will come back to shoot us or not depends on the level of frustration, as well as the person's values. But there is certainly evidence to suggest that when threatened with sticks, people are likely to go into some form of resistance—stubbornly refusing to do what's asked, pushing back or arguing, taking the issue to human resources, legal or union representatives (in other words, fighting); or quitting and leaving, quitting and staying, withdrawing from active and productive involvement in the team and tasks, and doing only the bare minimum to keep the paycheck coming in (in other words, *flighting*).

Purchases are all about need satisfaction. Savvy marketing people understand that. On the box of the packaging for Windows 95, it didn't say, "Buy this because it's great software!" Do you know what it said? "More Power, More Fun, More Freedom." Three of the five basic needs, right on the box. Microsoft understood people buy need satisfaction, not software.

Wow moments, too, are all about need satisfaction. Think about wow moments from your own life, what comes to mind? Falling in love? Birth of a child? Winning a contest or prize of some kind? A great trip or adventure? Beating out others for a promotion? A superb meal? Surviving a close call? All wows will be the result of a major satisfaction of one or more of those five basic needs.

Conversely, all ow moments are a result of a profound or chronic frustration of one or more of those needs. The death of a loved one, divorce, losing a job and being unable to find a new one for a long period of time, being forced to move from our home, and chronic pain or illness are some of the examples of need frustrating situations that will produce an inner or psychic pain, sometimes as a companion to a physical one. The pain is our system's attempt to get our attention and focus it on doing something to make things better. If we don't make things better, life and health are at risk.

I call the five basic needs the hidden fundamentals of all behavior because everything we do is ultimately an attempt to satisfy or protect one or more of them.

Survival Needs

These are the physiological needs for air, food, water, shelter, and safety. Can't breathe? Get to where there is air. Hunger pain tells us to eat, or we'll die. Too cold? Find a way to get warm or we're at risk. Everybody understands physiological needs for survival. Maslow presented the needs in a hierarchy, with survival as the bottom line need, but if that were true, how would we explain suicide or martyrdom? We do have a powerful need to survive, but sometimes when one of more of these other potent needs are at stake, we'll give up survival in an attempt to satisfy those.

Love and Belonging Needs

Have you ever known or heard of couples who have lived together for their entire adult life, and then husband or wife passes away? Sometimes within two or three weeks, the other one, who had been healthy up to that point, dies also. Without the person through whom he met his need for love, he faltered and died.

Loneliness tells us to seek companionship, or else we suffer. I remember reading in my Psychology 101 textbook about an orphanage during one of the world wars where babies were dying. The staff couldn't figure out why they were dying because their survival needs were being met—the babies were being fed, the temperature was fine, and the sanitation was good, yet they would become morose, give up on eating and literally starve themselves to death. Why?

While many babies were developing this moroseness and dying in cribs throughout the nursery, the staff began to observe that it wasn't happening in one corner of the room. In that corner, the babies were doing fine. So what was going on there? They watched and noticed that the maid who cleaned the nursery had her cleaning supplies in a closet in that corner of the nursery and when she'd go to her closet, she'd stop at the cribs nearby. She'd pick up those babies and coo at them; she'd spend some time with them. And those babies were thriving. Life was worth living. But for the babies without that attention, life wasn't worth living . . . they gave up on survival, and died.

Love and belonging is a need that must be satisfied throughout our day, whether at work or outside of it. How do we know people care about us? It's when people spend time with us, touch us, or at least are in touch with us—giving us praise once in a while. This need is so powerful that, statistically, if we join a new organization and don't connect with anyone in the first three months, we won't stay. According to research done by the Gallup organization, the number one reason people leave a company is a bad relationship, or no relationship, with the boss. Was a lack of relationship one of the missing ingredients in Susan's job at Office Connection? Absolutely. Remember the three rules in managing people from Chapter 1? Relationship, relationship, relationship.

The need for belonging must be met at work if people are going to perform well. Just like most people take a lunch break to feed their survival needs at work, they also take a phone-home break some time during the day to feed their belonging needs. Because there is a need for love and belonging, successful management requires that managers build and maintain good relationships.

But what does that mean? The definition of a manager/employee relationship isn't one where managers have to invite employees over for a Sunday afternoon barbeque. I define a relationship in the work context as one where the other person believes the manager cares and is credible.

As already mentioned in Chapter 1, the two requirements in a relationship that facilitate great performance-changing conversations are care and credibility. The people we manage should believe that we care about their need-satisfying wins (as well as the company's and our own) in any of our communications; and we should be credible, which means we should have both integrity and competency. Our employees should believe that we tell the truth, that we make and keep promises, and that we know what we're talking about. When those conditions are met with those we manage, addressing and improving behavior without the use of carrots or sticks will be much easier and more successful than when those conditions are not met.

Where else does the need for love and belonging surface? Think about the last meeting you went to. Did you look around for a familiar or friendly face so you could sit with someone you'd be comfortable with? If you don't remember, keep that question in mind for the next meeting you go to. If you do find yourself looking for that familiar or friendly face, you'll realize that the need for belonging is alive and well in you, too.

Will people kill and die over love issues? I already mentioned the young mother who was willing to kill her own children in her tragic attempt to be loved by a particular guy, but she's far from the only one to have been driven to that extreme in her quest for love. What would you do if something threatened the people you care about most? The need for love is a powerful driver of our behavior and we will go to great lengths to satisfy or protect that need. Thinking it's not a factor in the workplace would be folly indeed.

Power Needs

Power is about achieving and winning. It's the reason we compete and compare. Power is the reason we criticize, too. Karl Menninger, considered by some to be the dean of American psychologists, points out that criticism is never about the criticized; it's always about the power needs of the critic. George Carlin has a comedy routine about oxymorons, where he talks about words that we put together, but when looked at individually, they cancel each other out. Examples include: jumbo shrimp (big littles?); honest politician (name three); military intelligence (weapons of mass destruction?); white chocolate; overeaters anonymous; and Victoria's Secret (not much stays secret). To this list, I've added constructive criticism. Constructive is building up, criticism is tearing down. Ironic, isn't it? Synergy may be the highest form of power there is and that never comes from tearing down, yet we sometimes tear others down in an attempt to feel powerful. In Australia they call that the tall poppy syndrome. If you're the tall poppy in your field, the other poppies, rather than try to grow to match your height, will instead, try to cut you down to equalize power.

With power needs at work, we compare to see who's best, who's wearing what, who's invited, who's in, and who's out. We compete to be the best, to be number one.

There are shabby ways we pursue power, and there are sensible and heroic ways also. Power needs drove Attila the Hun and Julius Caesar, but they drove Gandhi and Mother Theresa, too. Power needs drive selfish decisions and selfless ones. They drive terrorists, soldiers of fortune, and mercenaries, but they also drive defenders of freedom and of homelands. They are driving our leadership, as well as driving the leaders of our current enemies. Power needs drive us to accomplish and to win. When power needs are harnessed, they can serve an organization well; when they run amuck, they can be the organization's internal undoing.

Jefferson Welch, a great friend and successful CEO of an international construction company, used to drive home the idea that "in this company, we collaborate internally and compete externally." Knowing that love and power needs are both in play at all times, he helped focus people on the best ways to meet those needs for the good of the organization.

That brings up another key insight about power. Peter Senge, author of *The Fifth Discipline*, once said the problem with selfishness is that we're not selfish enough. If we were really selfish, if we wanted the biggest wins possible, we'd learn to synergize. In Chapter 1, I talked about the three possibilities when people come together: synergy, samergy, and lessergy. To meet power needs, synergy is the ultimate goal.

Fun Needs

There's plenty to suggest that we are driven to have a good time, to do things just for the joy we get in doing them. The billions of dollars spent in pursuit of fun every year is strong evidence that there is a powerful need to have some once in a while. Joy in the workplace is the sign of a successful operation and once it's gone, an organization is in trouble.

Will people risk their lives in pursuit of fun? They'll not only risk it, but some people have lost their lives in attempts to have fun. One winter not too long ago, both Sonny Bono and a Kennedy clan member died in skiing accidents, and there are many other examples. From the class clown getting kicked out of school to the adrenalin junkies of the X Games, fun is so important that people believe it's worth the risk.

And there may be an additional payoff to fun. William Glasser believes that fun may be an inherent reward for learning. He said that when he was watching the animal channel, he noticed that animals that were born knowing it all, like turtles, didn't have to learn anything to make a living, so they didn't play. Once hatched, they went directly to work. They didn't slide down little sand dunes on the way to the sea, they didn't tell little turtle jokes or romp and wrestle with other little turtles, they just got busy avoiding predators and seeking food. Since they already knew what to do, they didn't have to learn. On the other hand, tiger cubs and wolf pups—animals that had to learn how to hunt if they were going to survive—seemed to learn through play. People who enjoy learning are usually much more fun to be around than those who know it all.

Additionally, learning, or continuous development, is critical if we're going to keep up with the changing demands of life and business. Senge, in *The Fifth Discipline*, says that learning disabilities are tragic in human beings, but often fatal in organizations. The need for learning is life long and the immediate payoff for learning is fun, while the long-term payoff for accumulating knowledge is power. Many people report that the best years of their careers were the ones where they were learning and developing the most. Joy in the workplace is one of the hallmarks of organizations that produce quality products or services. When morale is high, fun flows easily. But if that need goes unmet for too long, morale and retention go down, and quality suffers.

Freedom Needs

Freedom is perhaps as obvious as survival itself. Without a certain degree of liberty, or physical freedom, we could not move around enough to find the food, relationships, accomplishment opportunities, and fun activities to meet our other needs. But freedom is about more than liberty. It's about intellect, creativity, and spirituality as well. It's the reason Patrick Henry declared that life without freedom wasn't worth living and demanded liberty . . . or death. It's the reason Maya Angelou wrote, "I know why the caged bird sings," and Solzhenitsyn triumphantly declared, "You can lock up my body, but not my mind."

The need for freedom is strong and people will kill and die in their attempts to meet it. This need is strongest in our most creative colleagues: designers, engineers, artists, and writers. It's also strong in salespeople, entrepreneurs, and others who prefer jobs where they don't have to answer to others or sit behind a desk or at a workstation all day.

So which need is the strongest? The one that's not being met at any given time.

Need Profile

But while all of us have all these needs to some degree, we each have a different need profile. On the A-HA! Performance Edge map of Intrinsic Motivation Points, I represent these five needs as the points on a five-point star (Figure 2.5).

Each of us has a unique star profile—the longer points representing the strongest needs in us. In some of us, the love and belonging need is strongest and we'd risk survival and give up freedom to defend and take care of those we love. Some of us care more about freedom or fun than relationships and will sacrifice friendships for the open road. The need star in others of us may have the longest point representing a strong need for power. A great salesperson may have a strong power need and a strong freedom need. Human resource

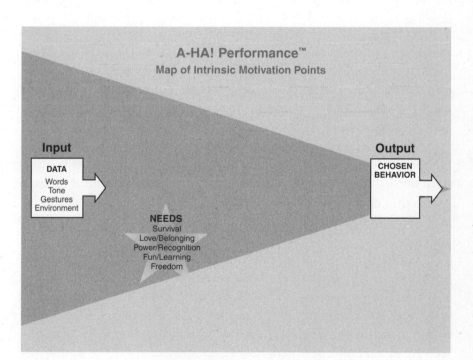

FIGURE 2.5 IMP 1—Needs

professionals, customer care professionals, and teachers—especially those who teach elementary school kids—probably have strong love and belonging needs so their star would show that point as the longest.

What the A-HA! Performance manager learns to count on, regardless of an individual's specific need profile, is that each person he manages does what he does to satisfy or protect one or more of those needs. To manage someone successfully through change requires that we focus on finding need-satisfying wins for that person.

> If we're going to find the payoff—the strong motivator for people—so that they are willing to do what we want them to do, we have to think about how the individual's needs will be met.

When needs are being satisfied, morale and motivation are high. We are energized and are willing to do more. On the other hand, when needs are chronically frustrated, we expend energy without satisfaction. We get worn out. When we are unable to feed our needs, strength and enthusiasm dissipate, effectiveness diminishes, and accomplishments decrease.

Morale in our organizations is directly traceable to need satisfaction or frustration. If morale is bad, one or more of the needs have been suddenly or chronically frustrated and individual and organizational performance will suffer. If morale is good, needs are being satisfied, enthusiasm is high, and productivity and creativity are flourishing.

Cisco Systems Chief Executive Officer John Chambers was once written up as the best boss in America and featured on the cover of *Time* magazine. Why? Because he did a lot of things right when it came to satisfying the needs of his employees. One simple thing he did was on Fridays, he would walk around the office with an ice cream cart and personally serve ice cream to all the employees who wanted some. He talked and listened to them. Through this consistent routine, he was available to them on a regular basis. There is even a name for this process; it's called Management by Walking Around (MBWA).

What he was doing was satisfying his employees' needs for survival, power, fun, and belonging. Ice cream is food/survival; knowing and chatting with the boss is power, especially if he's actually listening to ideas employees might have; ice cream and good times on Friday is fun; and being included in the party and in happy conversations with the boss is belonging. And his employees were happy because of it. Great bosses find ways to satisfy employees' needs.

Needs must be met or morale will be low and productivity will suffer. But just how each of us should best do that in our own companies will be something we each must figure out for ourselves. There isn't a one-behavior-fits-all solution. What I call the Myth of Best Practices is rampant in the workplace today. The implication is that someone has figured out the best way to do something and that all the rest of us have to do is copy that. Did John Chambers figure it out? Should all bosses serve ice cream to their employees on Fridays? It won't work for others the same way it worked for him. Best practices are best for certain people because of their unique combination of personality, expertise, experience, education, and energy. But for those of us with different personalities, expertise, experience, education, and energy, those practices just won't fit.

Getting clarity around best paradigms and best motivators is much more useful than copying others' best practices. Far more beneficial than learning someone else's seven-step shtick about how we can get the results we need is learning the A-HA! Performance Intrinsic Motivation Points.

Where as the practice that works well for one doesn't work as well for others, best understandings and best motivators allow each of us to comprehend the bases that need to be covered, and apply individual creativity and style in figuring out how to cover those bases.

The important thing here is to develop a deep understanding that satisfaction or frustration of these needs is what determines the state of morale in the workplace. If employees can meet these needs through their performance and the relationships they have with managers and other colleagues, morale is good. If they can't, morale is bad. When morale is bad for extended periods of time, quality and efficiency suffer and retention becomes an issue.

With the baby boomer generation about to leave the workforce, retention of top performers is going to become an increasingly important focus. The manager who understands the power of the needs, and the absolute requirement that they must be satisfied to retain and maximize talent, will have The A-HA! Performance Edge over managers who don't.

The payoff piece for any desired change of behavior always taps directly, or indirectly, into these needs.

> When looking to get an employee to do something, utilizing the A-HA! Performance vested interest approach—tying desired behavior directly to need satisfaction—is the most effective way to get buy-in and compliance.

So understanding our employees' needs and, in particular, their unique need profile allows us to not only make sure their needs are being met—and thus morale is high—but it also gives us the ability to focus quickly on what is most likely to be an intrinsic or vested interest payoff for them in doing what we want them to do.

Summation

Needs are the hidden fundamentals of all behavior. Through employees' needs, we can work directly with the source of motivation—why people do the things they do and don't do. So whether we're looking to get an employee to shape up or simply improve an already good performance, understanding their needs is crucial to building and managing a self-motivated workforce.

3

Wants: The Not-at-All Hidden Fundamentals of Motivation and Behavior

n Chapter 2 we revealed the needs: Intrinsic Motivation Point 1 of A-HA! Performance. I said that they were the hidden fundamentals of motivation and behavior—the invisible drivers, the foundational motivators, the primary reasons for everything we do. There are very few, only five in fact, and while every one of us has a unique need profile, all of the needs are present in each of us, at least to some degree. Love, power, fun, freedom, and/or survival are at the core of every wow, every ow, and every action we take.

But since needs are the hidden fundamentals of motivation and behavior, we don't satisfy them directly. Instead, we satisfy them through wants: specific preferences that are tied to our needs. Based on five general needs, people develop an infinite number and wide variety of specific wants. And it's our wants that make up Intrinsic Motivation Point 2 (see Figure 3.1).

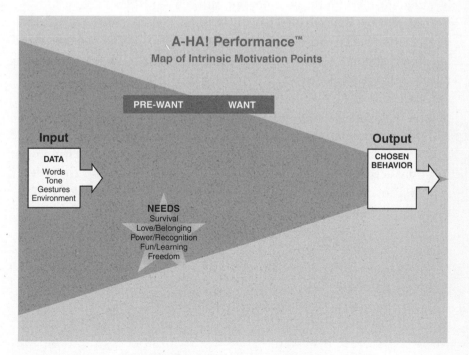

FIGURE 3.1 IMP 2—Wants

Wants are our individual and unique preferences for how we protect and satisfy our needs. Wants are the not-at-all hidden fundamentals of behavior, as they are the identifiable, perceivable, blatant, tangible, describable, definable, immediate, and clear motivators of behavior. Before output, there is a want.

We may not be aware of our needs, but we are aware of our wants. We don't say, "I miss love," we say, "I miss my significant other, my kids, or my close friend from high school." We don't say, "I want survival," we say, "I want chocolate, a steak, a burrito, or tofu." We don't say, "I want power!" We say, "I want to win that account" or "I want management to listen to those of us on the front lines" or "I'm right and you're wrong!"

We meet our needs through getting some specific thing we want. And the good news is that if one of our wants is impossible to get, we can, whether through a conversation with someone or through a painful process called grief, switch to another want that will also satisfy the same need. Needs are fixed, but wants are flexible, changeable, and to some degree, interchangeable.

When my mother died nearly 30 years ago, as much as I wanted her alive and in my world, there was nothing I could do to make that happen. Grieving is the difficult process we go through in order to let one important want go and find other wants that can take its place in meeting that need. We do that by changing from wants that are impossible and unattainable to wants that are possible. Fortunately, I had other people in my life who loved me and whom I could love; my family, my father, my siblings, and great friends. No longer able to meet my need through my mom, I found that I've been able to meet it very well over the past 27 years through other loving people. When we can't change reality, we can change what we want from reality.

Job loss is another example of times where changing our wants is the key to satisfying our needs. With downsizing as the norm in business today, the average job lasts three years. That means a lot of us have lost jobs we liked.

So what happens when the environment changes, when the opportunity to meet our needs by continuing to work for the company we loved, is gone? If we can't stop wanting to work for the company that laid us off, we're going to suffer because we'll go on wanting something that's impossible to get. But if we change our preference to wanting to work for any of several new "target" companies, we can develop the skills and work the processes that lead to employment in one of those organizations. We can't change our needs, but we can change our wants. And the new want will change our behavior from moping around due to the loss of the old job to active pursuit of a new position.

Knowing that we have the ability to change wants empowers A-HA! Performance Managers. For example, Hector was an excellent supervisor in a government agency. He had just been promoted to a position he liked and was feeling quite comfortable in it. Although he was only in his forties, he'd be eligible for retirement within five years, so he figured he had the perfect position in which to ride out his career.

His manager, however, thought Hector had the kind of talent the organization was going to need, especially in light of the baby boomer exodus and a talent pool that was shrinking. But when his manager sat down to talk to him about any plans for promotions into the next leadership position, Hector, while flattered, told her that he loved his new position and didn't have a desire for an increase in scope, title, or pay. Just the opposite from being on the fast track up, Hector saw himself on that final glide to an early retirement (he started with the agency at 18 and was eligible for retirement at 48).

So how could Hector's manager get this talented guy to go from not wanting to put effort into further development to considering that there might be something in it for him to go on learning and becoming an even more capable professional?

For starters, Hector was not stuck wanting to glide through his last five years of work. If he could be convinced that other wants were just as need satisfying, he could give up the glide want and start wanting to grow and develop additional leadership skills because that would increase his ability to get other things he wanted.

When Hector's manager approached him a second time, she was well equipped with the A-HA! Performance Edge. And an important feature of the conversation between Hector and his manager was the manager's focus on this Intrinsic Motivation Point 2—

knowing that Hector's specific wants were tied to powerful needs, and that his wants, like all wants, were changeable. So the manager addressed Hector's needs by probing for his preferences that were related to each of those needs. She knew that we don't meet our needs directly, but indirectly through our own unique wants.

> Getting what we want is the tangible way we satisfy our needs.

The manager also understood that having more than one want for each need allows us to meet that need through a different want. Since we're able to satisfy needs through more than one want, all we have to do is switch or change our want in order to get what we need.

Once the manager figured out what was important to Hector, she helped Hector change some of his wants; she tied professional development to specific future wants, thereby helping Hector realize he might meet his needs better by doing what the manager was suggesting, rather than if he ignored the opportunity to grow and develop new skills. Knowing Hector wanted a comfortable future, and knowing he wanted to be a great role model to his kids, the manager worked at getting Hector to want to take advantage of the organization's professional development opportunities as a great way to get those other wants.

She tied the payoff to his needs by pointing out how leadership development would satisfy Hector's particular wants. The following are some reasons that the manager used to tie into Hector's specific wants:

- "You may want to buy more things, maybe take more trips some day, so an increase in pay couldn't hurt."
- "If you got bored and decided you were ready to take on exciting new challenges, you'd be in a position to do so. Doing the same old thing can get stale."
- "You're a good dad. It will always be important to you to continue being a great inspiration and example for your kids."

Just like that, the manager had tied development—something she wanted Hector to get involved in—to Hector's needs for:

- *Power:* Through wants for buying stuff and taking on exciting new challenges
- *Fun:* Through his desire to experience the opposite of being bored, to take trips, to do new things
- *Freedom:* Through his hopes for options in retirement and dreams of travel
- *Love and belonging:* Through his plans for spending time with his wife and kids

The first two points to remember about Intrinsic Motivation Point 2, the Wants, are:

1. Based on five general needs, we develop a wide variety of specific wants.
2. These wants are the particular motivators of our actions, our behavior. The wants are the conscious reasons we do anything. Before output, but based on the needs, we have a want.

Quality is the third point to remember. Quality is that which most thoroughly matches our strongest wants. Wants are our preferences for meeting our needs and when we find someone or something that matches our wants, we perceive that person, situation, or thing as quality.

Our wants represent an ideal state, the way things are supposed to be; they represent quality to us. The finest people we know are quality people, as they are the people who represent the way we want people to be. A quality automobile is one that most closely matches our ideal wants in an automobile. Remember, wows come from getting what we want. The closer we get to what we want in terms of a particular product or service, the closer we'll be getting to our idea of quality for that particular product or service.

But what constitutes quality varies from person to person. We may both agree that Lexus makes a quality car, but which model is the best? That depends on the individual preferences of those doing the buying. While quality has some commonly agreed upon characteristics, such as the product or service does what it's supposed to do better than other similar products, quality mostly means what's best for us. And best for us is whatever closely matches our wants, or our ideal. Price range would be a factor, as well as intended use of the product. Lexus understands that quality is unique to each individual. Go to their website and click on the tab that lets us design our own Lexus with just the specific accessories we want.

To review, we've covered three important points about wants (there is also a fourth, how we form them—to be presented later). Wants:

1. Infinite specific individual preferences, based on one or more of the five basic needs.
2. The particular motivators of our actions, our behavior.
3. Quality, by definition, is that which most thoroughly matches our strongest wants.

Glasser refers to wants as quality world pictures or pictures in our heads of ideal people, situations, and things. He explains that it's like we have this photo album in our head where we keep all of our quality world reference pictures, what I call our wants. But prior to putting a specific picture in the album, there is a silhouette, a vague idea of the kinds of things we'd like for satisfying our needs.

When we're born, we are born with the needs. We need to be loved and to belong. We may have a silhouette of the ideal person, but not until we meet and experience our needs getting met by this person do we put his or her particular picture in our album. When we find that we want to be around this individual more than anyone else, it's because he or she is so need satisfying. Once that happens, his or her picture has been put into our album, in place of the silhouette. Now it's that person we want. As you can imagine, moms and dads, the primary caregivers and need satisfiers, get put into the photo album fairly quickly.

We may come pre-wired to have certain preferences for types of people, power, fun, freedom, and food, but it's through experiences that we actually lock someone, or something, in as being the specific want.

We're exposed to many people as babies: siblings, grandparents, aunts, uncles, cousins, and friends. What are the particulars that have to fall into place before we'll lock in a specific person as a preference? My belief is that there are three particulars: clarity, attainability, and payoff. The next chapter covers this more thoroughly, especially in the context of managing people, but the reason it works in management is because it's the natural way we've been developing preferences since birth.

This brings us to the fourth point about our wants or preferences. We develop wants by experiencing someone, or something that meets A-HA! Performance Intrinsic Motivation Point 3, which is the CAP criteria: clarity, attainability, and payoff (explained more fully in Chapter 4). Once we experience a person, situation, or thing that is clear, attainable, and satisfies our needs in a powerful way (produces a great or wow feeling), we'll lock in that person or thing as a strong preference or want.

So how do we first develop our preferences naturally, and how do we use that knowledge as managers to get the people we work with to develop preferences for the tasks we want them to do?

We develop a want naturally because, having experienced it:

- It's clear.
- We know it was attainable at least once, so it should be again.
- The wow or great feeling was a wonderful payoff. At least one, probably more, of the needs was satisfied.

A romantic movie is a great platform to see this process in action. Boy walks into the room, girl enters from the other side. Everything goes into slow motion and soft focus, except the girl. She's well lit and crystal clear—clarity achieved. She looks at him, smiles, stops, and gives him enough of a look so that he thinks, "Wow, big possibilities here." Attainability or the belief that something can happen is locked in.

And then the music, the heartstrings amplified that reveal to the audience there is a wow that happened when their eyes met. His mouth dropping open is another clue. There is big payoff to being around this person. And so the puzzle has come together: clarity, attainability, payoff. The boy now wants to be with the girl.

And the rest of the movie follows a plot where the boy wants that girl and begins a series of sometimes effective, sometimes ineffective, sometimes funny, sometimes tragic attempts (behaviors) to win her . . . the chase is on. They even have a moment where boy starts to give up, maybe stops wanting the girl because something happens where he gets the false idea that she doesn't like him, that she isn't attainable anymore. But then, just in time, the misunderstanding is cleared up and boy and girl get together.

So how do wants get locked in? Through experiencing something that meets that CAP criteria: clear, attainable, payoff. It's very hard to want something we've never heard of or experienced before.

If we've never been in a leadership position, for example, how are we going to know that we'll like it? We may have a silhouette of leadership in our album, a fuzzy picture of just how great it could be, but until we've experienced it at some level, it's hard to lock it in with any specificity. If we then thrive as a leader, if we like it, that silhouette will turn into a specific preference around wanting to run a certain type of business, to play a particular leadership role and delegate other roles (ones that we don't want) to other people. All three pieces of that puzzle have to lock together before we want something. And experience is the natural way for that to happen, or not happen.

How many parents say that until they became one, they had no idea how much they'd like it? Through experience, we develop wants.

How do companies leverage this natural process to get potential customers to buy their products? They give out free samples of their product. They want potential customers to experience how satisfying that product is and to want more of it. They want people to place a picture, a mental picture, of that product in their internal photo album as their preference. Marketing is all about getting a company's product to be "top of mind," the number one want. In other words, companies want potential customers to prefer their product, to want their product more than they want the competition's version of it. If they can get people, through experience, to be clear about their product, realize that it's very attainable, and to experience a wow payoff (tastes great, does the job great, makes us more attractive to others, is fun) then we'll want it. How did that campaign for Alka-Seltzer go? "Try it, you'll like it!"

Why do companies have their best people interview highly qualified job candidates for key positions and bring these qualified individuals in for a tour of the facility, and wine and dine them and their spouses? They want that candidate to place the picture of working for their organization in their quality world photo album. They want that candidate to want to choose to work for them but they know that before that candidate will accept a job offer (take action), he or she has to want to accept that job. Organizations court prospects in an attempt to get that candidate to want to work there.

So preferences get into our heads through experience that produces clarity, a belief in attainability, and a wow payoff, a great feeling that comes from need satisfaction.

Before moving on, remember these four points about *wants:*

1. Based on five general needs, we develop a wide variety of specific wants.
2. These wants are the particular motivators of our actions, our behavior. The wants are the conscious reasons we do anything. Before output, but based on the needs, we have a want.
3. Quality, by definition, is that which most thoroughly matches our strongest wants. Wants are our preferences for meeting our needs and when we find someone or something that matches our wants, we perceive that person, situation, or thing as quality.
4. We develop wants or preferences by experiencing someone, or something that meets A-HA! Performance Intrinsic Motivation Point 3, the CAP criteria: clarity, attainability, and payoff. Once we experience a person, situation, or thing that satisfies our needs in a powerful way (produces a great or wow feeling) we'll lock in that person or thing as a strong preference or want. We do that because, having experienced it:
   - It's clear.
   - We know it was attainable at least once, so it should be again.
   - The wow or great feeling was a wonderful payoff. At least one of the needs was satisfied.

Summation

Wants are our specific preferences for meeting our needs. They are the not-at-all-hidden fundamentals of all behavior; what we do, we do to achieve a want. Wants, unlike the needs, are changeable, re-placeable. We're willing to reset our wants when something new is Clear, believed to be Attainable, and Pays Off better than a current want is paying off. This knowledge gives us a real edge in building and managing a self-motivated workforce. After all, when employees want to take action for their own reasons, they are intrinsically mo-tivated to perform.

4

CAP: Aligning, Setting, and Managing Self-Motivation

When I first greet my audience at A-HA! Performance trainings, instead of saying, "Good morning," I begin with, "Be honest. How many of you drove here today thinking to yourself, 'Gosh, I hope he lets us sing!' ?" As you can imagine, if any hands go up at all, it's only one or two.

So I point out that we have a very interesting management challenge here: The manager, in this case, me, wants to get 100 percent of the team participating in this song and only very few early adapters want to do it. So I suggest we try the Nike approach.

I pull out a guitar from behind the podium, and say, "Okay, here we go, let's all just do it," and I start singing a song no one has ever heard of before. No one is singing with me. So I stop after about two lines, point out that no one is singing, and ask, "How come?"

"We don't know the words," one participant will say.

"So if I teach you the words and the tune, how many of you will be ready to join in?" I usually pick up one or two people here . . . not many. Still, I make my point: Even those who are willing to sing can't do what I want them to do if they don't know the song.

"Anytime we want to get people to do what we want them to do," I continue, "we'll have to put three pieces of a puzzle together. If I don't put these three pieces together, you won't do what I'd like you to do. In fact, anytime people are not doing what we want them to do, we can take a look at these three pieces of the buy-in puzzle.

"The first piece of the puzzle is clarity. You can't sing a song you don't know. For most of us, it's very difficult to hit a target we can't see" (see Figure 4.1).

My job at this point is to teach this audience the song I want them to perform, not just tell them, but teach them. Teaching includes telling, but more than that, it often requires demonstrating or showing them as well as giving them a chance to try it out for themselves. It meets the hear-see-do criteria for new learning.

So the first base that I have to cover, and that any manager has to cover in getting buy-in, is clarity—what, who, when, and where.

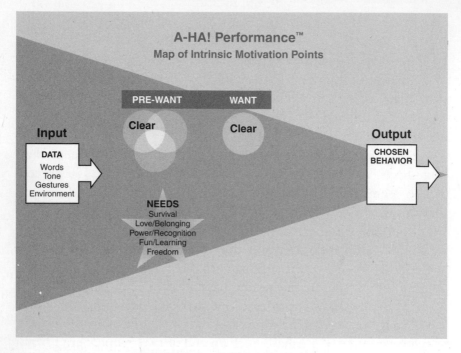

FIGURE 4.1   IMP 3—CAP: Clear

For some, that's all they need. They like singing, they like having fun and being part of a group activity. They just need to know what the leader wants, and they are ready to go. They are ready because, whether we've discussed them or not, the other two pieces of the puzzle are already in place. For others (and it's always true in the performance of this song exercise), they need more than clarity; they need one or both of the other two pieces put in place as well.

The next piece of the puzzle is attainability. Before people will do what we want them to do, they have to believe they can do it. So at the trainings, I ask, "Are any jaws wired shut?" This eliminates any "can't" excuses. Unless their voices don't work or mouths don't open, what I'm asking them to do is possible (see Figure 4.2).

Then I ask, "Now that you know it's attainable, how many are ready to join in?" I still get only a smattering of hands.

"What's the third piece?" I ask. "It's the what's-in-it-for-me (WIIFM) component, the payoff piece. And the payoff for you to

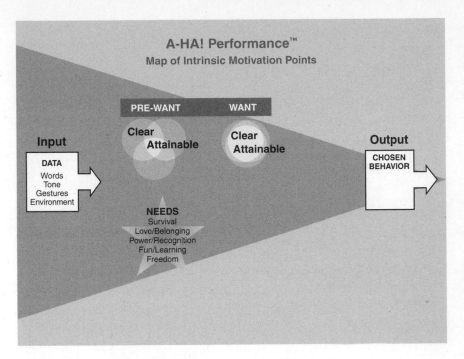

FIGURE 4.2   IMP 3—CAP: Attainable

join in has to be greater than the cost, or you won't join in" (see Figure 4.3)

Next I go into a series of options for people in an effort to reduce or eliminate the cost to them of joining in. "Some of you are saying, 'There's no way I'm going to sing, I tried singing out loud once in second grade and my teacher encouraged me to do that only in the shower at home.' So if you don't want to sing, would you be comfortable rapping or speaking the song?" I proceed to play the guitar and talk a line or two as an example (remember, hear and see), and then I ask again for volunteers. A few more hands go up, but not all.

I then ask "how many would be comfortable being part of the performance by lip-syncing the song?" By this time, most hands go up. Some will sing, some will rap or talk, and the rest will at least lip-sync. The point is that I've removed the cost of singing and offered people a safe way to be a part of the activity.

In the event that there are still people who are hesitant to join in, I say, "I know, some of you are holding out for kazoos." You'll

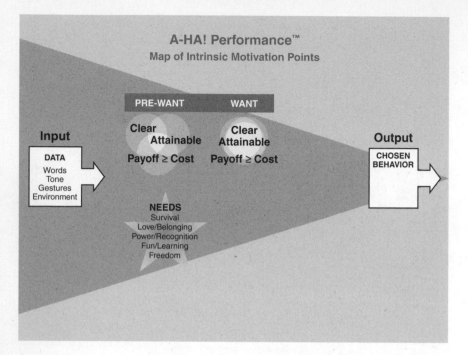

FIGURE 4.3   IMP 3—CAP: Payoff

have to attend a training to see how that unfolds, but the bottom line is, within eight minutes or so we've gone from no one wanting to be a part of the performance to everyone being willing to join in.

Clarity, attainability, payoff ≥ Cost (CAP)

Put all three of those pieces together and people will want to do what we want them to do.

Fail to put all three pieces together, and they won't. If they want to join in, they will. If they don't want to, they won't.

Wants precede performance. CAP is the formula for setting wants.

When the three pieces of this CAP puzzle—clear, attainable, and payoff—come together around new levels of performance, people will want to achieve those levels enough to do something about it.

When people are not doing what we want them to do, one or more of those pieces is missing.

Whenever we're not getting the behavior we want out of another person, a simple assessment exercise is to ask which piece of the CAP puzzle is missing. Have we not been clear enough for them in our request? Do they not believe they can do what we're asking? Is the cost for them to do it greater than the payoff? If we can cover these three pieces, then we can get a want locked in, and once we can get people to want what we want them to want, it will always lead to performance toward that want.

The better we get at utilizing this CAP Intrinsic Motivation Point (IMP), the better we'll be at getting buy-in and action from others.

Whether we are managing down, up, or sideways, our ability to get buy-in and desired performance from others is directly related to our ability to cover these bases.

While CAP is my preference for remembering these essentials used for getting buy-in from others, another way to think about them is: What (Clarity)? How (Attainability)? Why (Payoff)? Whether we think CAP or what, how, and why, our requests should cover these three points or we're unlikely to get the compliance we seek.

If we are managing sideways—trying to get our peers to do something we'd like them to do—we'll be most successful at getting their buy-in if they know what we think should be happening, how it could happen, and why it should happen.

If we are managing up—trying to get our bosses or upper management to buy into a proposal of ours—our proposal should be:

- Clear (Concise and complete are great companions of clarity.)
- Attainable (The organization would need to have the talent, resources, and systems to make it happen, and the bosses would have to be convinced that success was possible in their environment or marketplace.)
- Payoff ≥ Cost (If this is going to cost the organization more than it brings in, it's probably not going to be a proposal that leadership adopts.)

An added feature of mastering this CAP puzzle is that if we want someone to stop doing something, we can utilize this CAP knowledge, but in reverse. We know that if someone is doing something, they want the results that the particular doing will produce. If they want those results, then in their mind, the results meet the CAP criteria. They are clear, believed to be attainable, and payoff for that person. To get them to stop doing, we have to get them to stop wanting.

We can learn to remove one or more of these CAP pieces from the person's current thinking, thereby getting her to "un-want" it. We can try to convince her that the cost of what she's doing is greater than the payoff, that it's not attainable, or that the goal is not as clear as she thinks it is. In other words, take one or more pieces out of that CAP puzzle and the person will stop wanting it, and therefore stop behaving to get it.

The three CAP pieces can be covered in any order. Let's say an employee knows the payoff for doing what her boss wants her to do. Perhaps it's job satisfaction, she's good at what she does and likes being recognized and appreciated for her work. Payoff is about satisfaction of the needs and can come in a variety of ways, but let's say in this case that it is covered. Let's also assume that she believes the task must be attainable or else her boss wouldn't have asked her to do it; she also has faith in her ability to take on new challenges and get them done. But there's one component she is missing: She doesn't understand what it is her boss wants. It's not clear.

Clarity

Not too long ago, I chatted with a man who owns a business in a suburb of San Diego, where they make those giant inflatable objects that sit atop of buildings as advertising for businesses, as well as the inflatable jumps often rented for kids' parties. He had a client who ordered one and asked that it be designed as a big scary dragon. So this owner constructed the dragon, then went to his number one artist and told him to paint the scary face on it. Well, the artist kept delivering the wrong look. He just couldn't paint the face right, which really means he couldn't paint the face that the owner had in mind. The owner was so frustrated. "This kid just can't get it right," he lamented.

Remember, if someone isn't doing what we want him to do, one or more pieces of the CAP puzzle have not come together. So I talked my friend through the three pieces. I asked, "What's the payoff for him to get this done right? Does he have pride in his work? Is he getting paid enough? Does he like doing his part for the team?" His response was yes to everything—the designer wants to please and he's happy with his compensation.

Then I asked, "Is it attainable? Does he have the airbrush, the paints, the computer program, the skill-set, the budget, and everything else he needs?" Again, the answer was yes—the owner even said that this kid was the most talented artist he'd ever worked with. Skills and resources weren't the problem.

That left one question: "Is it clear what you mean by a scary face? Have you sketched it out for him?" That question seemed to hit him with the force of a blow to his chest.

"No." he said, "I just keep telling him scary. I've never sketched it out for him. I guess I thought he should just know what a scary face was." The word "scary" meant two different things to those two different people and until a shared clarity was covered, the artist could not possibly (well, maybe accidentally) paint the picture that only the owner had clearly in his mind.

> Communicating the job accurately and completely is a key aspect to putting the CAP puzzle together.

If an employee is trying, but doing it wrong, then we can assume she believed it was attainable and that there was a payoff for her to do it, but her understanding of what the manager wanted was incorrect.

Attainability

If an employee doesn't believe the task is possible—if she believes it's unattainable—then desired performance won't occur either. Attainability is about a belief that something is possible; that's what drives behavior. It doesn't matter whether something is or isn't possible. What matters is the person's belief.

How many attempts did Thomas Edison make before the light bulb worked? He is said to have tried over 6,000 different carbonized plant fibers, looking for a carbon filament for his light bulb. Why didn't he give up? He believed it was possible to create a light bulb that worked, that's why.

In 1960, when President John Kennedy declared that we would put a man on the moon by the end of the decade, it was clear and there was an obvious payoff to beating the Russians, to being first, but the piece that had to have been in place for us to accomplish landing a man on the moon in 1969 was attainability. The scientists and engineers who worked on that project believed it was attainable and thus made it happen.

Here's another example about the importance of having our employees believe in attainability if we want buy-in and action. Years ago, when TWA was last in their market in on-time arrival—tenth out of 10 airlines—Dan Tegel, PhD, was hired to see if he could help. Dan and I met several years ago while serving as consultants at the same company. He was doing the process redesign work there, while I was doing the A-HA! Performance individual coaching piece and we connected almost instantly. In fact, I created the A-HA! Performance Quick-Hits Process Redesign application for managers to use in improving the quality or efficiencies their teams produce based on Dan's Breakthrough Process Redesign.

When Dan's engagement at TWA was finished, TWA had gone from tenth to first in on-time arrival, contributing to a $50 million savings in costs in the first year alone. But in the beginning, Dan, who went on to serve as the head of 6 Sigma at Motorola, could only manage to get the TWA team to aspire to going from tenth to fifth in on-time arrival. The team wasn't even sure tenth to fifth was attainable, let alone tenth to first. People were saying, "From tenth to fifth? What an achievement that would be! We think we might be able to do that." So when Dan suggested they reach for the number one slot—not surprisingly—they were resistant. They simply didn't think it was possible and thus didn't buy into trying. Being first was clear, and the payoff would be huge, but the missing piece was the belief that it was possible.

It took some time, but Dan's paradigm-busting exercise helped the team discard faulty assumptions and replace them with accurate ones about real options they had, and they began to believe they might be able to achieve first in on-time arrival. They became convinced that they had the same resources as their competitors, and that by deploying those resources differently, they could become number one. And that was the clincher. The moment the team members understood they had the talent and the resources, they began to believe that being number one in their market was attainable. Changes in both effort and results started happening, almost like magic after that.

This is what attainability is about: believing that something is possible. There are people, like the fictional Don Quixote, who dream the impossible dream, who battle windmills, who go after impossible things because they believe it's possible to attain them. The belief is what matters when it comes to driving behavior.

So as managers, we'd be well advised to work on convincing our employees that the desired results are possible so that they will engage in the required tasks. Busting assumptions that things aren't possible and challenging beliefs that they can't achieve something is sometimes what this exercise is about. In fact, anytime we hear the word "can't," remember that the can't belief is based on a set of assumptions—likely an erroneous set of assumptions and faulty paradigms that keep us from realizing something is attainable.

It's our belief about attainability that plays a key role in determining whether or not we'll act.

If we're addressing the attainability piece with employees, some questions we can ask include exploring whether enough of the A-HA! Performance 10 Es are in place to be able to accomplish what we're asking people to do. The 10 Es are:

1. Expertise
2. Experience
3. Equipment
4. Education
5. Empowerment
6. Ethics
7. Expenses
8. Energy
9. Enthusiasm
10. Environment

To convince people that what we're asking them to do is attainable, we can demonstrate that they have the expertise and the experience needed. Then take a look at the equipment and tools available to determine whether or not we have what's needed. If employees don't have the expertise, maybe education or training could be provided. And what about empowerment? Does the individual have the permission and delegated authority? Are lack of ethics in any way thwarting the attainability? Do we have the expenses covered; is the budget adequate? How do the energy and enthusiasm levels measure up—does the individual have enough to do the job? And, is the task possible in that particular environment?

Payoff

The third piece of the CAP puzzle is payoff—which must be greater than or equal to the cost of getting something, or we won't put forth the effort to try to get it.

Payoff is about need satisfaction.

Think about a wow moment from your life. The good feelings wows produce are the payoff we get for satisfying our needs. The times we satisfy them best are the wow times. When love, power, fun, freedom, and survival needs are met to the max, we experience a wow. When they are frustrated of course, we experience ow.

So if payoff is about need satisfaction, how do we leverage that when trying to get buy-in to new and better performance?

I got insight into ways to tie performance requests to employee need satisfaction from my son Todd when he was about five years old. It was the end of the day and getting close to bedtime. I was upstairs and wanted him to come and take his bath. "Todd!" I called to him. It took a couple of repetitions, each louder than the last, but after about the fourth call, he finally replied, "What Dad?"

"It's time for you to come up and take your bath," and what I wanted him to say was, "Well certainly, Dad, I'll be right up."

Although he didn't say that, he didn't really argue or resist either. He simply asked, in a very reasonable tone, "Why should I, Dad?" The old, WIIFM, what's-in-it-for-me? And it occurred to me that there are really only four possible answers to that question. Two are based on avoiding pain, two on approaching pleasure.

1. Avoiding the Pain of Force (Figure 4.4)

I could have said, "You should come up here and get yourself into the bathtub so that I don't come down there, pick up your little body, carry it upstairs, and put it in the bathtub for you." In other words, he should do it to avoid force. Do people like to be forced by other people to do things? Not really. Will we sometimes comply with a request in an effort to avoid being forced? Sometimes we will; sometimes we'll risk our lives resisting it. Payoff is about satisfying or protecting our needs. Because our needs are the hidden fundamentals of motivation—the ultimate reasons we actually do anything—sometimes the payoff

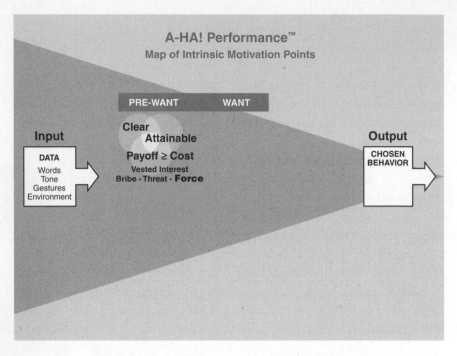

FIGURE 4.4 Pathways to Need Payoff: Force

for doing something has to do more with protecting our needs, than satisfying them.

Force frustrates all of our needs. When someone else physically controls us, we don't have the ability to move around to get what we need. Assuming we are being overpowered physically, we'll be going wherever that force takes us. It could be life threatening if we're restrained without the ability to get to water or food for a long period of time. We may comply to keep that from happening. We do have to protect our survival need.

Force frustrates our love and belonging needs too. When we're being moved against our will to a place we don't want to go, we're not feeling the love. Although a loving parent may physically restrain a young child to keep her from touching an electric socket or running into the street, the child rarely appreciates being forced at the time.

When we're being overpowered, our power needs are also frustrated; our ability to achieve our own purposes is shut down. We feel powerless. It's the opposite of winning, and losing isn't the way we meet our power needs.

Fun needs take a beating when force is applied. With the possible exception of some deviants in our society, there's nothing most of us find fun about being physically forced to do something. Force frustrates our freedom needs. Being restrained is the antithesis of being free. Being picked up and held in, or transported to, a destination we didn't choose frustrates our liberty (physical freedom) and our choices (mental freedom).

Because force is so threatening to all of our needs, the frequent counter is to struggle against it. Fight it or get away from it. We see that outcome when force is applied in homes, and with police or military force, too. People don't like it. It frustrates and threatens their needs past the point of toleration and they fight back with force of their own to try to escape or oppose it. Force is applied to get people to do something. And if people are fighting back or running away instead of doing what we want them to do, then the force isn't working.

Still, it was a possible answer to my son's question, "Why should I, Dad?" I could have said, "So I won't force you." But I didn't want to deal with the probable repercussions, so I passed on that option.

Force is an answer available to parents, to the military, and to our police forces, but it's not really available to managers in the workplace. Not only does it not work well in the workplace, but there are also way too many attorneys around, at least in the United States. The cost to managers for using force in the workplace is too much. It's clear and may be attainable, but the cost outweighs the payoff so managers don't want to do it. It doesn't pass the CAP test. It certainly didn't for me as I stood at the top of the stairs thinking about my son's question.

2. Avoiding the Pain of Threat (Figure 4.5)

If I was not going to use force to get him into the tub, I could still use threat. I could still say some version of, "Do it, or I'll hurt you in some way." As a parent, my typical options included: I'll be mad at you, I'll ground you, or I'll take something away from you that you like. Threats, like force, are aimed at frustrating the

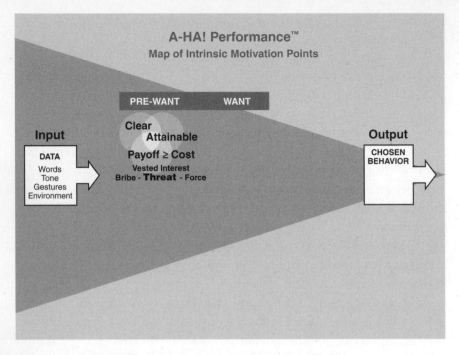

FIGURE 4.5 Pathways to Need Payoff: Threat

needs unless the targeted person complies. There is a payoff to protecting the needs. If you do what I tell you to do, your needs won't be frustrated.

Plenty of frustrated managers go right to the stick or threat approach. Coercion is the first choice of many, not necessarily because it's been well thought through, more likely because it somehow feels like it should work. But the fact is that it doesn't work that well, especially over time. People want to avoid the threat all right, but eventually decide to avoid it by getting away from the one who's doing the threatening. There are lots of ways managers can threaten or hurt people. They use sanctions that frustrate employee needs in a variety of ways: I'll fire you, I'll take you off that project, I'll demote you, I'll put you on probation, or I'll embarrass you verbally by dressing you down in front of others. The bottom line is, it's still a form of "Do it, or I'll hurt you." Businesses have institutionalized this approach in the form of sanctioned performance improvement plans (PIPs) that keep the company compliant with laws and regulations, but are still well articulated ways to hurt people when they don't comply.

The problem with using threats on people is; people don't like to be threatened. When threatened, we protect or defend. If we believe that obeying is the best way to protect or defend our needs, then we might obey enough to get by, at least until we can figure out a better way to get away from or neutralize that threat. Managers who use threats hope that we'll choose to protect our needs or avoid the pain of their threats by complying with their edicts or instructions. But we may have our own ideas about how we're going to protect our needs and compliance may not be among the ones we're considering.

Often employees don't comply when threatened, and when they do, never to the level of those motivated by their own sense of pride, joy, or team responsibility. Sometimes they may appear to be complying with a management threat, but what they're actually doing is quite different than what the manager intended. Sometimes it's subtle sabotage, done with a smile, hard to detect until things fall apart down the road. Sometimes it's saying the requisite "yes" then making no changes at all. Sometimes employees counterattack by going to human resources, an attorney, or to their union. Sometimes they go into push-back or active resistance mode. Threatened employees often try to undermine the manager's authority or simply go into passive resistance or avoid mode where they withdraw from active engagement in their work and do the minimum to get by. Or they quit.

If threats are our primary way to address and impact people's needs, and if payoff is only about protecting a threatened need, then retention will become a huge issue.

Employees will seek work environments where their needs are not constantly threatened or frustrated; they'll seek work environments where their needs can be satisfied.

And as retention is a growing concern in a shrinking workforce, coercion, sticks, or threats will be less effective and less acceptable ways to cover the payoff piece of the puzzle. Yet to some managers, if they don't have sticks, they have nothing. "How can I manage without negative sanctions?" some ask. Remember, those internal motivators are far more powerful and more omnipresent than any manager's stick could ever be.

I could have used a threat with my son and said, "Get up here and take your bath or I'm going to take your toys away." But after considering the flaws with that choice, I decided to consider my other options. There had to be a better way.

3. Approach the Pleasure Promised in a Bribe (Figure 4.6)

In addition to the avoid pain options (force or threat) of payoff, there are also two approach pleasure options. Bribe is one.

I could have said, "If you'll come up here and take your bath, I'll give you some M&M's." But the problem is that bribes

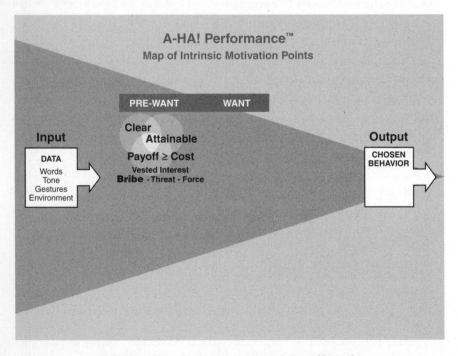

FIGURE 4.6 Pathways to Need Payoff: Bribe

are also short-lived. While M&M's might work this time, he'll demand more the next time I want him to take his bath. He'll want peanut butter cups for a while, then Godiva chocolates, and then the whole candy store. Getting the bribe just right is problematic.

Bribes work in the short term, and are effective at getting strangers to do what we want them to do, such as giveaways at trade shows or free products for consumer purchases.

> But bribing people we live or work with stops working over the long term.

Glasser calls bribes positive coercion and Dr. Thomas Gordon, author of the Effectiveness Training books: *Leader Effectiveness Training, Parent Effectiveness Training, Teacher Effectiveness Training,* called them seduction. The workplace calls them incentives or carrots, and they are utilized when managers feel they must sweeten the deal in order to get the performance they need from the people they manage.

Glasser, tells about people involved in county fairs who train little piglets to climb a ladder and slide down a slide. When the piglets slide down the slide, they trip a little lever and receive little piggy M&M's (or some equivalent). But what the trainers found was that the piglets would only go through the effort of climbing and sliding for about three months. After that, they just wouldn't do it. Glasser's explanation was that even piglets have a certain *pignity* and that they just won't allow the trainers to make a fool of them any longer for the extrinsic reward of a treat. The treat wasn't enough to get to the internal satisfiers of power, freedom, belonging, survival, and fun.

At the top of the stairs, I knew that, like the piglets, Todd would begin to resent being positively coerced, or seduced, into behavior he really didn't want to do and he'd keep upping his price if he were going to be willing to do it at all. I moved on to the only other option I had: Vested Interest.

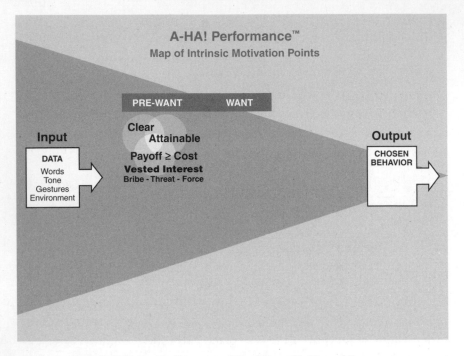

FIGURE 4.7 Pathways to Need Payoff: Vested Interest

4. Approach the Biggest Pleasure of All: His Own Vested Interest (Figure 4.7)

Most managers don't seem to know about this practical option. Not only do they not know that the vested interest approach exists and is viable, they don't realize that it is a more powerful one than carrots or sticks. So when managers have performance problems, discussion usually focuses on what they know: carrots or sticks.

Vested interest as an alternative to carrots and sticks is a major a-ha for a lot of people. Not only that, it's also a major differentiator for the A-HA! Performance approach. In one eight-week course on A-HA! Performance, students emphasized that vested interest was one of the a-has that made this course "transformational" for them. "Once you learn it," one said, "you can't not use it." I like that one. Worthy of Yogi Berra. "Once you learn it, you can't not use it!"

While carrots and sticks are indirect or extrinsic attempts to satisfy or threaten the needs, vested interest approaches are direct or intrinsic approaches to satisfying the needs.

Carrots and sticks are extrinsic satisfiers and frustrators of the needs; vested interest is intrinsic satisfaction or frustration of the needs.

A vested interest focus attempts to tie the desired task directly to need satisfaction. Vested interest payoff is the reason people volunteer their time to worthy causes.

I have a friend, Craig Blower, who goes to Children's Hospital every Wednesday evening as a volunteer. Does anyone force him to go? Nope. Threaten him that if he doesn't go, they'll hurt him in some way? No. How about a bribe? Does anyone offer him M&M's if he'd be willing to give every Wednesday, no matter what, to those kids? No. None of those motivators would have the power to get him to give up holidays that happen to fall on Wednesdays, or to go no matter what kind of a day he's been having. He goes because he feels good about going. And he feels good about going and helping others because it's need satisfying.

When we do things that satisfy needs directly, we're doing them for our own vested interest. Those are the things we do voluntarily—no force, no threat, and no bribe.

So there I was at the top of the stairs having asked my son to come up and take his bath. With vested interest in mind, I knew that if I could tie what I wanted him to do to his own need satisfaction, I wouldn't have to provide the force, the threat, or the bribe.

"You should take a bath because good hygiene leads to good health which is tied to your survival needs." Well, okay, I didn't use that one on a five-year-old, but it's true. Do it because it's healthy.

"You should take a bath because clean-smelling boys are easier to be around and love than stinky boys are, and being loved meets your belonging needs." I didn't say that either, but I did tie my answer to this need. I offered to stay with him in the bathroom while he took his bath. Adding a social element to the task often makes it better.

Doing something where we are likely to meet our love and belonging needs in the process, even if it requires effort, is worth it. At five, most children still like to be around their parents. And in the workplace, relationships are important, too. High performers often do what they do to support a great boss or to contribute to a super team.

"You should take a bath because big boys take their own baths without even having anyone remind them that it's time." With this effort, I was trying to tie my want to his power needs. Lots of recognition, too, goes a long way. "I was just talking to Granddaddy and telling him how many things you can do on your own now, he was so proud of you." Or, "Your sister said you weren't big enough to take a bath on your own, but I think you are. What do you think?" Meeting a challenge and achieving purpose is a common pathway to meeting the power need.

"You should take a bath because it's fun. We've got all those bath toys in there; you can use bubble bath, and draw on the tub with that soap chalk." My Uncle Maury once said, "Fun is more fun when you accomplish something." He was right. Meeting fun needs and power needs is a double win, but the reverse is also true: accomplishing something is more satisfying when it's fun, too. Do it for fun.

"You should take a bath because of all the choices you have. Do you want a bath or a shower? Bubble bath or no bubble bath? Soap chalk, toy boats, or a rubber ducky?" If I take away his freedom as to whether to take a bath, I'd be wise to offer other freedoms as replacements.

One machine shop improved production and revenue dramatically by allowing machine operators to choose their own machines, rather than having a purchasing agent make the decision on price. Freedom to choose. Do it because you have lots of options.

In the end, to get a person to do what we want him to do, we first have to get him to want to do it. To get him to want to do it, we have to CAP our request.

Clarity is about the details of the desired end state.

Attainability is about the belief that the end state is possible.

Payoff is about need satisfaction, or need protection, as reasons to pursue that end state.

The four pathways to the needs when covering payoff are vested interest, bribes, threats, and force. Bribes, often called carrots, and threats, known as sticks, are alive and well in workplaces and homes around the world. But when we use the vested interest approach, people will do what we're asking them to do because it feels good; it satisfies their needs intrinsically. As the most powerful of the options, vested interest is an a-ha for many of us, and because of its superior results, it's one well worth learning.

Summation

Locking together the three pieces of the CAP puzzle is what buy-in is about. It's how we get employees to want to perform the tasks we believe need to be done. Once we really grasp the CAP buy-in puzzle, we can leverage it to both spark motivation and thwart it, when necessary. The magic is in getting our employees to want what we want them to want because it's clear to them, they believe it's attainable, and their own needs will be satisfied in the process (Figure 4.8).

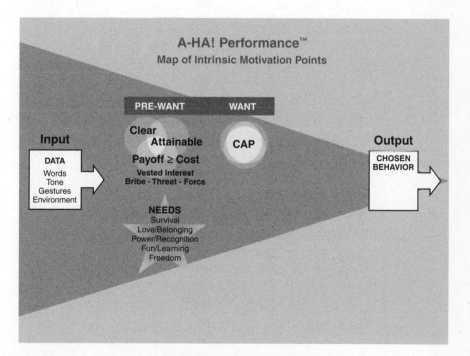

FIGURE 4.8 IMP 3—CAP

5

Got: Our Baseline for Knowing Where We Are Relative to Any Given Want

Have you ever engaged in a conversation, probably in high school or college, about whether the basic nature of human beings is good or evil? The arguments almost never convince others to change their minds. Some claim people are one way, some the other, but whichever way the argument is made, the counter to it is: "Well if people are basically evil, how do we explain a Gandhi or a Mother Theresa?" And "if people are basically good, how do we explain Attila the Hun or who ever the leadership is of the group one's country is currently fighting?" There are plenty of examples of human heroics and just as many examples of human atrocities. Whether we label an act heroism or horrifying depends less on the act, then on the person doing it and the context in which it was done. So are people basically good . . . or basically bad?

I had participated in more than one discussion/argument on that question, never reaching a satisfying conclusion. I've finally decided that people are neither good nor bad, intrinsically, but that we are basically needy and that in an attempt to satisfy these unrelenting needs, we are capable of great good or great bad.

We have needs, based on those, an infinite variety of wants. The ones we act on are the ones that are clear, attainable, and have payoffs by meeting or protecting these needs. We satisfy needs by doing something to get what we want.

Whether what we do is classified as good or bad depends on how our behavior impacts needs; other peoples' and our own. Bad behavior, at least from the other person's point of view, is behavior we engage in that satisfies our needs while frustrating or negatively impacting theirs. It's when we gain at their expense. Good behavior, or at least acceptable behavior, is when we satisfy our needs without frustrating or negatively impacting the needs of others. Great behavior is when we meet our own needs while helping others meet theirs.

So what does that say about bad managing versus good or great managing? Bad managing is when we try to meet our needs or the company's needs by getting our employees to do things even at the expense of their own needs. They hate that and, if we continue doing this kind of managing, retention will be an impossible issue for us. Good or acceptable managing is when we try to get our employees to do things that meet our needs or the organization's needs in ways that at least don't frustrate their needs. Great managing, the focus of A-HA! Performance, is when we try to get our employees to do things that meet our needs and the organization's needs in ways that satisfy the employee's needs, too. Great managers don't have an issue with retention.

Whether we choose great managing behaviors, good ones or bad ones, we will do something to get our employees working toward achieving our goals, but the urgency with which we do what we do will be dependent on how close we are already to our goals. If we're pretty close, and not much change is needed, we may not feel the urgency we feel when we still have a way to go to achieve those goals. Knowing how close we are to getting what we want—to meeting our goals—is important if we are to gage the amount of effort still needed to get all the way there.

Knowing how close we are to getting what we want requires that we know A-HA! Performance Intrinsic Motivation Point 4— knowing what we've got. That sounds simple enough, but for a variety of reasons, we don't always know. Sometimes we don't know because we're just not paying attention. We occasionally get careless or reckless about keeping track of important things. That can be a critical or fatal mistake. If we don't know what we've got, we have no idea whether we're getting what we want (need) or not (Figure 5.1).

Most of us want a positive balance in our checking accounts. But how many of us have not known what the balance was or wrongfully assumed it was something other than what it really was at some particular point in our checking career? When we don't know what we've got, our decisions can cost us.

An extreme example of the danger of not knowing what we've got would be the relatively unknown condition called "congenital insensitivity to pain with anhidrosis," referred to by some as CIPA. What happens is our nervous system cannot tell us, through pain, that what we've got is a serious injury, causing us to behave in ways that make that injury dangerously worse.

The life expectancy of people with this condition isn't very long. But it's improving because of a growing awareness of the condi-

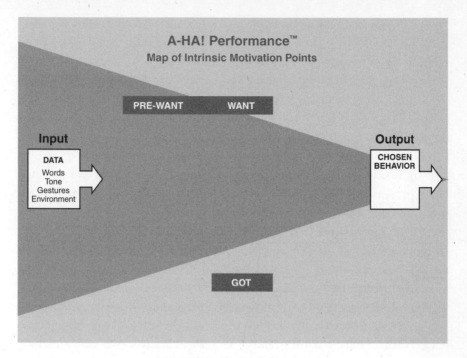

FIGURE 5.1 IMP 4—Got

tion, as well as resourceful remedies being developed that help overcome the body's inability to signal through pain when it has life-threatening conditions. Clearly, the challenges that come from not knowing what we've got are monumental—both for individuals and organizations.

Businesses sometimes lose customers. When they do, it's for a reason. The customer was dissatisfied with something, whether quality, efficiency, service, or price. If we don't know what we've got in terms of current levels of customer satisfaction, we may make a wrong assumption and neglect that customer. If we're not paying attention to what we've got in terms of customer satisfaction, we simply won't know enough to make the changes needed to preserve that customer relationship. The cost of losing a key customer can be substantial, sometimes enough to put us out of business.

What is the lifetime value of a single customer? It varies per industry, but it's always a lot more than most people realize. And customers bring value to our business in two ways: for the business they do with us and because of the other customers they send our way.

Delighted customers may tell 3 or 4 other prospective customers about us, while unhappy customers will warn 10 or 12 prospective customers never to do business with us—and sometimes they listen. So knowing what we've got is critical for success.

But knowing our current situation is easier said than done. Because it's so hard to "know what we've got," many assessment tools have been developed in an effort to help us know in a variety of areas. Hiring is one. We have assessment tools to help us know what we've got in terms of candidates for particular positions. If we Google "salesperson assessments," nearly 800,000 results come up. It's so difficult to know from a few conversations whether or not a new person is the right fit. These assessments were developed in an attempt to enhance our ability to quickly know what we've got before deciding what to do.

We also have a wide variety of 360 assessment instruments, which are designed to help managers and leaders know what they've got in terms of particular leadership competencies. By getting feedback from others through these 360 assessments, we get a clearer picture of what we've really got when it comes to those competencies. Without the feedback from up, down, and sideways, our belief about what's true may be skewed. Yet accurately knowing what we've got in terms of those competencies is crucial in deciding where to most effectively concentrate our development efforts.

Organizations that survey current levels of employee satisfaction understand that leadership has to know what it's got if it is going to know how to lead effectively. Our beliefs about what we've got, relative to what we want, influence how we proceed. Perceptyx is a good example of an organization that surveys employee satisfaction. Their business is based on helping leadership get real time, accurate information as to what they've got in a variety of employee satisfaction areas.

On their website, it reads, "Perceptyx understands that perceptions [beliefs about what we've got] affect attitudes. Attitudes behaviors. Behaviors performance. And performance success. We are masters in the fine art of corporate perception."

In other words, Perceptyx is rightfully recognizing that an accurate perception of what we've got is essential for making sound business and resource investment decisions.

There are plenty of assessments and tons of technology devoted to accurately letting us know what we've got—though, admittedly, sometimes we overdo it. A friend and mentor, Dick Hawes, shared a story with me once that illustrates this well. He told me about a man he knew and admired in Sacramento, Cotton Johnson, who made part of his living doing psychological testing. One psychiatrist in town sent all of his patients to Cotton for testing before he'd even meet with them. I imagine in the psychiatrist's mind, he wanted to be sure the "got" was covered; he wanted to know accurately what he was dealing with.

The psychiatrist sent one patient to visit Cotton because he suspected this patient had homosexual tendencies and he wanted to see if this psychological testing might bring that out. Because the testing took all day, during coffee breaks and a lunch break, Cotton and this patient chatted. By the end of the day, they were reasonably comfortable with each other so Cotton asked the man as he was leaving, "By the way, are you gay?"

"Yes. I am," the man replied.

After Cotton put together official reams of the assessment results, he then took out a blank sheet of paper and wrote across the top. "Cotton Johnson's Ask-a-Person Test. The Question: Are you gay? The Answer: Yes. I am. Conclusion: Tends to indicate the subject has homosexual tendencies."

The message? Sometimes good ol' fashioned asking does the trick. In-depth psychological testing or sophisticated business related surveys aren't the only means we have for determining what we've got.

> Accuracy in perception is the goal, not complexity in acquiring it.

Cotton Johnson's Ask-a-Person Test sometimes gets us the most accurate information in the least amount of time.

How do we know the truth of something? Some people want to see research data, some people know intuitively. I've come to believe that there are four ways to test the accuracy of a belief about what we've got. The successful application of all four points will probably yield the best results in determining the correctness of our beliefs about what's true. I call it my R2E2 Criteria:

1. Research
2. Reason
3. Experts
4. Experience

What does the research say? Is it reasonable; does it make sense? What do the experts say? Is it consistent with our experience? Each of us may have a preferred means for determining truth about what we've got, but the prudent person will utilize all four criteria to make up for the vulnerabilities of any particular one.

A-HA! Performance passes these tests. Research supports it over and over. The Gallup organization confirmed our needs for love and power when it identified a bad relationship with the manager as the number one reason employees leave an organization, and identified lack of recognition for contributions to the organization as number two. If love and power are needs that must be satisfied, and they aren't in a particular environment, people are going to leave and find a work environment where their needs can be met.

Reason supports A-HA!—the ideas are relentlessly logical. Experts in the field of human behavior support it, too. Glasser and Powers, of course, agree with the A-HA! Performance principles, and authors Steven Covey, Peter Senge, and W. Edwards Deming are saying very similar things as well.

While using the R2E2 Criteria will help illuminate what the current reality is, remember:

> People act, not on the facts, but on their belief about what the facts are. That's what the "got" is, it's our belief about what the facts are.

All of us come to conclusions about reality through our own unique set of filters. I'll address these filters in a later chapter, but for now, it's important to note that our perceptions are filtered ones, and are therefore subject to inaccuracies.

The stories about witnesses who offer differing accounts of the same event are evidence that our ability to know with certainty what we've got is not highly developed. Therefore, our proclivity to act on what we believe we've got and our inclination to argue that our perception is fact should be tempered by an awareness of the weakness of this skill in human beings.

When I was a kid growing up in the mid-1950s, Disney introduced us to Davy Crocket. A line attributed to Davy Crocket sums up what we're talking about here: "Be sure you're right, then go ahead." So we should be as certain as we can about what we think we've got before acting on it. The closer our belief is to what reality is the more effective we'll be in life and in the skill of managing others.

What we've got includes details: the what, who, where, and when. It also includes an internal judgment about whether or not those things are good or bad. So not only do we know what the situation is, we know how it impacts us. The total of what we believe we've got—in business and in our personal lives—always has some pluses, some neutrals, and some negatives, as things in our lives are either want/need satisfying, want/need neutral, or want/need frustrating or threatening. What's interesting is that the things we pay the most attention to are the things that are need frustrating—what seems "not right."

Occasionally things are so dire that finding anything positive seems to be impossible. Some lives seem to be filled with chronic pain; everything they've got, physiologically or psychologically, seems bad. Very few people, on the other hand, complain of chronic pleasure. But in order to maximize the good, we need to be keenly aware of the bad so that we can act in order to change it. If we are going to be successful in life or business, we need to know with as much certainty as possible what we've got.

If I'm a cook, I want to pay attention to what's simmering on the stove. If I have a baby, I want to pay attention to what's going on in the crib. If I'm a student, I'll want to pay attention to my grades. Knowing what we've got tells us how close we are to satisfying our wants, which of course is really all about satisfying our needs.

So if I'm a manager, what should I be paying attention to? Which are the most important things to keep track of? Which can sneak up and bite me if I'm not watching?

The details managers should pay attention to are the ones you may know as either the balanced score card or the service profit chain. We can think of the balanced score card or service profit chain as links in a chain that connect in the following way.

If we want the money, it comes from delighted customers. Customers are delighted by quality in a product or service. Can quality be delivered over time by disgruntled employees or only by gruntled employees? Only by gruntled (and it is a word, I looked it up) employees.

Whether we are the leader of the entire organization or the supervisor of a team, someone is paying something to keep us afloat. And all of us have to please or delight that someone in order to keep our piece of the funding going. In the for-profit world, the customer pays. In the nonprofit world, the funding source pays. Within companies, it's our boss who determines whether to continue to pay us or whether to increase what we're paid. If we want the money, we have to please and delight who ever that someone, the source or determiner of the funding, is.

So what have we got in terms of the money coming in and what have we got in terms of customer satisfaction or delight? We need to know these things. If the customer is upset and we don't know it, how would we know to rectify the situation? And if we don't rectify the situation, how much longer will that customer continue to give us the money?

If a customer is not happy, it's because the quality of the product or service we're producing is not what she wants. (The A-HA! Performance definition of quality is that it's the ideal want in the customer's head. The product or service matches or positively exceeds the customer's highest want.) So what's the current level of quality we've got to deliver to our customers? Are we delivering what they want? Are we exceeding their expectations and satisfying their dreams? Knowing whether we've got the kind of excellence that delights our customers will be the difference between correcting any deficiencies or failing to do so. If we think we've got what they want, or that it's "good enough," we won't do anything about it. We need to know if the quality we've got is the same as the quality our customers want.

> So for the money, delight the customer; to delight the customer, deliver the quality; and to deliver the quality, keep our employees gruntled.

An example of what disgruntled workers can do to adversely impact quality comes from one of the big three automakers. When some customers were bringing their cars back to the dealer, complaining of a rattle in the car door, the dealers would diagnose the problem by taking the door apart. What they saw was a bolt or nut sitting in there, not attached to anything, just free to roll and rattle as the car moved. But the catch is that it wasn't a bolt or nut that had come loose, it was there because a ticked-off worker had dropped it in there as a way of striking back at a boss who had treated him badly.

> A-HA! Performance Managers know about the needs and they know that employees come to us self-motivated to meet or protect those needs.

When this worker's power needs had been frustrated by a boss who embarrassed him—obviously not understanding the A-HA! Performance insights into managing a self-motivated workforce—he figured out a way to strike back and to even that power score. The worker was self-motivated, like all workers—self-motivated to meet and protect his needs.

So do you think that customers who have a rattle in a brand new car are going to return to the same automaker next time they purchase a car? Not likely.

If we want that money next time, we've got to delight the customer this time. To delight the customer this time, we've got to deliver rattle-free quality the first time.

> To deliver rattle-free quality the first time, we've got to treat our self-motivated workforce in a way that they can meet their own needs by meeting the customer's needs . . . which loops us back to how we meet our company's needs for revenue.

When companies have to enact major reductions in workforce, they try to retain the talent that is crucial in sustaining their ongoing ability to deliver quality products or services to customers. But in doing reductions in workforce, morale almost always suffers and companies have now come to expect that after a reduction in workforce, there will be some further attrition. And if the wrong people leave as part of the aftermath, such as the ones who delivered the quality the customers were willing to pay for, customer satisfaction and revenue generation take a hit.

How gruntled are our employees now? This is very important to know because disgruntled employees leave, under perform, or screw up. What have we got in terms of current levels of motivation and morale? It's extremely important to know what we've got in these areas or we won't take any corrective measures to make them what we want.

So:

- Take care of the employee (or the quality stops).
- Take care of the quality (or the customer leaves).
- Take care of the customer (or the money stops).

Summation

In building and managing a self-motivated workforce, knowing A-HA! Performance Intrinsic Motivation Point 4—which is what we've got— is critical if we want to make the midcourse corrections necessary to build and maintain success. We know and understand that we have to

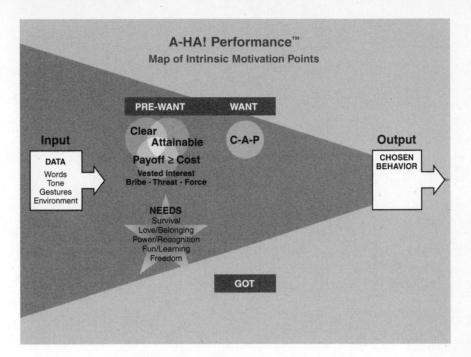

FIGURE 5.2   IMP 4—Got (in Context)

meet needs—the company's, the customers', the employees', and our own as managers. We also recognize that we all have particular goals, wants, or preferences for meeting those needs. But unless we know clearly what we've got, we won't know whether we're meeting those goals, getting what we want, experiencing our preferences, and satisfying our needs . . . or not (see Figure 5.2).

6

The Gap and the GapZap: Underwhelmed, Overwhelmed, Whelmed Just Right

How do "want" and "got" interact to initiate a behavior? When want and got match, life is good because we are getting what we want and don't have a problem. But when want and got do not match—when there is a gap between them—we do have a problem . . . or an opportunity. All problems and opportunities are gaps between something we want and something we've got. Whenever there is a significant enough gap between want and got, there will be a signal within our brain, a zap—felt as pressure or urgency to act, to do something quickly or methodically to maximize that opportunity or to solve that problem; to close that gap. Remember, gaps between a want and a got are what provide the energy, the GapZap, that drives all behavior (Figure 6.1).

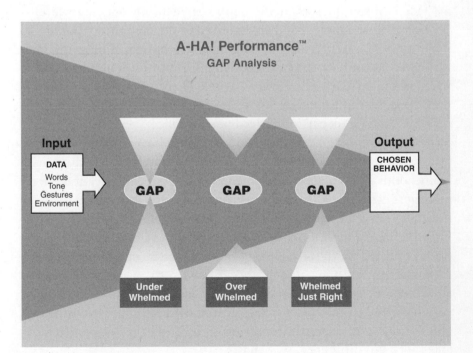

FIGURE 6.1 IMP 5—Gap and the Three Whelms

No gap, no behavior.

Gaps come in all sizes. We experience small insignificant challenges and irritations and huge dramatic debilitating dilemmas. As a gap widens between something we want and what we've got, increasing amounts of energy are added to the impulse to do something about it. When the gap is small, we may be aware that there's an issue, but we're underwhelmed by it. The gap doesn't generate enough energy—enough of a zap—to make us do anything.

On the other hand, if the gap is too wide and we're overwhelmed by the challenge we've got, the energy generated can escalate to such intensity that we're unable to think or figure out anything that makes sense to do. Super high voltage GapZaps knock us on our rears; they don't power productive progress.

Fortunately, though, there are those times where the problem we face is just right, when the gap is open to an optimum level—enough that we notice it and are inspired to do something, but not so much that we can't figure out what to do to close it. Optimum gaps are exciting and motivating challenges that we experience when we're whelmed just right, producing the energy we need for sensible well-thought-out behavior. Those are the GapZaps that produce the right amount of energy for desired performance.

Understanding how to utilize Intrinsic Motivation Point 5, how to fine-tune gaps in others, as well as in ourselves, will give us a tremendous edge in managing people and a strong advantage over managers who do not grasp gaps and GapZaps as a place to focus their performance management conversations (Figure 6.2).

William Power's book, *Behavior: The Control of Perception*, explains how all behavior happens in an effort to close that gap. He calls that, countering a disturbance, between the want (what he calls the reference condition), and the got (what he calls the controlled variable). We act in order to zero out the difference between the two perceptions; the reference condition (want) and the controlled variable (got). No difference, no behavior.

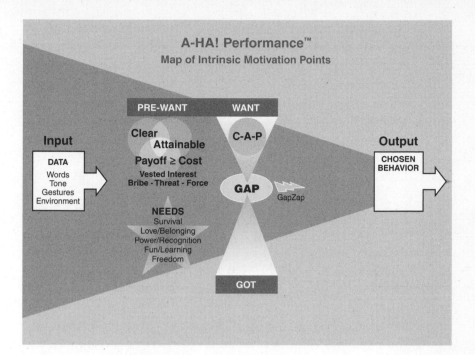

FIGURE 6.2   IMP 5—Gap and GapZap

> So behavior is always purposeful. And its purpose is always to close a gap between something we want and whatever it is that we've currently got.

According to Powers, our brains work very much like control systems, such as thermostats or autopilots. A thermostat gets set for 70 degrees. So the thermometer, which is the perceiving part of this system, measures the existing room temperature to see what temperature it's currently got. Let's say the current temperature is 60 degrees. The system wants 70, yet it's got 60. What is it going to do? It's going to behave to close that gap by activating its heating behavior until it gets the room to match the 70 degrees it wants, then it will stop. No more gap, no more behavior.

A thermostat is a fairly simple control system; an autopilot is a little more complex. An autopilot can be set on a destination, or at least a direction point on the compass. Ships and planes have this kind of control system. A course is set, and thus dictates what the autopilot wants. It has sensors that tell it whether it's got the course it wants. When there is a difference between the course it wants and the course it's got, it will move the rudder and the flaps and do what it has to do to get back on the course it wants.

> When it comes to gaps in human beings, size matters.

If a gap between what we want and what we've got is small, we are underwhelmed and are unlikely to think much about the situation or do anything about it at all. When things are good enough, we leave them alone. The attitude is, "If it ain't broke, don't fix it." No significant gap, no action. When the GapZap barely produces a tingle, we don't notice that there's an issue and don't feel that internal zap to do something about it. By the way, if it ain't broke don't fix it can be a dangerous philosophy. We don't want to wait until an engine seizes up before we change the oil. We don't want to wait until metal breaks of fatigue before changing out parts on an airplane. In those areas, rather, we want to create gaps that trigger behavior before things break. We set our oil change wants at 3,000 miles (okay, for the synthetics maybe 6,000 miles) and we set our change-out-parts-on-an-airplane wants at a prescribed number of flight hours. Once we start exceeding those miles and hours, the gap widens, the GapZap intensifies, gets our attention, and we act to make the changes that close our gaps and keep us safe and operational.

It's the size of the gap within an individual that supplies or generates the energy, the zap, to drive a behavior. Most households provide an example of how this works. Remember, it isn't what we've got that triggers behavior, it's the gap between what we've got and what we want that sparks it. Let's say that a husband's idea of an acceptable garage is one where he can walk between the piles on the floor in order to retrieve tools and other items he wants. His wife's idea of an acceptable garage is one where there are no piles on the floor. But the husband barely sees the piles. So long as he can navigate between them, he's fine. What he wants is the ability to get around and retrieve things in the garage and that's what he's got. No pile gap for him. No GapZap energizing him to clean it up.

But it's a different story for his wife. She wants a pile-less garage. When she sees piles starting to form, her gap widens enough that her GapZap is significant and she has to do something about it. So she does. She tells her husband to clean up the piles. Although he doesn't have a gap about the piles, he does have one between the happy and cheerful wife he wants and the grumpy wife he's got in moments like this. That GapZap intensifies and gets his attention. So to close that gap, and quiet the zap, he cleans up the piles.

Looking at the piles didn't produce enough of a gap to energize him to clean them up. He was underwhelmed and didn't act. But looking at his gonna-get-really-cranky-if-those-piles-aren't-cleaned-up wife activated a different gap. He was whelmed at an optimum level for action when what he wanted was a happy wife, but what he had was a wife who was about to be really grumpy. He cleaned up those piles.

Sometimes we do what we do because it's intrinsically satisfying to do it. It just feels good. Sometimes we do what we do because it's extrinsically satisfying, or need protecting. If we clean up piles because we want to clean up piles, we are intrinsically motivated to do it. If we clean up piles because we want to please somebody else, we are extrinsically motivated to do it.

The reward for being intrinsically motivated to behave is that we close a gap directly. We want the piles clean. We clean them, that closes the gap and we feel good. The reward for being extrinsically motivated to behave is that we close a related gap. We want our spouse pleased, so we clean the piles, and the spouse is pleased. Either way, it's about the good feeling that comes from closing one gap, or another.

You've no doubt heard or read about how if a frog is in hot water, it will jump out. The gap between the pleasant temperature it wants and the hot temperature it's got is significant enough that it creates a zap, an urgency to act, and the frog jumps. But if we put that same frog in cool water and slowly heat it up—so that from moment to moment there is no significant gap—there will be no discernable zap and the frog will remain underwhelmed and do nothing. It will sit in that water and slowly boil to death.

Sometimes gaps grow slowly, so slowly we barely notice them. We recently adopted a new puppy. My oldest daughter Darcy and her husband Drew were at the house a day or two after the puppy arrived. Two weeks later, they were at the house again and commented how much the puppy had grown. We hadn't noticed. The change from day to day was not as significant as the change over two weeks and the daily change didn't get our attention.

> Sometimes gaps are small; we're underwhelmed, barely notice, and rarely act on those.

But when the gap is huge, when the difference between what we want and what we've got seems impossible to overcome, we feel overwhelmed and succumb to the realization, or belief, that what we want is not attainable. Once that happens, the CAP puzzle has been pulled apart and we stop striving for the goal.

> When we are sufficiently overwhelmed, we give up trying because we don't believe we can achieve success anyway.

So how do gaps, whether big, little, or just right, impact us at work? In many companies, employees have dealt with the implementation of a new technology, such as a new software application that senior leadership purchased, hoping for increased efficiencies, but, which requires employees to navigate and endure a major learning curve. Learning takes time and energy, and for people who are already swamped with a full workload, the time to learn and implement the database and the time to deliver on their main job add up to more hours than they have. New systems—designed and purchased to save time—often require more time, especially in the beginning of the learning phase. When the gap grows too big, and the GapZap is too intense, people become overwhelmed. Something will stop. Doing it all in the time available is perceived as unattainable. Either the customer service stops or the utilization of the new system stops.

In one example, the employees at a company I'm familiar with simply did not enter the data they were supposed to be entering. Two gaps were generating a GapZap, an impulse to act: One was the gap between wanting to serve clients really well and knowing they weren't being served; and the other one was the gap between wanting to serve the company through learning and implementing this new technology, yet not getting that done either. High degrees of frustration and barely acceptable levels of compliance were rampant. Morale was sinking and productivity was shrinking.

Finally, in an effort to reduce the gap from overwhelmed to a more manageable and therefore motivational one—one where employees were whelmed just right—management said, "Let's bring our expectations in a bit, closer to the reality around what's happening." In other words, they figured they'd reduce the size of the gap, not by getting what they really wanted, but by resetting the want to one that was still clear and had payoff, but also met the attainable criteria. Let's reset the want to where the gap is closeable, to where people believe it's possible so they'll be willing to try again. What they did was eliminate the need to fill in the more time consuming data, which wasn't really utilized in delivering the service anyway. With a more reasonable gap now, both performance and morale improved.

> Resetting what we want is often the way we have to deal with overwhelming gaps.

That's one reason mega projects are broken down into achievable milestones. The gap between where we are and the next milestone is not as huge as the gap between where we are and the final destination.

Sometimes, however, there is no way to reduce a gap to the point where we can achieve the want. In this case, the only way to close a gap is to accept what we've got.

The death of someone, for example, or the loss of a job or a relationship are situations where we are powerless to get what we want. Just like when I struggled with the death of my mom. I've discovered that anytime doing won't do, anytime there is nothing that can be done to change things from what we've got to what we want, we are stuck with thinking and emoting. Eventually we'll heal or close our gap by accepting what we've got and focusing on new wants that are attainable. But when what we've got is the death of a loved one, and what we want is for the individual to be alive, the gap is enormous. There are times when we can't get what we want. Sometimes the only way to close a gap is, over time, to accept what we've got (see Figure 6.3).

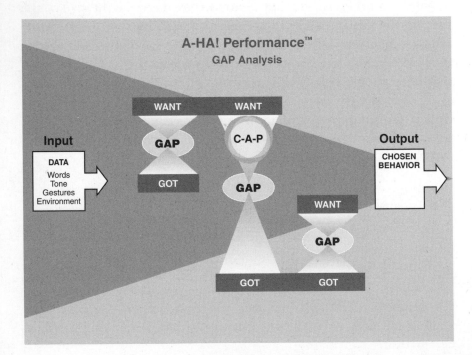

FIGURE 6.3   Getting Wants—Accepting Gots

Not all impossible situations are as powerfully personal as death, but there are still only two options in any truly impossible situation. Continue to try to make the impossible happen—and if it's really impossible, it won't—or give up and turn our energies to that which is possible.

A company I worked with recently wanted to hire a particular person into a key position. The interview went well, as the candidate's expertise, experience, education, and enthusiasm were a perfect match for the job. But the gap between the salary the company wanted to pay and the salary the employee wanted was too great. The company had to give up wanting that particular person and move on to identifying and wanting a different candidate.

Salespeople experience this, too. A sale they've worked really hard to close ends up going to a competitor. They can go on wanting the sale, but if it's gone, there's nothing they can do to get it. If they keep wanting it, they'll be stuck with a lot of thinking and a lot of emoting. This could lead to spending counterproductive time pondering the loss, even though they'd be better served accepting what they've got—that the sale is gone—and moving on to the next opportunity. We can close impossible gaps, overwhelming situations, by accepting what we've got.

With a small gap, we're underwhelmed and don't do much because there isn't a great payoff. With a huge gap, we're overwhelmed and don't do much because we don't think closing the gap is possible.

But the gaps that produce the most effective action are the optimum gaps—the ones where we are whelmed just right.

They might be significant goals, even Big Hairy Audacious Goals (BHAGS),* but they are ones that meet the CAP criteria; they are clear, we believe they are possible, and they have a huge payoff for attaining them. Or some gaps may be huge goals that seem overwhelming at first glance, but can be cut down into whelmed just

*Jim Collins, *Good to Great: Why Some Companies Make the Leap . . . and Others Don't* (New York: HarperCollins, 2001).

right chunks. Huge undertakings are often achieved by breaking them down into smaller goals or milestones.

I have a friend who wants to complete her bachelor's degree. Although she has finished some college courses and doesn't have to go through a four-year process, even two and a half or three years of classes is daunting to a parent of two who is also working full time. Add the money it costs and the time it takes, and her gap is pretty big. When she envisions doing the entire stint and paying the entire cost, it's too much—it's overwhelming, she is GapZapped on her rear and she's unlikely to get started. So how would an A-HA! Performance Manager leverage the insights about gaps to help her buy into starting on the next steps in working toward her degree?

First, a quick summary (see Figure 6.4):

- *Gap is too small.* We're underwhelmed and won't do much.
- *Gap is too big.* We're overwhelmed and won't do much.
- *Gap is optimized.* We're whelmed just right and move toward the goal.

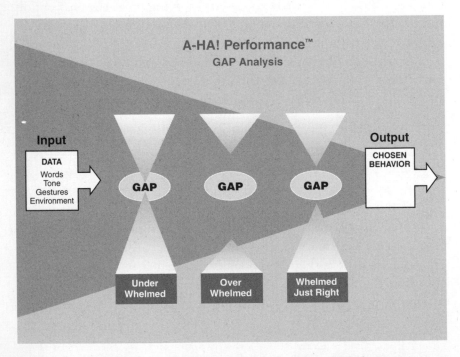

FIGURE 6.4   IMP 5—Gap and the Three Whelms

The manager's task in getting someone whelmed just right may be to comfort the afflicted—to reduce the gap to where the individual is whelmed just right for action. Or, if a person is underwhelmed, the manager's task is to afflict the comfortable in an effort to increase his or her gap.

A tool that salespeople are taught to use in dealing with customer objections can serve managers well in any circumstance where a gap makeover is needed.

The sales tool is called "feel, felt, found." The basics are: "I understand how you could feel that way, my other customers felt that way at first, too, but you know what they found was . . ." What a nice method for connecting in an understanding way and turning the conversation in a more productive direction. A salesperson is affirming he can understand the current conclusion, but still pointing out that as unimportant as the underwhelmed person might think it is, or as unattainable as the overwhelmed person might think it is, others have found that it is both worthy and doable. Here are some examples:

- "I understand how you could feel that six guitars is a little excessive, there are other spouses who felt that way, too, but what they found was different styles of music work better with different kinds of guitars. And husbands who make part of their living using their guitars seem to be happier and perform better with the right instrument for each job."

- "I understand how you could feel that getting to work before 8:00 A.M. is a hardship. Joe down the hall felt that way at first, too. But what he found was that by getting here early—he now gets here at 7:00 A.M.—he gets a ton of work done while it's still quiet, before others even get here and he gets to go home earlier, too. He loves it."

- "I can see how you would feel like the old database was just fine for serving our client population, I felt that way, too, but you know what I found was that this new one just took some getting used to. Once I got past the learning curve, data entry is not as difficult as I thought and this new one can produce more useful reports, in real time, than the other one ever could."

Comforting the Afflicted: Reducing the Gap

So how would we use that tool in comforting the afflicted, in helping the woman who is currently overwhelmed by the investment of time and money required to meet her long time goal of getting that degree?

With the feel, felt, found approach, a manager could say, "I understand how you could feel that way. It is a lot of money and would require a certain amount of time. With the demands of a growing family and a full-time job, finding the time to do it would require a slight shift in priorities and an adjustment on everyone's part to be sure the important stuff still gets done. Many people have felt the way you do about the costs of taking on a worthy endeavor, on top of everything else they're doing. But do you know what many of them have found? That by taking a hard look at what was really important to them, and a hard look at how they actually spent the hours in any given week, they were able to let go of some less important pursuits to focus on the more worthy one. They carved out chunks of time in ways that still allowed them to cover most of the important items.

"And although money can be an issue, most of us spend a lot on far less worthy pursuits than a degree. Others found that a close look at the budget revealed a few places where spending could be redirected. They found that there are scholarships and low cost loans available as well. Often the workplace will reimburse tuition and some companies even give time off to take courses. The point is, they found that with a little research, a little creativity, and a little willingness to sacrifice some of what they were currently doing, for the greater satisfaction of having that degree, they could at least get started.

"Three years from now, we're all going to be three years older. Would you rather be three years older with that degree, or just three years older? If you want it enough, then let's break it down into bite-size chunks. You can't take three years of courses in the next four to six weeks, but you could take one course. Maybe you could take a fun and easy course, just to ease back into that academic groove."

If we can comfort the afflicted, we may help her decide that a degree is attainable. So the objective is to get her locked in on the want by putting the CAP puzzle together in order to make this happen. To review, two of the puzzle pieces are already in place: a bachelor's degree is clear, and the payoff is certainly obvious.

Her love and belonging needs would get met because a major source of motivation to get a degree is her two kids—wanting to guide them by example, not just words. Another source is her other family members. In particular, her mom and siblings who have degrees. She knows they'd be proud of her, too. Power needs? She'd absolutely be achieving purpose, considering she's wanted to get her degree before her kids do for a long time, largely to demonstrate her conviction that a degree is important. She has also shared that she's slightly embarrassed to not have a degree when so many people around her do. She'd feel more powerful with it than she currently does without it.

What about fun/learning needs? If she believed there were professors who made learning fun, she might be more likely to sign up. Freedom? There is a certain freedom to having a degree that doesn't exist for her now. So with her love and belonging, power, and freedom needs, there is a payoff.

The missing piece of the CAP puzzle, however, has been the attainability piece—she's been overwhelmed. The clarity and payoff pieces are in tact and if we can coach her around ways to make this happen in doable steps, we'll have helped comfort the afflicted. Perhaps so much so that she'll believe it is possible and with that belief, enroll in her first class.

Afflicting the Comfortable: Widening the Gap

We can also use the feel, felt, found tool on Hector, the government agency supervisor who wanted to retire early. In essence, Hector was underwhelmed and didn't have the motivation to continue working after he was eligible for retirement. But his boss couldn't stand to see such a talented professional, who was an integral member of the team, leave so soon or avoid fulfilling his potential as a higher up leader in the company.

Unlike my friend who was overwhelmed by the notion of getting a bachelors degree, Hector knew that staying with the agency longer than he had to was attainable and what his boss was asking him to do was clear. But he was missing the payoff.

Using the feel, felt, found approach, his manager could say, "I understand how you could feel. You've worked hard to retire and now that retirement is approaching, you want to take advantage of it. Having entered the workforce at 18, you've spent your entire adult life working. A lot of people in your position have felt the way you do about wanting to let go of the pressures of work once and for all. But do you know what many of them have found?

"When they actually stayed on longer than their eligibility date for retirement, they were able to save up money to take more mini-vacations during the year, and then splurge on an exotic trip down the road—thanks to further promotions and increases in pay. Some have even found that after retiring, they were bored and ended up rejoining the workforce in order to take on new challenges. These people found that having too much free time got boring.

"But most important, you're a good dad and it's vital for you to set an example for your kids. By retiring exactly on the date that you're eligible, it may send the message that hard work isn't important and they should only aspire to retire, and nothing past that."

In optimizing Hector's gap—from underwhelmed to whelmed just right—Hector's manager would use her knowledge of his wants relative to his basic needs and, just like she did in Chapter 3, tie the payoff for professional development to those needs through his specific preferences. If she is successful at optimizing his gap, amping up his GapZap, then he'll be energized to engage in professional development activities.

Managing the gap is critical to getting action. Remember, when it comes to gaps, size is important. The size of the gap can tell us:

- The level of motivation
- The degree of frustration
- The scope of the problem
- The intensity of the urgency to do something
- The obstacles that need to be overcome before action will occur

If you are underwhelmed, belief that there is a payoff needs to be increased. If you are overwhelmed, belief in attainability needs to be increased.

How big are the gaps, problems, and challenges that we're currently facing? What's the distance between what we want and what we've got with people at work? And what should we do about these gaps?

If they are small or petty and we are underwhelmed, we can let it go and not worry about it. We can accept "close enough." Or we can redefine it as something worth pursuing by either redefining the want as something more and better than what we've got or realizing that what we've got is not really as close to the want as we had first thought.

If gaps are humungous, immense, or monstrous and we are overwhelmed, we can be consumed by painful emotings and hopeless thinking; we can give up on it and let it go, accepting what we've got; or we can chunk it down into doable goals and optimum gaps that can be closed with creative and productive effort.

If gaps are important, exciting, and we are whelmed just right, we can start working on closing them by doing something productive to take us from got to want.

So we can manage gaps in two ways:

1. We can manage their size for optimal motivation, best possible GapZaps.
2. We can work at getting what we want. But if that's impossible, we can learn to accept what we've got (see Figure 6.5).

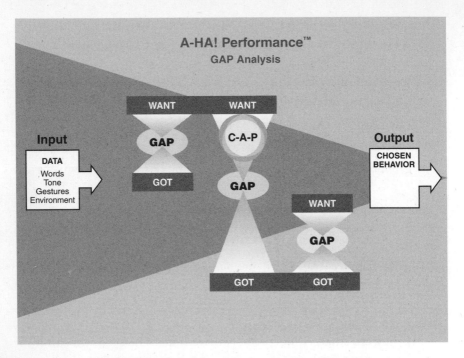

FIGURE 6.5 Getting Wants—Accepting Gots

The successful manager spends a lot of time in the "Drivers" section of the A-HA! Performance Map, on these Intrinsic Motivation Points 1 through 5.

Rather than going straight to telling employees what to do, or advising them on what their output should be, the manager with the A-HA! Performance Edge skillfully addresses the drivers of behavior; the Intrinsic Motivation Points that culminate in the gap: needs, wants, CAP, and got. (See Figure 6.6.)

Summation

Gaps are what produce the energy and urgency to do something. Think of it as a GapZap. It's the gap that zaps our brain to come up

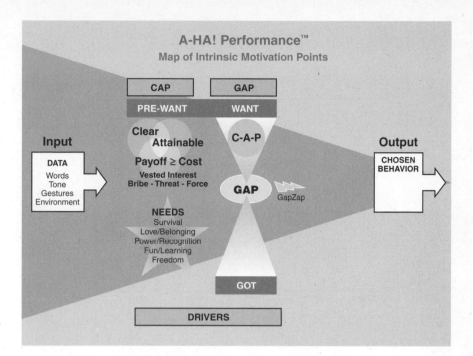

FIGURE 6.6 Drivers of All Behavior

with a behavior. The intensity of this GapZap will not only be the difference in whether people act at all, but also the difference in whether they act in a productive or panicky way. Gaps can leave us underwhelmed, overwhelmed, or whelmed just right. To establish an optimal gap—one that leads to a self-motivated workforce doing what   we'd like them to do—we develop skills at creating gaps in employees' minds where they are whelmed just right for productive action. Weak GapZap . . . no behavior. Overpowering GapZap . . . shorts out productive options and jolts us off our feet. Optimum GapZap provides just the right amount of urgency to rationally and productively perform.

7

Options: The ABCs of Choices—
Choosing Our Own Behavior
Means a Whole Lot More than
We May Think

All of the pre-behavior buy-in functions covered in Chapters 2 through 6—the needs, CAPped want, got, and gap/GapZap—are what I call the Drivers of behavior. And until these Drivers are in place, people won't go on to the next step, which is accessing an area of the brain where our behavior options are stored. As we know, once the Drivers are in place—where we want something that is an optimal difference from what we've currently got—we'll figure out what to do to go after and attain it. So where do we go to figure out what we're going to do to get what we want? Intrinsic Motivation Point 6: Options (Figure 7.1).

The behaviors we choose on a daily basis have four possible sources within the options area of the brain: (1) automatic behaviors, which are our habits or comfortable way of doing things; (2) a back-up repertoire of things we know but may not be comfortable with or

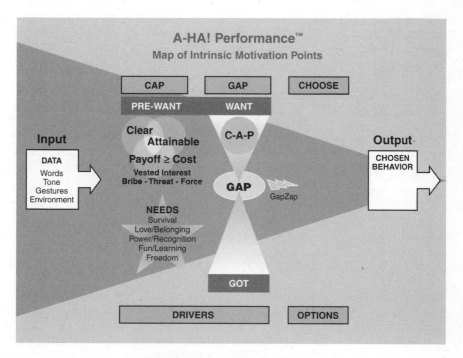

FIGURE 7.1 IMP 6—Options

accomplished in; (3) a creative zone, which is our ability to come up with something new from behaviors we have already used; and (4) a new learning capability, which is the ability to learn a new behavior from outside of ourselves.

Automatic Zone

We all have our automatic habits, our comfortable way of doing things. Whether it's the way we brush our teeth, the steps we go through to begin our day at work, or the way we deal with performance issues when managing others, having routines allows us to do things without much thought (Figure 7.2).

The simple act of brushing our teeth illustrates how habits work. Some of us brush our teeth with our right hand—it's auto-

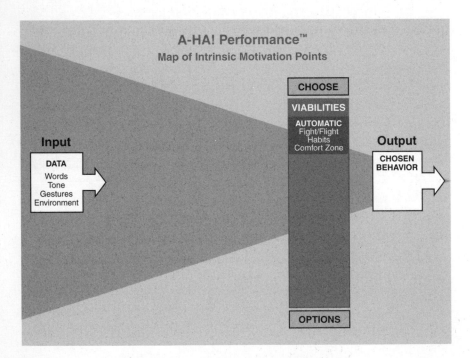

FIGURE 7.2   Options: Automatic Zone

matic and we don't think much about it. Yet, if something were to happen to our right hand, we're capable of using our left hand, which would be a back-up behavior. Although we're not accustomed to using our left hand and we may even be frustrated by it, we know it's there and can tap into its resources if need be.

Another habitual behavior is getting dressed in the morning. What's your routine? We all have one. There was an *All in the Family* episode (for any who don't know, it was a popular television series from the 1970s), where the son Michael was putting on his shoes: a sock and a shoe; a sock and a shoe. His father-in-law, Archie, said, "That's not the way it's done; it's a sock and a sock and then a shoe and a shoe." Obviously, there's no right or wrong way to put on our shoes, but both Archie and Michael had different automatic ways of going through the motions. Our automatic behaviors are the things we've done the most and know the best. They're comfortable. They're habitual. They require almost no thought.

The automatic zone is where we go first to come up with a behavior, especially if we're under time duress. Pressed for time, we'll quickly come up with something from this automatic or habit zone—whether it's right or wrong. For example, I'm going to ask you a question and I want you to be aware of the first answer that pops into your head, even though you know it's wrong. Are you ready? What's the moon made out of?

Cheese? Green cheese?

That's how this automatic zone works. It uses answers that we've rehearsed—answers that were once the right or effective ones for a period of time. When something works, we do it over and over again until it becomes the automatic thing we do in that situation.

That's what our automatic behaviors are: behaviors that we have done over and over again to the point where they are cemented into our automatic area and come out of us so fast that we experience them more as reactions, rather than what they really are, which are pro-actions. They pop out of us quickly because they are well-rehearsed actions for dealing with common situations. With the moon question, many of us came up with the "cheese" answer because it was put into our automatic zone when we were kids. It was the right answer then and even though it's not right now, it's still right there, ready to go.

At the top of the automatic zone are our fight or flight impulses. Once a filter in our brain picks up a threat, it shuts down the rest of our options and we're left with our fight or flight behaviors. Whether it's a school boy throwing a punch at a bully who threatens him or an employee quitting on the spot after being threatened by a manager, these are fight or flight behaviors that are stored in the automatic zone.

Emotings are also among the behavioral choices in our automatic zone.

A lot of times people emote to close gaps. A child who cries so she can get her mom to buy her something or a girlfriend who sulks so her boyfriend will apologize are examples. We emote to control people. How else can babies get full-grown adults to get out of bed to feed and comfort them? They emote at their parents and it works. We've been using our emotions to close gaps since we came out of the womb. And since we've been using emotions for such a long time, they are well entrenched into our automatic zone.

Whether we cry, beg, yell, or sulk, we are using emotional behaviors that we probably haven't really thought through, yet they pop out of us because they are easily accessible from our automatic behavior zone and we are way too comfortable using them.

If an employee does something that is different than what we want, which creates a gap for us, what's our comfort zone behavior? Is it to attack back, sulk, ignore it, write him up, take the issue to human resources, or have a rational discussion? Some of us immediately fight back, emoting through anger and words we may regret later.

This often happens in intimate relationships as well, where we say all kinds of things based on the heat of the moment; things we wish we hadn't said and that we'd like to take back if we could. These quick behaviors are all emotings coming out of our automatic zone.

And as much as we may believe we don't have any control over these emotional displays, we do.

Because the behaviors that come out of our comfort zone happen so fast, they don't feel like choices at all. They feel more like someone made us do them.

Remember, over time, we've put those behaviors in our automatic zone. Yet, if the behaviors stop working for us—if they are doing us and others more harm than good, we can learn to put new habits in their place. That's what disaster training is designed to do. Practice something over and over until it becomes the new habit—the behavior we choose automatically when there's no time to think about other choices. To get something into our automatic zone requires repetition and practice.

That's why schools do fire and earthquake drills, so kids not only act immediately, but act with the right set of behaviors. When the bell rings, teachers don't want students to have this big gap: I want to be safe, I'm not safe; I need to run out the door. Instead, in an effort to give everyone the same behavior, teachers and students practice an earthquake drill. And they practice this behavior over and over so when the time comes to act quickly, students don't have to think about it; they just do what's in their automatic zone.

An important thing to realize is that we're not stuck with unproductive behaviors.

Back-Up Zone

If we take the time to think of a different behavior—possibly because the automatic one isn't working, we can access our back-up repertoire. Let's say we are going to apply for a job at NASA, and on the

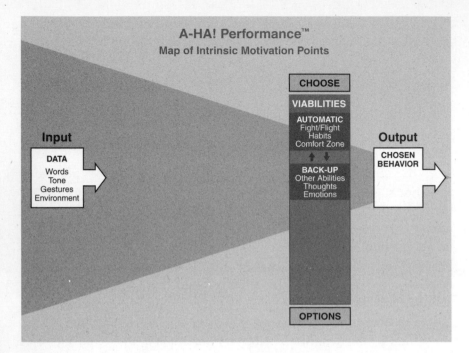

FIGURE 7.3 Options: Back-Up Zone

application form is the question: What's the moon made out of? Are we going to go with our first automatic zone answer? Or are we going to go deeper into our options zone and come up with a better answer? Probably the latter (see Figure 7.3).

On school playgrounds, a teacher may tell a student who is fighting with another student to stop and count to 10. Take a time-out. That allows the child to take the time to think a little deeper and come up with something from his back-up zone that won't get him into trouble. If the student doesn't take the time to go into his back-up zone, then his automatic action might be to throw a punch or mouth off. Again, not necessarily the best behavior, but, without the reminder to count to 10, this might be his instantaneous action, based on previous learning as to what was okay in dealing with threats or difficult people.

The important thing to realize about unproductive automatic behaviors is that we're not stuck with them. We not only have a back-up repertoire that we can tap into, but we also have the ability to think of something completely new; something we've never done before, yet it just might be the most effective way to approach a particular situation.

For example, take a manager who time and again gets irritated by this one employee. Out of her automatic zone, she's exhibiting impatient and emotional behaviors. And instead of the employee improving and getting less irritating, he is getting worse. But the manager is not stuck with her bad attitude or impatience, as she's able to ask herself, "What am I doing, and how is it working? Since it's not working, what else can I do to improve the situation?"

Albert Einstein understood the concept of digging deeper to come up with better behaviors when he said, "Insanity is doing the same thing over and over again and expecting different results." Basically, we'll never solve problems by doing what we've been doing that made the problem in the first place.

Even though we're comfortable with our current habits, when they stop working, we have other choices. This is a valuable lesson not only for employees but also for us as managers—we all have the ability to think our behaviors through and come up with better ones if the current ones aren't working.

Though it's so easy to do what we're comfortable doing, there are no excuses anymore. With the A-HA! knowledge of our back-up collection of behaviors, the creative zone, and our ability to learn entirely new behaviors, we have tremendous capability for solving all kinds of problems. If we're doing things that aren't working, we have it in us to access alternative behaviors, ones that might work better.

If I'm talking to an employee who is constantly gossiping about other employees, and he is telling me that there's nothing he can do because he needs to vent, I know that's not true. Because of his back-up zone, I know that in his system, there is more he has to draw from than what I'm currently seeing.

Creative Zone

I know that he has the ability to be creative. When I was a counselor at the Los Angeles Job Corps, I counseled a student who wasn't going to class. In addressing the issue, I started with all of my automatic behaviors: I talked to her about it, I pointed out the virtues of class, I shamed her for not going to class, I begged, I pleaded, and I tried to get her to want to go to class. But to no avail. I then went to the organizationally proscribed and sanctioned coercion or stick mode, threatening to take her before the review board. Still, nothing worked.

That's when I tapped into my creative zone (Figure 7.4). Asking myself, "What else can I do?" it occurred to me that I could do exactly the opposite of what I had been doing. So instead of talking about the problem every time I saw her, I wrote a letter that said, "I know you're avoiding me, and I know why. I've been pounding this thing too much. So I want to let you know that if you want to come by and talk, feel free, and I promise not to talk about the fact that you're not going to class."

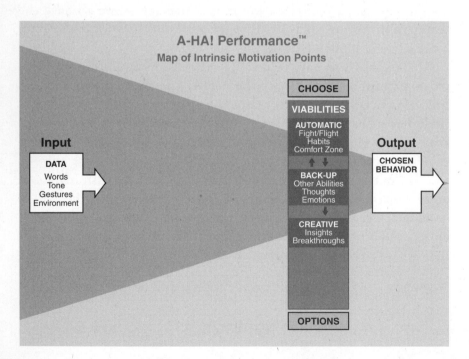

FIGURE 7.4   Options: Creative Zone

Although I had never written a letter to one of my students before, I came up with this completely new behavior as a creative new way to handle the situation more effectively. Clearly, what I had been doing wasn't working. Creativity boils down to taking behaviors that we already know and mixing them up differently, which produces something new. I knew about letter writing and I knew about not talking about sore subjects, but I had never combined these behaviors in working with my students. In that context, writing a letter saying I wouldn't talk about the very issue I wanted to solve was a creative idea.

In fact, all of the Intrinsic Motivation Points that I'm sharing in this book are subjects that have been addressed before, but I'm packaging them together in a creative and unique way to come up with the A-HA! Performance Model. Likewise, Albert Einstein may have known about E and M and C separately, but when he came up with $E = MC^2$, he was putting them together in a new way.

Using our creative zone means creating never-before-used combinations or configurations of behaviors to handle a challenging situation. Whether we create from things we already know or from a combination of what we know and what we learn from others around us, creativity is rearranging or repackaging.

> Creativity is a rearranging or repackaging exercise.

That's the advantage of talking to many people: we learn new things and add more raw materials to our reservoir of creativity.

So if we have nothing in our automatic or back-up zone, the purpose of our creative area is to tap into resources we've seen or used before and package them together differently.

The outcome of my letter? The day after the student received my letter, she peeked her head around the corner to my office and, with a grin on her face, said, "Have you heard from the teachers? I got your letter yesterday and went to class today."

New Learning

We also have the ability to learn something entirely new. That's why self-help books are widely used. People are able to reach outside of themselves and learn new behaviors that they have never utilized before. Employees do this often when they take seminars, go on business retreats, take courses, or read books like this one— all in an effort to learn new behaviors that might prove fruitful in their professional and personal lives. The new learning option is our ability to learn something new that we've never known about or done before.

We Aren't Only Automatic Beings

Knowing that we have our automatic, back-up, creative, and new learning options for behavior empowers people; it opens their eyes to a whole new realm of choices. People become open to other possibilities—something that proves useful in managing them.

The opposite situation, where people aren't aware of these alternative behavior zones, is self-limiting. If people only operate in their automatic zone, then they're limited to a narrow vision of themselves and their possibilities.

The Myers Briggs model of personality is one assessment tool that, though thought to be a powerful personality test for senior leadership in the workplace, produces this limited outlook. It measures personality preferences using E for Extraversion or I for Introversion, S for Sensing or N for Intuition, T for Thinking or F for Feeling, and J for Judging or P for Perception. From a set of questions, the Myers Briggs assessment combines people's preferences to give their personality type, with 16 different combinations (Having preferences for E and S and T and J results in a personality type of ESTJ).

Many professionals take the Myers Briggs assessment and think they are the personality profile that's identified by this instrument. But here's the danger: Myers Briggs is only measuring people's automatic or comfort zone behaviors. Some people think they are that profile and lose sight of what the A-HA! Performance Model teaches, which is that our automatic behaviors aren't all of who we are. We also have our back-up, creative options, and new learning capabilities.

In recognizing that we aren't only our automatic behaviors and that we are capable of putting something else out there that may be more productive, managers and employees alike realize that even our attitudes, our emotional outbursts, are behavioral choices and there may be better ones available to us simply by accessing back-up, creative, or new learning capabilities in our existing options system.

> Emotions are choices we make.

An employee didn't make us act the way we did. We chose to act that way. Actually our brain registered a gap; the difference between the behavior we wanted from that employee and the behavior we were getting from him. That gap signaled an urgent need for action—a GapZap—and the brain chose a behavior that was high in emoting. It may have happened so fast it didn't seem like a choice, but it was. And we have the ability to choose a better way.

For example, when we go into a situation where we're trying to change the performance of somebody else, we start with the gap: We want an employee to be different than we're experiencing him now. So we then have to go through our own behavior options to understand what we can do to get the individual to be the way we want him to be. In looking to create the gap in our employee's head, we first need to explore our own options for how best to approach this particular situation.

This includes digging deep into our options zone to ensure we don't approach an employee in a way that his brain chooses defenses. If we want full access to our employee's behavior options to the point where we're both actively engaged in figuring out the best solution to a gap, we should choose our approach carefully so that defenses don't get generated that cost us time and energy.

And if we find ourselves in an adversarial situation, where we're making demands and the employee is fighting us, then why not back off? As soon as we're in any sort of argumentative place, our employee won't buy into our want. He's too busy protecting his own. We want to ask ourselves, "What's the vested interest win for this employee to do what I'd like him to do?" When the defenses go up, think payoff. We can use our own options to come up with a different approach that finds the payoff for our employee to do what we'd like him to do.

I had to do this recently with my daughter, who had just finished her first year of college, but didn't want to show me her grades. I figured she was embarrassed by them because as soon as I brought them up, boom, her fight or flight kicked in and she was defensive. But as her father, I didn't want her to continue the same pattern in her second year of college. So I thought about payoff for her. How could I convince her that getting good grades would pay off? Knowing that she has preferences for feeling proud of herself and accomplished based on her need for power, and a preference for recognition based on her need for belonging, I said, "If you improve your study habits, you'll be happier and prouder to talk about your grades than you are now. You won't be embarrassed by them." She's already intrinsically motivated to do well. She is amazing at doing favors for other people and at skillfully taking on physical chores that need to be done. She is constantly thinking of other people and what she can do for them. She loves to accomplish and she loves to belong. She's pretty fond of fun, too. Why not tap into that? She'd feel better about accomplishing good grades, sharing it with those she cares about, and celebrating in some fun way than she's feeling now.

When we change from an adversarial approach and start to point out the wins for our employee—how she can actually feel good about this change in performance—then the defenses settle down and she begins to listen. When she can trust that we're not trying to hurt her, but instead looking out for her best interests, then she will open herself up to the gap and will be willing to engage her options for closing the gap.

And our goal is to get employees to the point where they are navigating their own options—without us telling them what to do or how to do it. As we'll see, telling people what to do will never have the same result as when people make their own decisions.

Internal versus External Control

That's one of the major a-has in the A-HA! Performance Model: No one makes us do anything.

We choose our own behaviors. Yet, most people aren't aware that we have behavior choices. Many people really think that other people made them mad, or made them sad or made them love another person—Remember that old song, *You made me love you, I didn't want to do it.*

Have you ever blamed someone else for your behavior? Anytime we blame someone else for what we do, we're demonstrating a belief in external control; that forces outside of us controlled us. But this book is all about how that's not the way things work. We are internally motivated and, because our brain chooses it, we are responsible for our own behavior. (I know, what a concept, right?)

Let's use a couch salesman to illustrate. A couch has been sold and the delivery service should deliver the couch in two weeks. But two weeks rolls around and the couch hasn't been delivered. So the salesman gets on the phone, fuming with irritation, and yells at the delivery guy, demanding that he stop what he's doing and deliver the couch immediately. He then slams down the phone and storms onto the sales floor. Later, he laments to his coworker, "The delivery guy made me so mad because he didn't deliver on time."

He blames the delivery company's failure to deliver for his anger, which means it's not his fault, but the delivery company's fault. Yet, the salesman had a choice; he didn't have to use his angry emotions to deal with the company's failure to deliver on time. He could've dug deeper into his behavior options zone, called the company, and politely, but firmly, negotiated a clear, attainable, payoff-greater-than-cost time that that couch would be delivered. He chose to anger instead of negotiate. No one made him be angry.

"With A-HA! Performance, people begin to take responsibility for their own situations," says Bryce Whiting, a sales trainer, business coach, and a student of A-HA! Performance. "And in today's society, we all do it: it's woe is me, or it's somebody else's fault. But the more we understand this model, the harder it is to blame others for what we do."

Many managers, like Richard Harper, are promoted to a managerial position and think it's their job to make their employees perform a certain way—betraying a belief in external control. "I have to make my salespeople hit their numbers," might be a typical thought of an external control-oriented manager. This manager would try to make his employees hit their numbers by either bribing or threatening them; using carrots or sticks. But even that is really another way of saying: You have needs inside you that I can try to extrinsically satisfy or frustrate in getting you to do what I want you to do. Yet, the manager believes it's the external control of the threat or the bribe that's going to make his salespeople hit their numbers, not understanding at all that it's really need satisfaction or protection that's going to make that salesperson perform.

What A-HA! Performance introduces is a huge paradigm shift from external control to internal control, with the pictorial map illustrating the internal process. Here's how it works in a nutshell:

> Everything is about protecting or satisfying our needs, and we satisfy our needs by getting what we want, and the way that we get what we want is by choosing appropriate behaviors. The Drivers (motivation) and Options (viable choices for that person) are inside. And as managers, we don't make the Drivers, and for the most part, we don't load the Options; they are already there.

When we are aware that people's motivation and choice of behavior are internal events, not only will we see that our employees are accountable for their own actions (they can't blame others for making them do something), but as managers, we also realize that we can't control another person's behavior—as much as we may think it's our job. The real control is inside each individual.

Fortunately, we're now starting to learn how to access and work with those internal control factors.

> With external control, managers believe it's their words, gestures, and emotions that control other people's behavior, but in reality, the words they use are just input and the degree to which their input covers the Drivers will determine whether an employee will perform.

So managers are accountable at some level for a team's performance, because they're responsible for thinking of the best ways to influence a team's behavior in order to get what they want, but they can never control the behavior. Once we're able to shift gears and stop trying to control other people's behavior, our reputation as a manager, and the strength of our relationships (care and credibility), improves dramatically. We go from being a manager that was known for saying, "Do it my way or the highway," to, "I'd like to meet the customers' needs, the company's needs, and my needs, but I'd like to do it in a way that helps you meet your needs as well."

> Not only do we earn respect and form practical working relationships from our caring and credibility, but we don't have to do nearly as much hand-holding when we utilize internal control insights as we would if we thought it was our job to control employees.

It takes all of the pressure off of us to provide answers, and instead, allows us to help employees uncover what they see as their best options.

It's Their Options Zone, Not Ours That They Will Draw From in Choosing and Implementing Their Behavior

Because we have to engage our employees' Drivers first, before they will be willing to look at their behavior options, we must resist the temptation of giving advice. In fact, if we catch ourselves arguing or in some adversarial posture in a conversation with our employee, we should ask ourselves, *Am I exploring this person's drivers for doing what I'd like him to do, or am I arguing about the specific way I want him to do it?* For example, if I'm talking to an employee who is coming in late and I am an external control-minded manager, I would go straight to advice: Get up earlier and get here on time. In telling an employee what to do, I'm focusing directly on her output—all the things she physically does to close her gaps. I refer to output as Chosen Behavior, which is the Intrinsic Motivation Point that we'll cover in the next chapter.

What we don't want to do is go straight to an employee's output by telling her what she can or should do to close the gap. In doing this, we're ignoring both the Drivers of buy-in and her Options; what's viable for her to do. We're telling her what we would do; what's in our options zone. But what if our employee, who we just told to get up early, already does get up early? What if she has kids that she needs to tend to and drive to day care, which prevents her from getting to work any earlier because day care doesn't open early enough? So to tell her to change what she's doing without changing her Drivers or Options won't do us any good. If she doesn't believe she can change, if she doesn't believe that what we're asking her to do is attainable, she won't do it.

Richard went straight to Susan's output. He went right to demanding that she answer the phones the way he wanted her to, not to exploring whether she could do it or whether she wanted to do it—he just said, "Do it."

I'm guilty of this, too. When a sales manager recently approached me with a problem he was having in a certain division of his company, I said almost immediately, "I can fix that. Here's what you do." In other words, I went straight to output. The look on his face told me I hadn't impressed him. I hadn't understood the issue. My advice missed the mark. But with the A-HA! Performance Map, I had a quick assessment tool to figure out where I went off the map and tried to short-circuit the process. Anytime we find ourselves veering off track and going nowhere in a performance conversation, we can pick up the pictorial map as a reference to see where we've gone astray. It helped me get back to the Drivers and Options in that conversation: *What do you want to have happen? How close are you to that now? What have you tried so far?* And it can help you do the same.

And here's another feature of the Options zone: If we have nothing in our automatic, back-up, or creative zones, we can learn something new. If I find that that sales manager does not have the behaviors to solve his problem, and he agrees with me that he doesn't, perhaps he'll be open to learning something new that might (Figure 7.5).

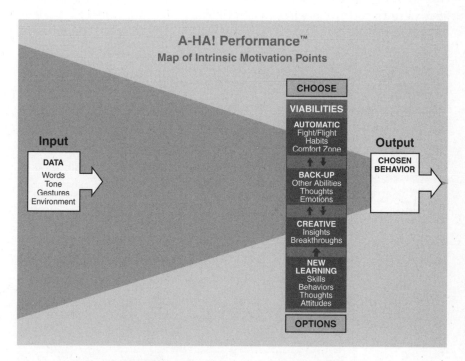

FIGURE 7.5 Options: New Learning

Thanks to the A-HA! Performance Map, I had a quick assessment tool for figuring out where I went off track. Anytime we find ourselves in a conversation where the other person is resisting our efforts to manage their behavior and we are arguing or in an adversarial posture with them, we can pick up the pictorial map as a reference to see where we've gone off the buy-in and performance decision process. It provides a shortcut to getting back on the path that works (Figure 7.6).

> In bypassing the Drivers and Behavior Options zone in an effort to dole out our sage advice, we're also missing an opportunity to enable employees to figure out their best options by themselves.

If employees know that the solution for closing the want/got gap was their idea—it was their choice out of their viable options—they're much more likely to implement the solution than if a manager were to tell them what to do. Why?

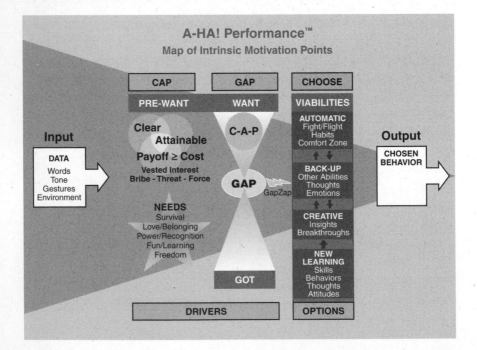

FIGURE 7.6   Drivers and IMP 6—Options

For starters, what works for one individual may not work for another individual. Remember what I said in Chapter 2 about the myth of best practices, the fallacy of thinking it's some specific way of doing things that is the reason for a person's success. When corporations release a list of best practices, they are displaying a belief that employees can watch what others do and, if it works really well for others, then it should work just as well for these employees. But there are too many factors, such as varying personalities and capabilities, for one option to work for everybody.

Remember that old joke about the guy who gets put into a prison where inmates are not allowed to talk? He's only there a few minutes when he hears an inmate yell out, "43!" and all the other inmates burst out laughing. Then another voice is heard shouting "27!" Again, lots of laughter. "What's going on?" he whispers to his cellmate? The cellmate quietly explains that because they're not allowed to talk, they've devised this system where all the jokes are numbered. The guys shouting out numbers are really telling jokes. "How cool!" says the new inmate, and wanting to be part of a good thing in a bad situation, he decides to shout out a number himself. "36!"—silence. "17!" he tries again . . . still, nothing. "How come no one laughs when I yell out the numbers?" he asks. "Well," answered the cellmate, "some people can tell jokes, and some people can't." Exactly. And that's how it is with so-called best practices.

The true factors for success include effective practices, but before we can implement effective practices, we need to access our personality specific skills and resources, ones that are viable for us. And before utilizing our particular viable skills and resources, we need to line up the Drivers of motivation, ones that create the GapZap that energizes an excitement to achieve. Better perhaps than best practices are best motivators. If we can get people to want it enough, and manage the gap for optimum GapZap energizing, then they will implement their own best practices. Once they want it enough, as Paul Simon writes, "there must be 50 ways." A-HA! Performance focuses us on managing motivation, not tasks or processes.

Years ago I was talking to a nine-year-old boy who was causing a lot of problems at home. At some point I asked if he wanted things to be better for him at home. He did. Next I asked what he could do to make things better there. "What's one thing you can do differently every day for the next week that you think will make things better?"

He said, "I don't know, you tell me." What a trap he was setting.

How am I going to know best practices for that particular nine-year-old boy in that particular household? If I told him what I would do, as a . . . well, let's say older than nine adult, would he be able to copy that? I told him, "there's nobody who knows better about what you could do differently than you." Here I was, an older guy who had just met him. I didn't have a clue about what this kid could or should do. I wasn't a nine-year-old in his environment, he was. And I knew that he had to figure it out on his own. I could support or challenge his ideas . . . maybe ask a "could you do something like X and if so, how would you do it?" kind of question. But if I had told him what to do, he wouldn't have done it exactly the way I had in mind. It probably wouldn't have worked and he would have been able to blame me for its failure. That's why managers shouldn't tell employees what to do either; rather, managers will get better results if they help employees explore their own ABCs of viable behavior choices.

In fact, there is a ton of research showing that when comparing solutions that management comes up with to what employees themselves come up with, employees' solutions are the best ones more than 80 percent of the time.

And part of this is that employees will implement what they create.

It's the people on the frontlines that know what's best and have the right ideas in their options zones to complete tasks successfully. So if managers don't do a little mining of what the person has in his option zone, they are going to miss out on what are probably the best ideas and the solution is not going to be as good.

It's possible that in having this discussion, an employee will say, "I can't think of anything." So that's when we can say, "Are you open to some ideas? If you can't think of any options, would you be willing to learn new ones?" Assuming defenses haven't kicked in, we can then help employees explore their back-up zone and creative options, or help put new learning into their options. Still, it's not providing the answers, but trying to uncover what the employee sees as his options.

Even when we're able to share new ideas, employees will still have to make the ideas their own before implementing them. They will have to take the new ideas in, add their personality to the situation, and create their own version of the behavior. But that's how it is with anything. Whenever we digest new information or learn a new skill, we'll never imitate the information or behavior precisely.

It's the same with the A-HA! Performance Model. I'm teaching it to managers, but when managers take all the information in and then attempt to share it with other professionals, it will inevitably come out differently. People will always add their own creative touch.

> Not only are employees much more likely to implement a behavior when it comes out of their own options, but when we choose our own behavior, we are also responsible for it.

So when an employee knows she chose her own behavior, she can never blame us for making her do something, especially if the solution doesn't work out. Rather, she will take responsibility for her own actions. And if one behavior doesn't pan out as expected, then she knows she has the ability to choose something that's more effective.

A-HA! Performance brings increased capability to the workplace on the part of our employees because it reminds us to mine back-up, creative, and new learning options for solutions as well as the automatic ones. This helps managers and employees know that they are plenty capable of finding better ways and that they are responsible for their current choices as to the performance they're giving. A-HA! managers understand that employees have way more capability than they may have previously assumed because employees' options include automatic, back-up, creative, and the ability to learn something new.

This is part of the internal control a-ha: We choose what comes out of us and are therefore responsible for it. And the resources we have aren't just our comfort zone behaviors, but we're capable of utilizing back-up, creative, and new learning options as well. Employees are therefore more capable than many managers think. Once we understand the A-HA! Performance Model, and the four viable sources of possibilities for new behavior, we'll trust our employees' capabilities much more than before we knew they had alternatives to automatic comfort zone habits. We may learn to trust our own capabilities more, too.

A bonus is that when we put our trust in employees, they feel more supported and empowered and are thus more able to be effective. They much prefer being allowed to come up with their own way of doing things. And when they do, they are much more likely to implement those self-created solutions. We're all like that. As may be obvious by now, sooner or later we realize that "they" are "us."

Beginning with the Drivers, our first challenge is to establish the gap that needs to be closed; to get our employee to believe there is a problem or challenge that needs to be solved. Until an employee buys into our gap, she won't realize that our gap is a problem or challenge for her, too. Once she believes there is a problem, or a worthy challenge, then she will feel the urge, the GapZap to solve it, too.

The next step is figuring out with her how. In other words, how is she currently addressing the problem? What are her current habit behaviors and how are they working? If they're not working, is she stuck with those behaviors? The answers to these questions, ultimately, have to come from her. She knows what she's currently doing and how it's working. Once we both agree on what we want that's different than what we've got, and we are both clear on what her current behavior is that isn't working, then we need to figure out a different behavior that might work better.

Here's the catch: We may have a great idea for her, but she's unlikely to be open to our advice right at the beginning. We'll want to explore what ideas she has, from her options zone—her automatic, back-up, or creative behaviors. If she comes up with something that sounds like it would close the gap, getting us to the new want, then we support her in doing those new behaviors. If she really doesn't know something effective to do, or asks for our input, then we can make some suggestions. "What do you think about this approach? Have you thought about doing X?" In other words, she's capable of learning new things, even from her manager, but she'll mostly open the door to new ideas when she's exhausted her own. And, once we make the suggestions, she'll still have to put them into her style, one that's consistent with her way of doing things and her personality. What we see her do won't look exactly like the way we'd do it. We may want to do some coaching, let her practice until she gets better at it, or closer to the way we want her to do it anyway, but at this point, she'll have bought into the need for a new way of doing things and some of the specific suggestions we make as to how to do them. She can't solve the problem directly from our options; she can't do exactly what we would do. But we can help navigate her through what her behavior options are.

As long as we stay in the Drivers and Options, without jumping over to output, we'll have a strong chance of closing our gap, by getting her to come up with her own solution. And with an employee choosing her own behaviors to solve the problem, we can sit back and watch as she implements the performance we want because she wants it, too.

Summation

Choices: Employees are capable of coming up with their own optimal performance options and can be managed in such a way that they feel responsible for what they come up with. Once the gap is established, once there is a perceived difference between a compelling want and the present situation, the employee will be motivated to act, to do something. If the employee knows what to do, or can figure out what to do, she should be encouraged to do it. If she wants to work toward a goal, but neither knows nor can figure out what to do, she might be willing to open up to new learning. The manager's job is to help a motivated employee navigate the ABCs of her behavior options; her automatic ones, her back-up ones, and her ability to create. If the employee can't come up with a good thing to do on her own, the manager should remember that that employee is capable of learning and should be prepared to teach, not tell, but teach, that employee what to do. Either way, through probing or teaching, it is the manager's challenge to help her come up with and commit to optimal behaviors for closing specific gaps. Choosing our own options makes for self-motivation at its finest. As a bonus, when enough employees are doing it, it breeds a culture of can-do responsibility and accountability and sustained morale.

Output: Chosen Behavior—
Doing, Thinking, Emoting, Physiology

Behavior is what we've chosen to do to get from got to want. When we don't have what we want, we act.

Examples are everywhere because all behavior is a result of this "gap" between something we want and whatever it is we've got. Look at your fingernails. If they look "right" to you, you will leave them alone. If they do not look right, or at least not right enough (too long, too rough, dirt under them, cuticle issues, chipped polish), you will do something.

Driving a car, we have wants to stay within the lines that are the border to our lane. We are constantly monitoring our car's position within those lines and then behaving by moving the steering wheel to reposition the car so that it does stay in the correct lane. Someone counted the number of movements we make each minute in this constant exercise of behaving to keep gaps closed between what we want and what we've got. The number of movements the observer counted was more than a hundred per minute, as we monitor the gap between where we are in the lane and where we want to be then choose and execute a corrective (gap closing) action—a slight turning of the steering wheel.

Even physiologically we are designed to work this way. Our eyes want a certain amount of light coming in to maximize a clear perception of what they're trying to see. Too much light, the pupil closes—not enough light, the pupil opens. Way too much light, the eyelid closes—nowhere near enough light, we turn on the lamp. Behavior, both consciously and unconsciously, is about closing gaps.

Think about the people we live or work with. When they are acting the way we want them to, we ignore or enjoy. When they are not acting the way we want them to, we do something. Sometimes our doing has a lot of thought or emotion tied to it. Sometimes, in fact most times, it has physical, observable action like conversation, words, volume—or some other form of communication; body language maybe, written notes, e-mail—as we try to get the person in the real world to match that person in our head. We do what we do in order to control or manipulate a situation so that we are getting what we want.

That means, of course, that we are all controllers, we are all manipulators, not only of cars in lanes, but also of the people in our lives. It's just that some of us have learned ways to do it so that the people around us say "thank you," while others of us do it so poorly people resist, fight, or leave us.

When we live our lives on automatic, it feels like other people make us *react* in certain ways toward them. But even what feels like a reaction (she made me mad) is really a choice our brain makes when it is not getting what it wants. This is a huge a-ha for many people. Because the brain makes its choice of behaviors so fast, it often doesn't seem like a choice at all.

A story I heard attributed to the well-known psychologist Albert Ellis makes this point: Suppose you have to take the bus home from work one day because your car is in the shop. The day has been particularly grueling, people coming to you with problems all day long, and you just want to get home to a place where it's quiet and you can relax. You get off work around 3:00 P.M., board the bus, choose a seat near the back door, and heave a big sigh . . . finally . . . no more commotion. Since you don't normally take the bus, it hadn't occurred to you that this bus goes by the local middle school and that those kids get out of school at this same time. The bus stops at the school, kids swarm on and the peace you sought is gone. You want to be left alone in a place you can relax; you've got loud kids shoving and pushing their way into the back of the bus when suddenly, Whack! You get hit on the back.

Does that hit *make you* mad?

Most of us would say, "You're darned tootin' that hit would make me mad! Those kids should be careful, more considerate of others. They have no right to be hitting people on the bus."

So let's say you did get mad, you swirled around to confront that adolescent thug who hit you and saw that it was actually a little seven-year-old blind girl who had accidentally fallen and hit you with her cane on the way down. Now, if that hit had *made* you mad, you'd *be* geared up for violent action. But it occurs to you that it's not really good to kick little blind girls on buses. Your brain has a want to stay out of jail and off the front pages of the local newspaper, so it quickly chooses compassion and lets go of the mad it had originally chosen. Mad wasn't a condition, it was a choice.

Sometimes the brain chooses so fast we're not aware it was a choice at all.

In this case, your brain chose angering—and we'll find that it's helpful to use the verb tense of emotions (emotings) in learning this concept because it helps us understand that emotings are behaviors chosen by the brain as the best option it can come up with in a particular situation, to help us get what we want. Emotings are not conditions or states of being—the brain saw angering as a good choice for moving those kids away from you. Angering, and the physical actions it supports, are sensible options for getting people away from us and settled down so we can get back to that quiet space we wanted in the first place.

Anger was a logical choice in some ways. It's a tool designed to energize our actions, to get the attention of the target, and to communicate danger—stay away. Isn't that the message you wanted these kids to get? The hit hadn't *made* you do anything at all. Your brain had just made a quick choice about what to do. Energized by the sudden gap between the peace and quiet you wanted, and the noise and pain you got, the brain chose from its options a well-practiced one, one that's nestled firmly in that corner of our automatic zone known as fight or flight. Counterattack a threat using ample amounts of emotion to help fuel the actions. Someone told me that emotion is energy in motion. That fits. Picture yourself angrily swirling to set these kids straight about your boundaries. Whether or not you see that as a pretty picture, does *energy in motion* describe it?

So let's rewind that story in a further effort to illustrate this point. Same beginning, same chaos at work, same bus at 3:00 P.M., but this time, instead of passing by the middle school to pick up kids, you pass by the local motorcycle shop where 30 or 40 members of a motorcycle gang have just dropped off their bikes for servicing. They raucously board the bus, shoving, swearing, loud . . . smelly, too. You still want to be left alone but as they swagger by you, Whack! You get hit on the back. Same velocity as in the previous example. Does that hit *make you* mad? For survival reasons, our brain would probably choose fear as the emotional behavior in this situation. Anger would make us want to attack; fear leads more to a speedy low-profile withdrawal. "Oh, I'm sorry sir, is your hand okay? Would you like my seat? I'm getting off at this next stop. . . . I kind of like walking the last 10 miles to my house."

Behavior is chosen by the brain as its best idea, from the options it knows about and, in that particular circumstance, to get what it wants. When we're first born, we have a limited range of behaviors. To get what we want, we may blink, wiggle, grimace, but when those don't work, we'll emote . . . tears maybe, maybe loud sounds. And when someone comes and does for us what we wanted done, we learn that emoting works. It gets attention, and it gets action from others. We get fed; we get comforted; we get changed. So we learn early that emoting is a powerful way to control other people.

> Emoting serves at least three major purposes: it gets the attention of others, it's a call for help, and it gets us off the hook to do something better.

"It's not my fault. She made me mad! I'm too depressed right now to do anything about it." Depressing has the added feature of keeping angering in check. Angering at the wrong time and in the wrong ways can land us in a time-out, either on the couch as kids or in jail as adults. Choosing to depress instead of anger will usually save us from the forced time-out, although one could argue that depressed is a time-out of its own. The skillful emoter will have a lot to choose from. In addition to angering and depressing, there's fearing, anxietizing, worrying, raging, sulking, pouting, fretting, grumping, testying, irritabling, nervousing, fussing—lots of choices. But people don't like being controlled by the emotings of others, at least once we get past a certain age. Controlling more through reasonable actions and less through emotional eruptions is what maturing is all about.

My granddaughter, Rylie, is learning this lesson early. She was barely two years old but my daughter Darcy figured that's old enough to be taking responsibility for how one chooses to behave in an attempt to close one's gap. Rylie had been staying at our house for most of the day one Saturday while her parents were out doing something. She's fun to have around. She gets lots of attention from her Aunt Courtney, 19, and Uncle Todd, 15, and was pretty worn out by the time Darcy and Drew returned to pick her up. She wanted . . . there it is—a want . . . she wanted to be picked up and held by her mother. However, she was still on the ground. She had a gap she wanted to close, so she fussed and reached up toward her mom but Darcy, to my delight, quietly said, "Rylie, I know you want to get picked up, but if you fuss, you won't get it. . . . I won't listen. If you want to be picked up, use your words."

In the blink of an eye, Rylie switched from fussing to, "Mama, would you pick me up please?" What was important to her was getting what she wanted. If emoting didn't work, she was more than willing to switch to another more effective behavior: reasonable requesting. Barely two years old and her parents are teaching her that, as a human being, she has choices when she has a gap between what she wants and what she's currently got; conditions don't make her fuss, she's not stuck with emotings.

> One of the problems we all face is that the brain, left on automatic, will often choose what seems like a good idea at the time but ends up making things worse. Then, of course, we'll blame our choice on something other than the fact that we chose it.

Road rage, currently so much in the news, illustrates this point. One man gets in his car and drives off, wanting to get someplace safely. Another driver cuts in front of him so recklessly close and slow that if our driver does nothing, he will crash. The brain knows what it wants. It wants safety and it wants cooperation from other drivers toward that end.

In an instant, the brain perceives that it's getting a real threat to safety and that the driver of that other car is not cooperating at all. Two gaps. The brain decides and acts so quickly that many people would say it is reacting to the situation. That that other driver makes us do what we do in those situations. Those people miss the fact that our driver began with a want, two wants really, a double desire for safety *and* cooperation from other drivers.

The brain doesn't react. It acts on the environment to get or preserve what it wants; to keep gaps closed. If a driver only wanted safety, and another driver cut her off, she might simply apply her brake until she achieved a safe distance between vehicles. If she didn't care about safety, hers, the other driver's or her car's, she might not even slow down—just plow on into that slow car that suddenly cut in front of her.

The other driver cutting her off is only information. It's information that lets her know what she's got. It doesn't cause her to do anything. She'll compare it to what she wants, experience some degree of an energizing gap, depending on gap size the energy the gap generates will compel her to choose a behavior out of one of her option zones. Her brain will choose something to do that it believes will close that gap, and out will come a behavior that has four components:

1. Doing
2. Thinking
3. Emoting
4. Physiology

Primed with the double desire of safety *and* cooperation, the driver in our story leaves a restaurant with his family and heads home. On the freeway, a second driver cuts him off. First, the seemingly automatic movement of the foot from accelerator to brake, then the seemingly automatic movement of the hand and extended middle finger from the steering wheel to out the window and, where do those words come from, a stream of loud vocalizations.

We have all heard news reports about how dangerous it is to leave the brain on automatic in situations like this. A recent story I saw on television chronicled the tragic escalation of just such an event. A series of gaps between wants and gots in each driver led to a series of actions, choices each man made, that resulted in the shooting death of one driver in front of his wife and adult son by the other driver in front of his preteen son. Two weeks later, the shooter went back to the same spot and shot himself. The brain is a dangerous thing to leave on automatic.

> Understanding how the brain works gives us the opportunity to take it off automatic in order to prevent disasters and optimize opportunities.

Understanding will help the cranky manager change from criticism, reprimands, and coercion to listening, supporting, and cocreating solutions. It will help the frustrated punitive parent change from ranting and rules to reason and relationships. Understanding will open the doors to more effective ways of getting or keeping desired results.

So what does the brain have to work with when making its output choices? In general, it has actions (doing), thoughts (thinking), emotions (emoting), and the physiology that makes it all work. Some combination of these four components is what we use 24/7 in our attempts to get the world to be the way we want it to be. These four components are the tools we have to get what we want from the world around us.

Our output 24 hours a day, seven days a week, 365 days . . . well, you get the idea . . . basically all the time . . . is a combination of doing, thinking, emoting, and physiology (Figure 8.1). The want/got gap is what drives us to come up with a behavior and whatever we come up with is going to have degrees of all four components in it. And all of these must be congruent and support each other in any given behavior. In other words, for me to behave angrily, I have to have angry thoughts, angry movements, angry physiology, and angry emotions.

If I'm going to depress, my doing will be sitting there listlessly, my thoughts will be negative, my emotings blue, and my physiology producing the blood and brain chemistry scientists measure to confirm that we are actively depressing. But if I change one component, then the rest will follow. They have to. These four must support each other. Let's say I get up and start jogging or dancing (changing my doing). My physiology will crank up the chemistry I need to

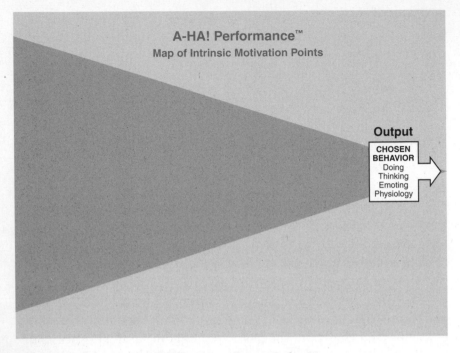

FIGURE 8.1   Chosen Behavior

support that, it's going to be hard for me to have negative thoughts or emote in a depressed way. As Steve Martin once said, "You can't play the blues on the banjo."

We change our doing, and it changes our physiology, thinking, and emoting.

On the other hand, take someone who believes that angering at his employees is the best way to get them to do what he wants them to do. Consequently, his actions will likely be animated, the tone of his voice louder (or, if he's really good at angering, softer) than usual, his thoughts will be on what a disaster the situation is, his emotings will look and feel like anger, and his physiology will be pumped full of adrenaline, blood coagulators—all the electrochemical activity inside the body that pumps us up enough to explode at someone.

When we're angry, it's hard to relax. Yet, if we divert our thinking to something more pleasant, perhaps remind ourselves of a good thing this person has done, that the sky isn't falling, then we can relax a bit, stop pacing, exhale, and let the anger change to a calm that allows rational thinking and productive conversations.

Or consider going on a job interview—some people are nervous (emoting); their hands are sweating (physiology); they can't sit still (doing); and they are wondering how the interview is going to go, whether they are any good, or if the interviewer is going to like them (thinking). Some people wonder why their hands instantly sweat when they walk into an interview. It's just their physiology staying congruent with their thoughts about what's going to happen, their emotings of nervousness and fear, and their doing of tensing up. If they change their doing and thinking, they may pull their physiology into a more relaxed state and the sweaty palms will dry. Thinking about the interviewer and how hard this may be for her gets our thoughts off ourselves. Or, remembering that humility is having a right view of ourselves and that the truth is we have a good combination of expertise, experience, education, and enthusiasm for this job. Those thoughts are going to be accompanied by relaxed posture, an easy smile, a calm voice, confident emotings, and a dry-palmed physiology. Change one component and the others follow.

Back in my counseling days, I had a client who came to my office one day saying she was so depressed she barely had enough energy to get to the appointment, but not enough energy to talk. She just wanted to sit in the chair across from my desk and stare into space. If I let her go on doing that behavior, sitting and staring, it would allow her to focus on woe-is-me thoughts and I'd be letting her maintain the components of behavior that enhanced her ability to depress.

She was depressing for a reason. She knew I was going to push her into living differently, more responsibly. I knew she had a better chance at happiness by getting involved with good people, working in a meaningful job, doing fun things. If she could do those things, instead of hiding out in her little apartment all day, all week, her life would be genuinely and intrinsically more need-satisfying. It would be better than trying to meet all her needs through coming to counselors. Coming to counselors was easy though—she knew how to do that. While better than struggling alone, and a Godsend through difficult times, counselors as a way of life are just not as good as the fruits of responsible living. But changing to living life like a responsible adult would take effort, both in the learning and in the execution. She didn't want to have to go through that effort. She wanted to control me into leaving her alone, into not pushing. If she depressed well enough on me, it might do what emotings are designed to do: It might get my attention, let me know she needed help, get her off the hook of having to do something different than she was currently doing (because she was just too depressed) and it might keep her from the angering that could actually make things even worse.

Her brain was choosing to depress to control me. But I knew that for her to continue to depress, she'd have to be allowed to continue to do what she was doing, sitting quietly and thinking negative hopeless thoughts. It's very difficult to will our emotings to improve; I could have said, "Hey, cheer up," good advice to a person who is depressing, but I didn't think that was going to work. Advice seldom does.

So here's what I was faced with: I knew that for her to change from a depressed recluse to a reasonably okay and functioning person would take effort. I knew that for her to be willing to put out that effort, she'd have to buy into the idea; she'd have to want to become a reasonably functioning person by getting *clarity* as to what that would look like, by believing that in spite of all she'd been through it was *attainable*, and that the *payoff* for it was well worth the cost. But to have that CAP conversation with her, she'd have to be willing to talk with me, and talking takes effort—energy. She is sitting in front of me saying she is too depressed to talk. What do I do?

If I believed that she was in a state of depression, I'd be stuck. Since I believe what A-HA! Performance claims, that emoting is a component of the behavior we choose, all I had to do was to get her to change her choice of behaviors from depressing to something better. I do believe that emotings are behaviors the brain chooses but that's not to say that we can volitionally just change them with ease.

It's possible to improve our ability at quick attitude changes, but for most of us, it's easier to change what we're doing, and then let the emotings follow, than the other way around.

Knowing that gave me lots of options. If I could get her doing something other than sitting, her emoting would change.

I happened to have a stack of foam rubber Frisbees on my desk from a recreation activity I had led the evening before. I reached over, picked them up, and asked, "Do you want to throw these or catch them?"

"What are you talking about?" she said. "Didn't you just hear me? I'm too depressed to talk and you want me to play Frisbee?"

"Throw, or catch?" I repeated, and picked up the first one.

"Sit down!" she said, a combination smile and scowl on her face.

I started tossing them; she raised her hands to bat them away and started laughing. Hard not to laugh when someone is tossing foam Frisbees at you. The point here is that she changed her emotings by changing what she was doing. Once we had broken the paralyzing chains of depressing, we could talk and plan. Had I not understood this Intrinsic Motivation Point, that we choose our behavior and that our behavior is made up of four components that have to support each other, I'd have been stuck, too. I wouldn't have understood that to change one, all we have to do is change a more changeable one. To change attitudes, sometimes it's easier to change actions. To change physiology, sometimes we change thoughts; the heart stops racing when we remind ourselves that there is lots that's okay. Some people choose to change emotings, thoughts, and behaviors by changing their physiology—living differently through chemicals, but the pros and cons of that approach will have to be flushed out in a different book. For our purposes, change one component and the others have to follow.

If we're not happy with the emoting component of the behaviors we're currently generating, our attitudes, for dealing with our management problems and challenges, we can change them. We can build more effective ones into our automatic options zone, new ones where the attitudes we use on our employees are the ones that support our best doing, our best thinking, and our healthiest physiology. When I taught these ideas in Australia, the vice president of an organization there told me three months later that no one yells in his organization anymore and problems have decreased dramatically. He even said his blood pressure had gone down 40 points.

Summation

All behavior, all output is chosen. Chosen behavior has four components: doing, thinking, emoting, and physiology. Most people are
willing to admit that they do have control over the doing component,
maybe some over the thinking component. Some people even acknowledge a modicum of control over their attitudes; their emotings.
The truth is, we can change any of them because, since they have to
be in support of each other, if we change one, the others will follow.
Managers who practice A-HA! Performance and utilize the Intrinsic
Motivation Points understand that all behavior (ours and others) is
chosen by the brain as the best thing it can come up with to deal with
a particular gap at a particular time. Because the brain chooses it automatically, we can take our brain off automatic and choose better
behaviors, intentionally (see Figure 8.2).

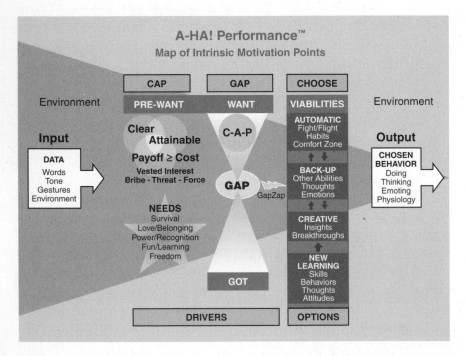

FIGURE 8.2 Drivers, Options, and Chosen Behavior

Filters: Coloring What's Coming In and Limiting What's Going Out

esearch, reason, experts, and experience all suggest that managers make their decision about a potential hire within the first three minutes, possibly the first few seconds, of a job interview. Why? Because of the effectiveness of our input perception filters (Figure 9.1).

Our perception filters include a knowledge filter, a valuing filter, and the amygdala. The knowledge filter recognizes things we've seen before. With people, it may be styles of grooming, energy levels, sense of humor, tone of voice, facial expressions, and candor in answering questions. So when we see it again, we know what it is and have a belief about what it does. The first time we're introduced to something, we may not have a clue about what it is, but we go through a process of storing what it is and what it does in our input filters so that the next time we see it, we recognize it without having

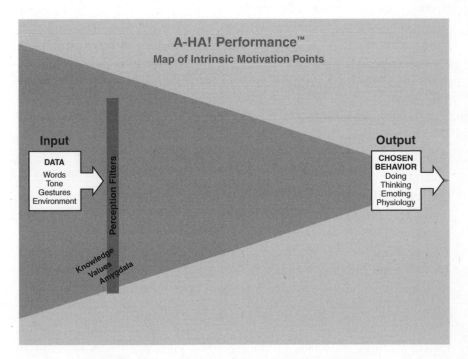

FIGURE 9.1 IMP 8—Filters: Input or Perception

to go through the time consuming process of learning about it all over again.

When I worked one summer on a dude ranch in Colorado, I was assigned fence-mending duty. The harsh winter weather breaks barbed wire and someone has to replace or reattach the broken wire to the fence posts. I was handed a tool that looked like a fancy pair of pliers. I had never seen anything quite like it before, but I was told it was a barbed wire fixing or tensioning tool—a combination cutter, gripper, stretcher, and hammer. It allowed me to grip the wire, stretch it, and keep it tight while I hammered in the staples to hold the wire in place. I had never seen one before that summer, but it's firmly in my knowledge filter now. When I see one again, I won't have to learn about it, I'll already know. We learn about something once and then recognize what it is thereafter.

The valuing filter lets us know the value of what we're perceiving relative to our needs; is it satisfying, neutral, or threatening to us? If we have a lot of barbed wire fence to reattach, that tool is very need satisfying. We'd want one.

We know what cheeseburgers are and we also have a belief about whether they're good or bad for us based on how we believe cheeseburgers impact our survival needs. If we like them, we'll set our values filter accordingly so the next time we see one, we'll know what it is and that it's good. If we don't like them, we'll still know what it is, but we'll see it as bad . . . probably unhealthy.

So while our knowledge filter tells us what something or someone is, our values filter tells us how that person or thing is likely to impact our needs. For example, when our employees see us, thanks to the knowledge filter, they know who we are and that we are the boss. And based on their experience with the way we treat them, they have placed a value on us as well. We are either a source of need satisfaction or need frustration for them and they will set their values filter accordingly. Once set, that's how they'll see us when we interact. Boss is almost never just boss. It's good boss or bad boss. And in fairness, employees are never just employees, either. We value them, too. We set our values filter to see them as somewhere on that scale that ranges from good to bad. Good bosses and employees are need satisfying bosses and employees; bad ones are need frustrating ones. So the first two filters—knowledge and values—help us know who or what something is, and how that person or thing is likely to impact our needs.

If you've ever called a company's customer service line and been frustrated by an unwillingness or inability on the part of the customer service person to resolve your issue, then you may have begun the process of calibrating your knowledge and values filters relative to frontline customer service people. From experience we know what a frontline customer service person is, and whether our needs are satisfied or frustrated when we talk to one. If we get a company script from that person that amounts to "sorry . . . your service agreement doesn't cover that," then we've started connecting customer service at the company with frustration, not satisfaction.

> So whether we view something as good or bad depends on what our experience has been with it and how we've calibrated our filters for the next time we see it.

The third filter, the amygdala, is the part of the brain that detects threat to the needs, and when it does, it shuts down the frontal lobe and activates our fight or flight behaviors.

In the book *Blink: The Power of Thinking without Thinking* (Boston: Little, Brown and Company, 2005), author Malcolm Gladwell discusses how we make decisions or recognize things and just know what to do in the blink of an eye. We bypass the "thinking it through process" because, in an instant, our input filters have already recognized what it is and calibrated whether or not it is need satisfying, need neutral, or need threatening. In an instant, a gap forms and a GapZap of energy is generated that signals the options zone to produce something, probably out of the automatic zone, to deal with that gap.

If we're hiking along a trail and see this elongated, tubular object that is about four feet long, maybe an inch or two thick, coiled up with a rattle on one end and a forked tongue flickering out of the other end, we would know what it is—a rattlesnake. What's happening in our brain is the image of the rattlesnake we're looking at hits our knowledge filter and we instantly recognize it. Then it passes through our valuing filter and gets labeled as dangerous. Now we see it as very threatening to our need for survival. In a nanosecond, we know what that tubular object is and its probable impact on our needs.

But my granddaughter, Rylie, wouldn't recognize this long, tubular object, nor would she place any value on it, because she has never seen a rattlesnake before. Our knowledge and valuing filters get calibrated and updated through experience.

By the time we're adults, most of us have set our filters to recognize a rattlesnake and to see it as a threat. And if it's a big enough threat, our amygdala will pick it up and send an urgent signal directly to our fight or flight options to act. Kill the snake, or get away from it.

Do we kill or flee the snake because it's intrinsically bad? No. In the real world, a rattlesnake is just a rattlesnake. Good and bad exist only in our internal world of filtered perceptions and since we each have our own filters, we sometimes disagree about what's good or bad. What if we were snake ranchers? We'd look at that snake, and through filters calibrated differently than those who loathe snakes, see it as cha-ching; an opportunity, rather than a threat. We'd activate our snake-handling skills so as to capture the snake, secure it, and then harvest its venom for profit.

The late Steve Irwin, known as the Crocodile Hunter, saw snakes as gorgeous . . . and he did a lot to help the rest of us see snakes that way, too. His mission was to help people all over the world calibrate their filters differently toward animals—to see their magnificence, their beauty and, while respecting them, to fear them less. He knew that we had choices as to how we saw things and that how we saw things would have everything to do with how we behave toward them.

My daughter, Courtney, a big fan of the Crocodile Hunter, has calibrated her own filters regarding animals in a similar fashion. In addition to the four dogs, a bird, a turtle, and various fish she cares for at home, she volunteers at the wildlife rescue facility in San Diego. How we see things will determine how we behave toward them.

We not only see a person we recognize, but we have also valued that person one way or the other: as one of the good guys or one of the bad guys. And that judgment determines how we'll behave around that person. Diversity training is all about recalibrating our filters so that instead of seeing differences as bad, we begin to see them as good, perhaps even as opportunities for synergizing.

Input filters—knowledge, values, and amygdala—help us know what things are, whether they're need satisfying or threatening, and how imminent or serious a threat is (Figure 9.2).

By determining that information almost instantaneously, we shortcut the decision-making process as to what to do.

A key a-ha for managers around input filters is that if our employees see us as need threatening, and their amygdalas kick in, employees will go into some version of fight or flight. Yet, if we have a significant challenge with them, we don't want them fighting or

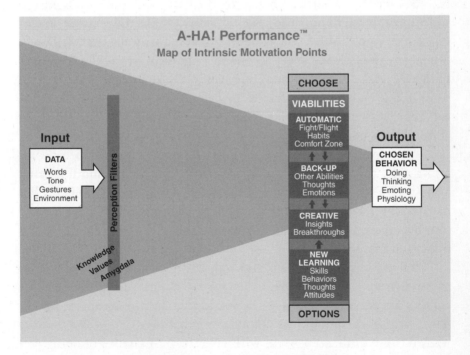

FIGURE 9.2   Input Filters—Options

fleeing . . . we don't want their automatic, back-up, or creative options zones to shut down. We'll want access to all of their best thinking in solving the problem (see Figure 9.2).

In addition to input perception filters, we have output filters. Technically there's more than one, but the one that's important for managers to know about is the values output filter. This is the ability we have to determine—before it's too late—whether or not the behavior we've just thought of will meet our needs in both the short and long term.

The output values filter sets the limits within which we will behave, as we believe that if we behave outside of those limits, our needs will not be met in both the short term and the long term. It's like a quality check on the behavior we're considering. So while our behavior options zone is responsible for coming up with a behavior it thinks will close a gap we're experiencing, our output values filter is responsible for looking over those options carefully so that we don't select one that is actually going to make things worse (see Figure 9.3).

Sometimes what we choose to do will meet our needs in the short term, but will hurt us in the long term. Take moderation in eating, for example. With the value of behaving in ways that will meet our needs in both the short term and long term, we will eat enough to where we're satisfied now but won't eat so much that we gain weight and endanger our future health. If we didn't have the value for health, then we'd eat as much as we'd want without thinking about what's going to happen to our health and weight later on.

Or consider a salesperson who is less than honest in order to win a sale, revealing that she doesn't have a strong value for being honest. She may get the sale and meet her needs in the moment, but in the long term, she will not only lose that customer, but she will also lose many other customers because she will get a reputation for being untrustworthy.

Yahoo! has a list of their core values on its website. The title on the web page is: "What We Value versus What Sucks!" Core value statements are declarations to the world that at "our company, we behave within certain limits because we believe that if we behave within these limits, our needs will have the best chance of being met over the span of time." Need satisfaction is valuable. Need frustra-

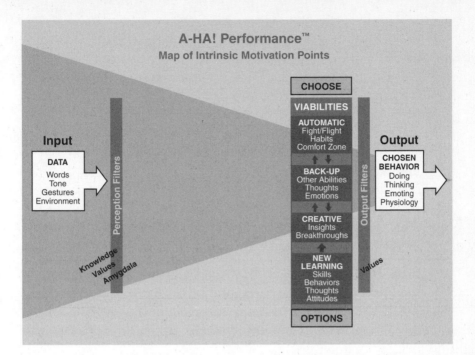

FIGURE 9.3   IMP 8—Filters: Output

tion sucks. Whether or not Yahoo! realized it at the time, values always apply directly to need satisfaction.

> Values are always the specific limits or parameters that keep us behaving in ways that most satisfy or protect our needs both short term and long term.

So before Yahoo! employees choose a behavior in any given situation, their output values filter will screen that proposed behavior for potential need satisfaction in both the short term and long term. If the filter picks up a behavior that is not within those values, it will reject it, and send that person back to his or her option zone to come up with something better; something that is consistent with the values. Values will allow some conduct, and disallow others.

Yahoo! What We Value versus What Sucks!

- *Yahoo! values Excellence:* "We are committed to winning with integrity. We know leadership is hard won and should never be taken for granted. We aspire to flawless execution and don't take shortcuts on quality. We seek the best talent and promote its development. We are flexible and learn from our mistakes."
  Need Translation: We value excellence because Yahoo! and its employees meet power needs better that way. We win and achieve more through striving toward excellence than through accepting "good enough."

- *Yahoo! values Innovation:* "We thrive on creativity and ingenuity. We seek the innovations and ideas that can change the world. We anticipate market trends and move quickly to embrace them. We are not afraid to take informed, responsible risk."
  Need Translation: Innovation helps Yahoo! and its employees meet their freedom needs; they avoid hardening of the categories and don't get stuck in doing the same old things in the same old ways.

- *Yahoo! values Customer Fixation:* "We respect our customers above all else and never forget that they come to us by choice. We share a personal responsibility to maintain our customers' loyalty and trust. We listen and respond to our customers and seek to exceed their expectations."
  And *Teamwork:* "We treat one another with respect and communicate openly. We foster collaboration while maintaining individual accountability. We encourage the best ideas to surface from anywhere within the organization. We appreciate the value of multiple perspectives and diverse expertise."
  And *Community:* "We share an infectious sense of mission to make an impact on society and empower consumers

in ways never before possible. We are committed to serving both the Internet community and our own communities."
Need Translation: Customer Fixation, Teamwork, and Community help Yahoo! employees meet their belonging needs with customers, colleagues and their community.

- *Yahoo! values Fun:* "We believe humor is essential to success. We applaud irreverence and don't take ourselves too seriously. We celebrate achievement. We yodel."
Need Translation: Humor, irreverence . . . and the occasional yodel, help Yahoo! employees meet their fun needs.

Companies and individuals alike should adopt values that create and maintain a culture where opportunities for need satisfaction are maximized in both the short term and long term. If we behave within effective values, we're much more likely to achieve what we want both now, and into the future.

Summation

Filters serve us in two ways. Input filters help us with instant accuracy as to our perceptions. We quickly recognize what we're experiencing and just as quickly determine whether it's good, bad, or neutral. Output filters help us limit the kinds of behavior we engage in to behavior that not only meets our needs in the short term, but also in the long term as well.

Input filters get calibrated through experience. A relationship between a manager and an employee will be maximized if the employee experiences care and credibility from the manager and thereby calibrates his or her input filters in such a way that "boss" is associated with need satisfaction. When employees value their bosses as good, they will be intrinsically motivated to do what their boss is asking them to do.

Not only is cooperation and compliance enhanced where bosses are liked, retention is higher, too.

Output filters get calibrated through R2E2; reason, research, experience, and experts. Creating organizational values that employees are willing to buy into because they are clear, attainable, and pay off by maximizing need satisfaction in both short and long term will benefit employee and organization alike. When we share the same vales, people can be counted on to perform within particular ethical parameters, not because someone is watching, but because their values filters wouldn't allow them to do otherwise. Shared values help minimize risk to the company and maximize the kinds of collaboration that only happen in high-integrity, high-trust cultures.

Addressing and Improving
Inadequate Performance Behavior

As a management level employee for over 20 years, Catherine Hopkins has had her share of management challenges. Whether it's a bad attitude or lack of work ethic, Catherine is no stranger to the daily struggles of managing a less than stellar employee. In fact, she chalked up one recent challenge she faced to the dichotomy between baby boomers and generation X.

Not only does Catherine think that younger employees are less concerned with loyalty to a company and more concerned with their own well-being, but she has also noticed a sense of entitlement. Before, people felt lucky to have a secure job, younger generations think a company should feel lucky to have them. "In hiring young people with advanced degrees, they tend to think, 'I've got an MBA from an Ivy League school so I should be able to get more money and rapid promotions just because I'm entitled to it,'" says Catherine. "But without any results or a proven track record, I don't believe they are entitled to anything."

Catherine adds that those employees don't always think they need to report to their managers just because they are their managers. Managers have to earn respect these days, it's far from automatic.

She ran into this situation when she was vice president of marketing for a software company. Samantha Flemmings, Catherine's underling, thought she was so good at what she did that she shouldn't have to be accountable to anyone and resented having to report to Catherine, who was her boss. "The whole time she was working for me, she didn't think she had to tell me what she was doing," says Catherine. "It never occurred to her that she should be sitting down with me to review what she was doing in the context of what I needed her to do."

Managing people is arguably the most difficult job in the world. How do successful managers have conversations with employees that result in the employee willingly, even enthusiastically, engaging in the desired activity? In other words, how do we address and improve behavior that is below the line of acceptability? And how do managers get talent that is already good to agree to do the work of learning and developing themselves into even better professionals? How do we address and improve behavior that is above the line of acceptability?

Another management challenge Catherine experienced was Samantha's unwillingness to do anything she felt was beneath her. Catherine says, "In a start-up, you have to wear a lot of hats—you have to do things that are below your title and not at all what you went to school for, like getting coffee or taking out the trash. With all the experience I had, I still did whatever was required to move the business forward." Samantha's attitude, however, was that she was too high level to do those menial tasks—and she made it known. "Why can't we hire someone to do the chores and administrative work?" was one of the ways she made it clear she didn't want to do anything out of her sphere of expertise.

Like Catherine, most managers at some point in their careers face the challenge of trying to improve the performance of one or more of their employees, either because it's unacceptable, or because they want to develop a promising talent into a leadership position. It's for both these kinds of situations that I am sharing an A-HA! Performance-based intervention called Address and Improve™, based on the work of William Glasser, MD. Addressing and improving a situation is not talking excessively about an employee's screwups or criticizing her performance. The objective of Address and Improve, rather, is to address the situation as it stands in the present and to engage the employee in improving it for the future in a way that doesn't ruin the relationship with that employee.

Just as there is a way to get a needle into a balloon without popping it, there is a way to address and improve difficult situations without blowing up the relationship between manager and direct report. Between the manager's input and the employee's output, there is a process. The process includes buy-in (or not), motivation (to do or not to do), behavior selection (good or bad choices), and behavior implementation (or not). Once managers understand the process the brain takes on the way to performance, managers can focus their conversations in ways that maximize buy-in and desired behavior choices.

The phases of Address and Improve are:

1. Assess strength of relationship between manager and employee:
   a. Care: Focus on need satisfying wins for all parties.
   b. Credibility: Integrity and competency.

2. Identify the gap: Both ends, want, and got, as well as size/scope:
   a. Identify your want/goal.
   b. Identify, as clearly as possible, what the current reality, or got, is.
   c. Identify the size of the gap, the intensity of the GapZap, the scope of the problem.
3. CAP the want:
   a. Clear: What? Who? When? Where?
   b. Attainable: What are the obstacles that need to be overcome in closing that gap and achieving the goal? Are we missing any of the Es of attainability?
   c. Payoff: Be clear about both payoff and cost involved in attaining the goal.
4. Examine current chosen behavior:
   a. What's the current behavior or behavior pattern; the current process?
   b. Identify the current mix of actions, thoughts, and attitudes or emotings. So what are you doing, thinking, emoting?
5. Evaluate how well it's working—Is the doing working in closing the gap and moving us closer to the want/goal?
6. Plan to do something that will work better:
   a. Criteria for a good plan:
      • Clear.
      • Attainable.
      • Payoff ≥ Cost (makes things better, not worse).
      • Measurable.
      • Do plan, not don't do plan.
      • Dependent on doer only.
      • Immediately implementable.
      • Repeatable.
7. Get/make commitment:
   • Review consequences of success/failure.
   • No excuses.
   • Never give up.
   • Give up (confer/refer).

To elaborate on each of these, I'll start with the first.

Relationship Reflection: Assess Strength of Relationship between Manager and Employee

This is a preliminary, introspective step to assess the strength of our relationship with the employee in question. As mentioned in previous chapters, the two criteria for a good relationship are care and credibility: Does our employee believe we care that her needs get met in improving the particular situation, and does the employee believe that we're credible—that we know what we're talking about and that we keep promises?

If an employee believes that we care about her win in improving an issue, then it's less likely that her amygdala will pick the conversation up as a threat and send her into fight or flight mode. If she doesn't feel she has to protect herself, she'll be more likely to have a rational discussion. Some managers have a history of working with people in this way and gain a reputation for care and credibility. Those managers have a better chance at a reasonable and performance changing discussion than those known for thinking about the company and themselves only.

A great manager doesn't have to be a close personal friend with each employee. The relationship required is a professional relationship based on mutual care for the other person's interests, career, and well-being.

> An employee needs to know that when we sit down to talk with her, it's not to berate or criticize her; rather, it's to figure out a solution to an issue.

In making a change, we want it to be one with which she is happy, too. When Richard Harper approached Susan Moore with the attitude that he was going to win and she was going to buckle under, look what happened. There was no win in it for her, so she left. Not only that, she left in a way where he lost, too. So we train ourselves to think about employees' needs as much as we do the company's and our own. It's a minor addition to the thought process, but it pays off in major ways.

The answers to the relationship questions give us a pretty good idea about how this conversation is likely to go. If the employee believes we care and are credible, it will go a lot better than if she doesn't believe that.

Identify the Gap

One way to open an Address and Improve conversation might be: "I have a concern that needs to be addressed and I'm going to need your help in solving it. I want to be able to improve this situation in a way that works for you, for the company, and for me. From my experience, I believe the best solution is one we'll work out together."

In sharing the gap, sometimes we'll start with identifying our want: "Hey Shelby, I could really use your help. I want you to be on-site by 7:30 A.M., in the customer's parking lot, ready to meet to go over our presentation; to be sure we each have the right materials and the appropriate samples . . ."

Other times it might make more sense to start with the got: "Shelby, in the past two days, you haven't been at the customer site until after 8:00 A.M. (8:05 A.M. yesterday and 8:15 A.M. today) . . ." The main goal at this point is to remember that every problem has two ends to it: the want and the got. To really understand a problem, it's important to establish the gap by identifying both ends.

Should I let the employee know how upset I am? Should I unload my frustration on her? I think that this is counterproductive and a self-indulgent luxury. Few businesses or business people can afford to even be upset, let alone to vent it. It's much more productive to solve the problem than to anger or complain about it. Besides, the past two days are gone. That water has long since passed under the bridge and the only place we can make changes is in the present or immediate future. Share enough of the past to establish the current situation, but don't add too much judgment to it. "You've been late the past two days," is better than, "I am so upset at you for being late the past two days that I'm considering . . ."

CAP the Want

The opportunity here is in optimizing the gap by establishing a compelling want that brings together the three pieces of the CAP puzzle: clarity, attainability, and payoff (CAP).

Clear

To get a person to do what we want her to do, we must be sure to communicate clearly: who, what, when, and where. For some, that's all they need. Once they understand what we want, they move forward in an attempt to deliver. "Shelby, to me, being at the customer's on time actually means getting here early enough so that you have time to review the plan with the rest of the team. You may need time to get updated on any changes that have come about since yesterday. Please be sure you have all the materials you need and that they are organized the way you want them so that when you're in front of the customer, you'll be perceived as prepared and professional."

Clarity covers the four Ws. Who? Shelby. What? Arrive for the final prep meeting. When? Thirty minutes before the meeting with the customer. Where? In the customer's parking lot.

Attainable

But clarity alone isn't enough. Sometimes employees are clear about what we want but they still don't deliver it. That's where we address the second piece: the belief as to whether they think our request is attainable. Belief that something is possible is the key to this piece of the puzzle. When people believe they can achieve something that's clear and pays off more than it costs, they'll strive to do it, even if it turns out later that it was never possible in the first place. If they don't believe it's possible, they won't put forth an effort. We could ask, "Shelby, is it possible for you to be here at 7:30 A.M.?"

We can explore the 10 Es of attainability:

1. *Expertise:* Does Shelby have the skill to be on time?
2. *Experience:* What's Shelby's on-time pattern?
3. *Equipment:* Does she have alarm clocks and reliable transportation?
4. *Education:* Does she have the training to be on time?
5. *Empowerment:* Does she have the authority to be on time? This could be a business issue, a domestic issue, or matrixed organizations, for example, sometimes have conflicts around who's really in charge.
6. *Ethics:* Are being on time and keeping appointments values of hers?
7. *Expenses:* Are there costs: tolls, parking, gas, public transportation? What about family costs? Childcare? Carpools? Morning routine?
8. *Energy:* Does she have the physical energy to get up on time and do everything necessary to arrive on time?
9. *Enthusiasm:* Is she eager to be on time?
10. *Environment:* What are the environmental challenges she'll face in getting there on time? Traffic? Construction? Train crossings? New address? Weather conditions?

Payoff

The third puzzle piece that has to be covered to get others to want what we want them to want is payoff. What that really means is that unless the payoff for them is greater than or equal to the cost, they won't do it. For Shelby, the payoff for getting to the site early has to outweigh the cost of waking up early or of changing her usual routine. If she likes her sleep or routine too much, this might be an issue. We should be prepared to answer the question, "Why should she?" The "What's-In-It-For-Me (WIIFM)" piece is an important one.

As I've already discussed, the most powerful motivator in getting the WIIFM question answered is vested interest payoff. Not force, threat, or bribes, but tying the desired performance as directly as possible to one or more of an employee's basic needs:

- *Love and belonging:* "Shelby, don't you feel better when you support your team by being on-time as opposed to letting them down by being late?"
- *Power, self-worth, and achievement:* "I know it's a challenge sometimes to get up and going that early, but don't you feel better about yourself when you show up on time?"
- *Fun:* "We'll get the materials organized and then maybe have time for some recreational complaining."
- *Freedom:* "Isn't there a certain kind of freedom that comes with being on time? Freedom from stress about whether traffic is going to cooperate or not; feeling more relaxed if you get there at 7:30 A.M.?"
- *Survival:* "I'll have donuts waiting for you . . . coffee, too, if you want it."

To get Shelby to want the on-time that we want her to want, we have to be sure that all three pieces of the CAP puzzle are in place. Sometimes it doesn't take much: just being clear. Sometimes it takes addressing the attainability piece: She may have childcare issues or oversleeping issues. Sometimes it's the payoff versus the cost piece that needs to be addressed. Regardless, once all three are in place, she'll lock-in on-time as the right thing to do.

Next, we have to be sure that we've optimized the gap between this new want and the current reality. If she's a little loose on whether 7:55 A.M. is the same as 7:30 A.M. . . . because they're both before 8:00 A.M., then there won't be a big enough gap between the 7:30 A.M. we want and the 7:55 A.M. she's giving. Or if she thinks there's no way she can possibly get there by 7:30 A.M. because it's just way too early to get up, get showered, groomed, dressed, eat. . . .

Two of the skills utilized by A-HA! Performance managers are: (1) afflict the comfortable—open the gap wider to get people energized—GapZapped—enough to move toward a want that is different than the current got; and (2) comfort the afflicted—reduce the gap and GapZap so that overwhelmed people can see that achieving the goal is possible. When we can go from underwhelmed or overwhelmed to whelmed just right, we'll have achieved the optimum level of energizing motivation to come up with something to do to move from got to want.

Once we've established both ends of the problem—identified and optimized the gap, and CAPped or re-CAPped the want—then we need to take a look at the behavior that has us where we are—late, as opposed to where we want to be—on time at 7:30 A.M.

Examine Current Chosen Behavior

What's the current process or behavior pattern? Identify the current mix of actions, thoughts, and emotings. "Shelby, what are you doing now that gets you here at 8:00 A.M. or after?" This can be a little tricky in that we don't want to be prying into an employee's personal life, but the fact is, there is a process, a current set of sequential behaviors, thoughts, and attitudes that result in her being late. Whether we ask for them in detail, or ask her to take a look at her current practice, being aware of the current routine is this next step.

Evaluate How Well It Is Working

Is the current doing working in closing the gap and at moving us closer to the want/goal? This is the pivotal question in getting people to be willing to change. Is it working? "I get up early, do this and that around the house. . . . I leave the house in what should be enough time." Then the rebuttal is, "Yes Shelby, but is it working?" As we've learned, for a variety of reasons, we human beings have an enormous capacity to do what doesn't work, and to keep on doing it until we make things worse.

Just recently, I got into my car, inserted the key and turned it, hoping to start the car. It cranked, *ank, ank, ank, ank,* . . . but didn't start. Had I had the sense of a machine, I would have realized that ank ank anking wasn't working and I would have stopped before making things worse. But given my enormous faith in tried and true behaviors, like turning a key to start a car, and my capacity for continuing to do what wasn't working because it should be working, I continued to ank, ank, ank until it no longer anked . . . it just clicked. I had anked fruitlessly until the battery died.

But what if someone had come along and asked me the following Address and Improve series of questions:

> *What do you want?*
> I want to get my car started.
>
> *What have you got?*
> A car that's not running.
>
> *How big a problem is this for you?*
> Pretty big, I have to get to work.
>
> *What are you doing?*
> I'm ank anking.
>
> *How's it working?*
> Hmmmm . . . hadn't thought about that but the fact is, it isn't.

Once we realize that what we're doing isn't working, it's awfully hard to say, "I know it isn't working, but I'm going to go on doing it anyway."

Instead, we conclude that we're going to have to come up with something else that might have a chance of working better. That's when we're open to change.

So what do we do to change? First we would stop doing what isn't working so that we don't make things worse. In the car, I stop turning the key and cranking the engine. Next, we figure out something that might work better—perhaps check under the hood, get a jump start for more power, call the mechanic and ask for tips . . . tow the car into the mechanic's. There are many options. Is it working? If it isn't, the trick is to stop doing that easy automatic one, the one that in this case isn't working, think of alternatives, choose one and try that.

Identify the Gap

Let's put the phases of Address and Improve to use. After assessing the relationship, we start by explaining both want and got—what we want the performance to look like compared to how it is now. Whether we start with the got or want is often a judgment call. Using Richard and Susan as an example, Richard might have started with the got: "Here's where we are—people are complaining about the way that you're answering the phone and it's starting to impact us as an organization. Are you aware of that at all?" It's possible she has no idea, but it's not likely. She might say, "What are you talking about? There's no problem, as I'm answering the phones just fine."

If she claims she had no idea that people felt that way, he might elaborate on the feedback he'd been getting, but only until she believes it (A-HA! Performance managers avoid criticizing employees as much as possible). Whether she admits to being aware of it or not depends on the strength of her relationship with Richard. If she believes he cares about her needs in solving this, and if she trusts his word and his competence, then he's got a pretty good chance. If not, this is going to be tougher.

There are a number of ways to get to an agreement about what the current reality is, such as further explaining what we're seeing, or doing a 360 evaluation, or simply stating the facts. For example, if Richard were having this conversation with Susan immediately following a customer complaint, it would be hard for Susan to refute that someone just called and complained about her attitude. Keep in mind that the purpose of establishing the got is to gain a mutual understanding of the current situation, and not to pile on offenses.

Next Richard moves to the desired performance, or what he wants in order to establish the gap.

CAP the Want

Richard uses the best method he knows to get buy-in to what he wants by covering clarity (what), attainability (how), and payoff (why). Richard could've said, "So I'd like us to get to the place where people aren't complaining (clarity) and perhaps, they're even complementing you and wanting to call in because you're so cheerful, helpful, and welcoming each time you answer that phone. I realize you can't control the comments people make, but do you believe that you are the one who controls your attitude, the tone of your voice, and the extent to which you try to be helpful when people call?

"Do you agree that it might be better for the company and the customer if you were answering the phone with a smile and a helpful tone? If you don't answer the phone in such a way that customers feel welcome, then you may turn them away. And without customers, you don't have a job. Not only that, but some of the people who call in are nice people and you might actually enjoy talking to them, making some friends while you're at it. Plus, if you start improving your performance now, you might enjoy working here more and you'd get a better reference for your next job if you wanted to pursue another vocation. If you want to be successful in any career, according to research, 80 percent of success in a career is how well you get along with people. So would you be against making some changes that result in better comments from callers?" Notice all the references to Susan's needs. Whatever our employee's strongest needs are, we're looking for reasons in them to want to be and do better.

> Once we come to an agreement as to what we've got and our employee buys in and wants to improve the situation, now the problem isn't just our problem, it's a shared problem.

At this point, we can look at how big that gap is, what the challenges are going to be in closing it and what our employee's behavior options are. What are the obstacles that need to be overcome in closing that gap and achieving the goal?

Examine Current Chosen Behavior

What we've currently got comes from what we're currently doing.

In Susan's case, the complaints come from the way she's answering the phone and treating clients. In this step, we would ask what the current behavior is, or some version of, "So how are you handling calls now? What's the current practice or process when customers call in? Are you putting a smile on your face when you answer the phone? Are you asking questions to determine the customer's issue? Are you handling ones you can and getting the customer quickly to the right person if you can't? What are you thinking when that phone rings? Are you thinking, 'Darn, another interruption,' or are you thinking, 'Oh boy, here's another chance to help someone'?" This step is a look at what the current chosen behavior is: the doing, the thinking, the emoting, and even the physiology (maybe how she's feeling physically). Although the physiology component is important to know about, examining the current behavior focuses mainly on doing, thoughts/thinking, and emotings.

Evaluate How Well It's Working

Are the behaviors she's choosing working? If you're having this conversation, they're not. In some ways, this question is so obvious many people don't ask it, but it is a turning point question.

People can go on doing what doesn't work seemingly forever. Ank, ank anking fruitlessly is rampant in businesses and homes around the world. But once our employee has actually said, "What I'm doing isn't working at getting to this better level," it's harder for her to say, "but I'm going to go on doing it anyway." This question, and her answer to it, opens her up to looking for a better way because it would be senseless to continue doing what isn't working. After she evaluates the effectiveness of current behavior and finds it lacking, she'll be much more willing to come up with something that might work better.

What we want the person to understand is that the options she is currently choosing have us in our current situation—getting complaints and customers that are unhappy. We may ask, "Is your current practice getting us to where we want to be or is that keeping us where we are?" Once we agree that the current practices are not getting us closer to the desired levels and that something could be done differently that could work better, then we move on.

Plan to Do Something That Will Work Better

Now we try to find out what can work for that employee. Given that everyone has unique gifts and limitations, we know that there's no such thing as a "best practice" in this or any other situation. Giving advice as to how we'd do it at this point is a waste of time because how we'd do it is dependent on who we are. They are not us and will therefore have to come up with how they'd do it.

Remember this quote when you're at this stage, "Never try and teach a pig to sing; it wastes your time and it annoys the pig." And please don't think I'm suggesting that we think of our employees as pigs. That quote is about the futility of advice, not the character of the target. So we want to help navigate through our employees' viable behavior options to see if they can come up with new things they can do that will be more effective at getting to where we want them to be.

What would the new performance look like? Is there anything in their ABCs of behavior—the automatic, back-up, and creative capabilities—that will achieve the want? Before going into the creative or new learning options, we'll want to tap into their current comfort zone or automatic habits to see what they already have stored in there. We may ask, "How do you answer the phone when your friends or family call?" Or, "When someone you care about needs help, what are you thinking and how do you respond to him?" What we're looking to establish is if the behavior we want from them is already in their comfort zone. "If it's not your automatic thing to do here at work yet, have you ever been in a situation where you've answered the phone with a smile? Do you do this at home? Is there anything in you already that we could go to that would work better than what's happening now?"

If new learning is required, then we may ask, "Do you know anybody who does this well that you could learn from, would you be open to some ideas from me or are there any books on the subject you might be willing to read?"

After our employee chooses an option that we both agree could work better, we have to make sure that changes will actually start to occur. For example, if our employee says, "Okay, I'll do better," what should we expect to see? We need to get specific. "What will you do? When will you do it?" Some employees will comply momentarily just to get us off their back. But there won't be any sustained changes if we leave it there. So it's good to nail things down by going through these criteria to know whether the changes have a chance of happening.

Clear

Is the plan clear?

Attainable

Is the plan attainable?

Payoff ≥ Cost (Makes Things Better, Not Worse)

Does the plan payoff for the needs of everyone involved?

Measurable

Because we're not going to watch our employee all the time, what will we look for to know that the new performance is being done? What will we use to measure the improvement? Richard might have used the number of complaints (or lack thereof), customer testimonies, or the number of times colleagues overheard Susan being nicer. Those are all measurable. We'll want to know what it is we're both looking for. And we'll want to encourage our employee to manage our perception that the change is happening. It's one thing to make changes; it's another to be sure they're noticed.

Do Plan, Not Don't Do Plan

A do plan is determining what's going to be done, rather than what's not going to be done. Instead of saying, "You're not going to frown anymore," the real question is, "What are you going to do instead?" So we want to establish what our employee is going to do, and not what she is going to stop doing.

Dependent on Doer Only

This is a plan that the employee is responsible for, regardless of the customer or anyone else in the office. For example, Susan couldn't say, "If the customer is nice to me, then I'll be nice back." Susan would have to agree to adopt the new performance regardless of outside influences. If an employee doesn't know how to perform independently of others' influences, then it may take some rehearsal on how to handle that. But, either way, this plan is dependent on the employee in question. Once we allow it to depend on someone else, the employee is no longer responsible for her own behavior. That's the opposite of A-HA! Performance, which teaches clearly that we are each responsible for the behavior that our brain chooses and that our values filters allow out. If other people's actions are needed for us to behave, then we have a valid excuse for something not to get done. It's the other person's fault.

Immediately Implementable

Can our employee start right away or does it have to wait until tomorrow, a week from now, or a month? The goal is to start immediately because if we put something off until the next day, the chances of the performance happening will decrease by 50 percent. In looking around at the clutter in my office, for example, I keep telling myself I need to clean it up. But the problem is I think, "I'll come in this weekend to do it." Right there, I've already decreased the chance of it happening by 50 percent. On the other hand, if I start right at the moment that I remind myself to clean my office, the clean-up has a 100 percent chance of happening.

So with Susan, if she wasn't comfortable with the new behavior, perhaps she would role-play with Richard. Or Richard would have a customer call in so Susan could put on her smile right away. Regardless, we'll want to figure out a way that the new behavior can be and is implemented immediately.

Repeatable

Through practice, can this new behavior become habitual? We'll want to ensure that the behavior our employee chooses to use to make the situation better is one that she can and will use again to sustain the heightened performance. A fix to important performance issues is about a sustainable fix, not a one time change, and then a return to old ways.

Get/Make Commitment

By now, we've covered many of the basics to make sure the new behavior can happen: We've come up with a plan, it's clear, it's attainable, it pays off, it's measurable, it's a do plan and not a don't do plan, it depends only on our employee, she can't blame anyone else if the performance doesn't happen, and she can start on it right away.

The next question is: "Will you really do this?" Sometimes just asking if our employee will make the changes adds the right degree of accountability. But other times, it takes a little more conviction. Maybe it's scheduling a review meeting in a week's time to create the accountability. Or with an employee who has a history of planning and not executing, a signed agreement or spelling out the

specifics might be in order. This is not to be confused with a performance improvement plan; it's simply a well-defined statement of the
agreed-upon plan and doesn't include negative sanctions as consequences for failure to execute. The consequences at this stage are
simply people having to face their failure to do what they agreed to
do; to experience the natural consequences, such as embarrassment
and disappointment that most of us would rather avoid. We can always escalate to threat later, but we'd better not do that until we're
prepared to lose this employee. Besides, if vested interest motivators
are working, why would we add threat? At some level, we need to
make sure that a reasonable commitment is made. If we feel confident
in the commitment we get from our employee, then the conversation
can stop there. But if we're still running into obstacles, then we may
have to cover the following:

- *Review consequences of success/failure.* Talk about the consequences of the changed behavior, both from the standpoint of
  success and failure. If our employee improves her performance,
  what are the consequences? Richard could point out to Susan,
  for example: "We begin to grow our relationships with our customers and thus our customers are happier. You'll feel better
  about yourself, you'll add the career enhancing skill-set of taking great care of others, and you'll be more comfortable with
  giving super service, which will serve you not only in your career here, but for the rest of your career period. You'll keep your
  job here because you want to, you'll avoid the pain of job hunt-
  ing, and you'll feel better about working with the team."

    The cost of not changing, on the other hand, should focus
  on the person's vested interest, too, not on the threats and sticks
  we can use or the pain we can cause them. We may point out
  that if she doesn't meet this challenge, she won't have as much
  to be proud of. We may also point out that her job could be at
  risk too (but then tie that back to whether that's important to
  her). In other words, we don't want to threaten her with being
  fired if she doesn't perform, although it may in fact be an even-
  tual consequence if she doesn't. Talking about that, and whether
  that's important to her, might be a good thing for us to do.

After all, if the change doesn't happen, then the position might not be the right fit for our employee. In that case, if an employee says she absolutely can't change or doesn't want to change, then the consequences might be working with that employee to transition out of our company and into another one, but in a way that works for everyone. It doesn't mean she'll be fired on the spot, but instead, we set a time line, support her in her job search, and she supports the company in her transition out.

- *Don't get sucked into excuses.* Sometimes employees will say, "I can't, because . . ." But as soon as somebody tells me they *can't because,* I'll ignore the because and say, "I was just going to ask you how you could. If you can't do that, what else could you come up with?" If an employee can't make a commitment to smile on the phone, then what else can she do to communicate care and service? We're trying to figure what she can do to make a commitment to the new performance, and it won't happen when we accept, "I can't because . . .", no matter what the reason.

- *Never give up.* Glasser says it best: "Never give up means hanging in there with people a moment longer than either they or you think you can." It doesn't mean hang in there forever, but at least a moment longer than our normal give-up threshold.

- *Give up (confer/refer).* If we get to the point where we are out of ideas, options, time, and patience, perhaps we should try to go outside of our automatic and back-up options to learn something new. We can confer with someone else, like a mentor or a coach. We can read books or take training courses. That way we may learn new skills and come up with a better solution for working with the individual. Additional competence can only help as we build our own careers.

Hopefully we don't have to get to the "refer" dead-end too often. This means that nothing we've come up with has worked and we're done. Typically we'd turn to HR here, but if we do that constantly, they'll wonder if we might need to be replaced by someone who has the A-HA! Performance Edge skills for effectively dealing with these performance issues.

Catherine Hopkins and Samantha Flemmings Have It Out

With a detailed explanation of how we can use the Address and Improve intervention, the final piece is seeing a conversation in action. This is where the story between Catherine and her stubborn marketing manager comes to life. If Catherine were to use Address and Improve in dealing with Samantha, this is how it might play out:

CATHERINE: Can you give me 15 to 20 minutes of your time? There are some things I want to talk about.

Catherine has made some off-hand comments in the past about Samantha's unwillingness to adapt to the ways of the start-up, but she has never directly addressed it. So Samantha may only have a vague idea of what Catherine wants to talk about.

CATHERINE: Do you know what I wanted to talk to you about?

SAMANTHA: No, I don't have a clue.

The relationship is not a solid one, so establishing the care and credibility is in order.

CATHERINE: I wanted to talk to you because I have a problem and I need your help in solving it. You're certainly not in any trouble and this isn't a scolding of any kind. First off, there are bunches of things you do extremely well and I appreciate your expertise around here. But there are some other things that I wanted to talk to you about, too. What I want from you in terms of you being a member of this start-up team is a little different than what I'm currently getting from you. If you don't see what I'm talking about and aren't willing to make any changes, then it's not going to be the end of the world, but I wanted to put these things out there and see what you think. Is that okay?

SAMANTHA: Yeah.

CATHERINE: One of the issues I want to improve is the frequency of our communication as well as the completeness or thoroughness of our communication. What I currently have is that we're not getting together much and I don't know what you're doing. I don't know which balls are in the air and which are falling. So what I would like is for us to get together more often and share more details about what's going on.

That's one of the reasons I asked you in here. The other is that we're a small operation, we're boot strapping and there are many jobs that need to get done. I'm certainly emptying trash, filing, answering phones, and making coffee, as is everybody else. Up to this point, my experience with you has been that you don't want to do those things, which I can appreciate. But I'd like to talk to you about what your willingness might be to do some of those things.

Maybe some of the tasks you absolutely hate and would not want to do at all. . . . I can understand that, but maybe there are others that you'd be willing to do if we talked about it a little bit.

Those are the two things I wanted to talk to you about, is that okay?

SAMANTHA: Sure.

CATHERINE: As far as meetings, can you tell me what your current practice is?

SAMANTHA: I'm perfectly capable of doing things on my own so I don't need to report to you. And the results are there, so it shouldn't matter.

CATHERINE: Okay, I agree that you're very capable, that's why you're here. There's no argument there. But there are some things that I need to know about and that's the missing piece. So if you can increase that part, letting your team members know what's going on, that's what I'm looking for. I don't want you to give up your current capabilities, those are good. But add to them the skill and practice of not doing everything on your own and sharing with your team a little. Let me ask you something, what would be the cost to you of sharing information with me?

SAMANTHA: I'm afraid of being second-guessed and I don't want my boss breathing down my neck.

CATHERINE: You don't want your boss breathing down your neck?

SAMANTHA: Yep.

CATHERINE: You're afraid I'll do what? What's the worst thing that I might do?

SAMANTHA: You'll micromanage me.

CATHERINE: Okay, so you don't like to be told what to do. What's your belief about synergy versus samergy or lessergy? In other words, you're afraid that if we get together, it's going to end up lessergy. Is that right?

SAMANTHA: Right.

CATHERINE: Have you ever synergized with people or have you mostly worked alone?

SAMANTHA: No, I've collaborated with people before.

CATHERINE: And did that lead to better results or worse ones?

SAMANTHA: Some of both, but mostly better. There have been times when other people have added good ideas or edited something I was working on where they improved it.

CATHERINE: Is it possible to do that alone?

SAMANTHA: No.

CATHERINE: Do you like collaborating and brainstorming with others?

SAMANTHA: Sure, but mostly with peers.

CATHERINE: Okay, but it's still true, you really need another person to synergize with and I'm not saying I'm the right one, but there's a possibility at least that if we got together and shared some ideas, especially if I promised not to micromanage you, then you might get something out of collaborating? For example, maybe you're headed for a wall and I can see the wall and point it out. And then I back off. But the point is if we don't talk, then synergy is impossible, right?

SAMANTHA: Yes.

CATHERINE: Could there be a payoff for you to brainstorm with me?

SAMANTHA: Sure.

CATHERINE: So if we're talking, there is a possible benefit to you in that we can collaborate, but you want to be sure that I'm not micromanaging you. Correct?

SAMANTHA: Yep.

Catherine knows that she can't get buy-in until she covers the payoff versus cost. So that's what she is currently working on—trying to see if Samantha is open to the changes. If she can get Samantha to see that there is a possible payoff and that the cost of micromanaging is lessened, then Catherine could get her to buy in. It's certainly clear what Catherine means by talking more—frequency and completeness of communication. And it's attainable in that they can set aside time to talk. So the payoff is the last piece that needs to be covered.

CATHERINE: So if I can try to shut off my tendency to micromanage, would you be willing to have more conversations with me?

SAMANTHA: Yes.

CATHERINE: Okay, so when could we meet because I'd like to get right on that?

SAMANTHA: Next week sometime.

CATHERINE: Well, today's Thursday, is there any way we could get together tomorrow? What does your schedule look like?

SAMANTHA: I have back-to-back appointments.

CATHERINE: Okay, next week will work. Let's do that. When?

SAMANTHA: Monday.

CATHERINE: Monday, first thing?

SAMANTHA: Sure.

CATHERINE: What time do you get here?

SAMANTHA: 9:00 A.M.

CATHERINE: Okay, let's meet at 9:00 A.M. on Monday.

SAMANTHA: Okay.

CATHERINE: That was the first thing. The other thing was out of all the grunt work around here, are there any pieces that you'll be willing to pick up? This isn't about making you feel less than worthy, because you're a tremendous asset to the company. It's just that it's hard to have a job where you only get to do what you want to do sometimes.

SAMANTHA: I don't like to get coffee for people, but I'll file.

CATHERINE: Great, you don't mind doing that piece?

SAMANTHA: No.

CATHERINE: Okay, I'll take it. And I'll get you coffee when you want it. So if that works for you, it certainly works for me too. It's just that I've got things to do too, and it's about sharing the load. I'm willing to do any of them—being the boss isn't the glamorous thing it used to be. But as long as you're willing to pick up something, that works for me.

As we just saw, Samantha went from someone who wasn't willing to do either of the tasks to now agreeing to do both. And it only took 10 minutes worth of dialogue. The beauty of Address and Improve—or simply referencing the A-HA! Performance Map when trying to improve the performance of our employee—is that it works. So before heading into your next Address and Improve with an employee, keep these guidelines in the front of your mind. You'll not only see improvement right away, but you won't have an employee leaving the conference room screaming obscenities at you. Now those will be worthwhile conversations (see Table 10.1).

TABLE 10.1 Performance Changing A-HA! Applications

Address and Improve	
Assess strength of relationship:	Care
	Credibility
Identify the gap between want and got	
CAP the want	
Examine current total behavior	
Evaluate how well it's working	
Plan to do something that will work better	
Criteria for a good plan:	Clear
	Attainable
	Payoff ≥ Cost (makes things better, not worse)
	Measurable
	Do plan, not don't do plan
	Dependent on doer only
	Immediately implementable
	Repeatable
Get/make commitment:	Review consequences of success/failure
	No excuses
	Never give up
	Give up (confer/refer)

11

Address and Improve: Excelling a Top Performer and Retaining Talent

Kyle Mackintosh, who is a sales manager at Regalo Golf, a leading producer of golf supplies, has faced many management quandaries. But not this year. Unlike Catherine or Richard, frustrating or underperforming employees hadn't been bogging him down. Quite the contrary, in fact. His sales team had just had a record year and everyone on the team was performing optimally. Not to mention that within his immediate environment, he was impressed with people's attitudes and willingness to work long hours.

He did face one impediment, however: Kyle was being pressured by the board of directors to increase revenue by 5 percent in the coming year. Though they were pleased with his team's performance to date, especially with the most recent year's accomplishments, they were looking to the future and they wanted more.

So it was now in Kyle's hands to motivate his already exceptional sales team to increase its sales by 5 percent. When he approached his team with this lofty goal, some employees said, "All I need to know is what percentage you want, boss, and I'll go after it." But others balked.

In particular, one employee, Scott Ferguson, Regalo's top performer, was shocked that Kyle was asking for more after an unprecedented year. He was blindsided by this notion because he already worked as hard as he possibly could to get to the prior year's numbers and he couldn't fathom working any harder. In other words, Scott didn't think 5 percent more in sales was attainable and the cost of working more hours and harder than he was already working outweighed the payoff of doing better.

It's not unusual for managers to find themselves in Kyle's predicament, where they're proud of their employees' performance, yet company circumstances require that even the cream of the crop deliver more. For this reason, it's not only important to see how we can address and improve a problem employee, but also motivate even the most conscientious and fruitful of them. Here's how Kyle's conversation might have unfolded with Scott had he used A-HA! Performance's Address and Improve:

Kyle and Scott's relationship is a solid one and because of his care and credibility, Kyle doesn't have to pad the conversation with pointing out that he has Scott's best interest in mind. While some managers may have to claim that they are looking out for their employees, the company, and themselves to try to establish care and credibility, Kyle had firmly established that by the way he managed Scott and the rest of the team during the previous year. He had the kind of relationship with Scott where he could jump right into his performance need.

KYLE: There's something I wanted to talk to you about. Do you have some time right now?

SCOTT: Sure.

KYLE: I realize we had a record year last year. And for that, I'm so grateful. I know you carried a lot of the weight. But I want to brainstorm with you about taking our record year and doing another 5 percent more next year.

SCOTT: What? You can't be serious. I already work 60 to 70 hours a week to get to the level we're at now. I just can't work any harder. And quite frankly, I have to start cutting back on those hours because we just had a baby.

KYLE: I understand. But if we could get 5 percent more this year without you having to work longer and harder, would you be open to the new goal?

SCOTT: Maybe.

KYLE: Would there be a payoff for you in terms of your family, your compensation, your professional growth, and your position in the company to figure out a way that we can increase our sales by 5 percent?

It was helpful that Kyle understood Scott's need profile so that he could tie the desired performance as directly as possible to those needs. For example, he knew that Scott's needs for love and belonging (family) and need for power (achievement) were really strong, so he tapped directly into those.

SCOTT: Yes, if we could do it without demanding more from me in energy or hours. Of course, I would benefit from getting 5 percent more. That would impact my paycheck positively and if I can accomplish that without letting it cut into my family life, it goes without saying that I would want it. But I either need to know how to do it better so I can do more in less time or I need a second personal assistant or we need to change our products . . . something has to change to be able to produce that increase, and it can't be my time.

KYLE: Okay, so you're not really against the 5 percent increase, you're just saying that we have to find a different way to get there than by adding to what you're already doing. You may not be willing to work longer hours to get there, but you're willing to work smarter?

SCOTT: Yes, so long as I'm not working longer hours.

Now Scott started buying in to the CAP puzzle, at least as far as clarity and payoff were concerned. The goal was clear—5 percent more—and there would be payoff for Scott, as long as he could mitigate the cost of working longer and harder. All that was left for Kyle to cover was the attainability piece and if Kyle helped lodge the belief that 5 percent more was attainable, then it too would be covered, and Kyle would have buy-in.

KYLE: I agree. That's why you're the top performer and you're terrific. I appreciate your expertise, as well as your dedication to our company. We're in agreement there. And if we can figure out a way to reach 5 percent more without you having to work harder and longer, you're open to that, right?

Kyle also has to be cognizant of Scott's power needs. If Kyle doesn't recognize Scott's power needs, he could go adversarial with his top performer. Kyle has to get his point across without blowing up the relationship. He wants to keep Scott's Amygdala quiet so he can have full access to the behavior options in Scott's brain. Not only that but he genuinely admires and appreciates Scott, so why not tell him?

SCOTT: Yes. But I know it's not in our budget to get me a second assistant or develop entirely new product lines, so how do we make this work?

KYLE: I'm not ruling out anything right now, we can talk about getting you another assistant . . . that could be one solution. But let's talk about our existing resources first.

When managers find themselves at an intersection—such as the one where Scott is requesting another assistant, albeit not having the budget for it—managers should let employees go down the road to see if it's a cul-de-sac or a legitimate detour. My belief with attainability, and it comes from years of experience with process redesign, is that if we change something about what we're doing with existing resources, we can figure out a way to improve without additional cost. So when employees try to convince managers that a task is not possible unless we add staff, managers may know differently, but why get into an argument about it? Why not set up an openness to checking out options? One process redesign team I worked with put it this way: "Let's test, not con-test."

The goal is to let employees see for themselves that the task is possible with existing resources. When that happens, attainability is covered.

SCOTT: Well, if I'm not working any harder or any longer, then the 5 percent is going to have to come from somewhere. If we put it in the hands of the guys who don't produce like I do, then you know who is going to be left with carrying all the weight again—me.

KYLE: But you're still thinking that the only way to do it is working longer and harder. What I'm suggesting is, I bet we can figure out some kind of way where you're not working longer or harder, but you're still at least 5 percent more effective. You've already said that if we can do it, you're not against it, right?

SCOTT: Not in the least.

KYLE: From your experience, could the market generate another 5 percent if we're able to figure out how to increase what we're able to sell, without working harder or longer, just more effectively?

SCOTT: Yes. The market can bear another 5 percent.

A-HA! Performance's Essentials of Success, based on the Map of Intrinsic Motivation Points, asserts that immediately upstream from current levels of success is the environment, in this case, the marketplace. When wanting to increase or set goals, the first question to ask is, "Can the marketplace yield another 5 percent?" Are there that many fish in that pond? If there are, then we have to admit the goal is possible.

But upstream from the marketplace are the processes and systems a company, or its salespeople, engage in to produce those results from the marketplace. Fish don't jump out of the pond. Bait has to be selected and attached to hooks, tackle has to be checked and adjusted, and lines have to be cast into just the right spots. Can the same processes that produced last year's numbers yield an additional 5 percent this year? Accidentally, maybe, but if we want to hedge our bets, the smart money is on a change or modification to the existing process.

Upstream from our processes are the skills needed to effectively implement those processes. Sometimes additional training is required. Most organizations get that the right processes are essential and more and more organizations are utilizing process redesign methodologies to maximize quality and efficiency. Most organizations also get that skilled people are required and that training, mentoring and coaching are often necessary. But not all organizations realize that upstream from skills is motivation and morale. They design, often top down, great processes, maybe even provide good training, but forget about the buy-in piece and wonder why success is not happening.

If Scott has the skills, and a good process already—accompanied by a skeptical willingness to examine that process for possible improvements—but doesn't buy into stretching for that extra 5 percent (in other words, he has not CAPped a want for that additional 5 percent), the goal will not be reached. Because an organization is made up of individuals, the psychology of an organization is the same as the psychology of people. Factors for success of one are the same as factors for success of the other. An A-HA! Performance manager understands these factors and focuses her conversations, her performance improvement efforts, in these areas:

Essentials for Success: Individuals/Organizations

For Individuals	For Organizations
Drivers	Motivation/morale
Options	Skill sets/resources
Output	Process
Environment	Marketplace

A-HA! Performance Success Essentials for individuals include Drivers, Options, Output, and Environment:

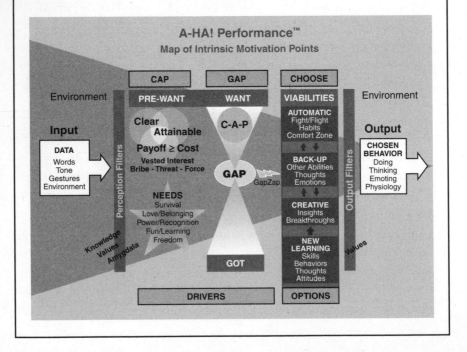

A-HA! Performance Success Essentials for organizations include Motivation/Morale, Skills/Resources, Processes, Marketplace:

A-HA! Performance Essentials for Success

	CAP	Motivation Morale	Skills Resources	Process	Environment Marketplace	Success Level
Current						
Plan 1						
Plan 2						

Once Scott believes 5 percent more is attainable in the marketplace and that it may be possible to redesign a process that doesn't require more cost from him (hours and energy) than the 5 percent payoff is worth, then we've covered CAP.

Now Scott is admitting the goal is attainable. Now onto behavior options: What are we currently doing, what's working, what isn't working?

Kyle: Can you think of anything you've done recently that seemed to be an effective sales strategy?

Scott: Actually, I saw a couple of percentage point increases from a change I made back in August. That could result in me getting 2 to 3 percent more.

Kyle: Good. So you've discovered something late in the year that was part of the reason for our increase last year and if you keep that going, it should keep our increase going. That's what we've been doing that's working; we don't want to lose that. Do you think this new found increase could bring even better results down the line?

SCOTT: Yes, but I don't think it's going to be responsible for the 5 percent. I found this one contact and she introduced me to another contact and through a chain of people I was able to produce more. I can't predict that's going to happen again.

KYLE: This reminds me of Malcolm Gladwell's book, *The Tipping Point*. Gladwell says that there are three types of people who speed up successful tipping points. One of those types he labeled as connectors. He said that in our networks, we want to look for and utilize connectors—people who are willing to connect us to other people. Is that what your contact did?

SCOTT: Yes. She just gave me the name of a guy in the forestry industry, who then led me to his contacts that use golf bags for an entirely different purpose than going golfing.

KYLE: How did you get her to share the information?

Kyle is still trying to explore the behaviors that are working.

SCOTT: I always ask people: Do you know anyone who may benefit from our 1,000+ products.

KYLE: How do you define the practice that you implemented four months ago?

SCOTT: Again, I just found this new market niche serendipitously. It has definitely paid off for me.

KYLE: It sure has. And part of your magic was getting networked into a unique function of this new industry? Almost discovering a new market?

SCOTT: Right. And the serendipitous part was I had no idea that these guys had a need for our particular product of golf bags.

KYLE: So one of your contacts saw what your product was useful for and connected you to the need? And having discovered this new vein, you're pretty sure you could do another 2 to 3 percent in sales, maybe 5 percent? You won't have to work longer or harder because you've got this momentum and you're past the cold calling, but you can continue to work this angle, right?

SCOTT: Yes, I can do my best to maintain this relationship. Perhaps to see what other market niches are out there, I can call my contact back and ask if she has anyone in her rolodex. Who knows what new connections that might produce, just like the last one did?

KYLE: Great. The bottom line is, you're willing to think of more connection ideas?

SCOTT: Yes, I'm willing to think and innovate, even test them out.

KYLE: Would you also be willing to use those gifts with other members of our sales team—if there was a way to do it that kept them out of the market niche that you're working in, but might give them ideas for pursuing ones where they have contacts?

SCOTT: Sure.

KYLE: Okay, because with your expertise and recent experience, I think that the notion of a focused networking approach is promising. You've overcome an assumption that you couldn't sell to a particular niche, so why not explore new niches? It's similar to how WD40 created its product for one use and now people have found many more uses for it. So maybe we could brainstorm on what the other possible uses are for our products. While you discovered one new vein by accident, the fact that you discovered a new vein proves that they're out there. Now as a team we might be able to figure out how to identify more of them. Does that sound right to you?

SCOTT: Sure, as long as it doesn't hurt my sales.

KYLE: That's fine. Rather than me bringing everyone together and delegating responsibilities, I'd like you to think of a way that you'd be comfortable sharing this with others; in a way that you'd feel protected. Then you and I can get together, structure it a bit, bring everyone together and then point them off to finding their own possible application of your idea. Would you be willing to do that in a way that you'd feel comfortable?

SCOTT: Yep.

KYLE: Well, I appreciate this conversation very much. Thank you.

Toward the end of the Address and Improve exercise, Kyle had to be, once again, sensitive to Scott's power needs. As a salesperson, Scott has a high competitive streak to the point where he didn't want to share his competitive advantage with his coworkers and Kyle, therefore, had to address Scott's inclination to compete internally. He had to make it safe for Scott to collaborate by emphasizing that he wouldn't lose in his efforts. Address and Improve lays the groundwork for getting our employees to do what we want them to do. Whether we're trying to mitigate a problem or develop a star performer is incidental.

> The key to Address and Improve is staying in the Drivers and Options zones and letting our employee determine the output.

Retention Mishaps to Avoid

While the A-HA! Performance applications, such as Address and Improve and Rapid Conflict Resolution™ (introduced in the next chapter), are great tools for leveraging self-motivation, sometimes we need only look to one area of the brain's functions (as seen on the pictorial map) to ensure success in our day-to-day operations. For example, there are many companies that overlook people's fundamental needs. And as I discussed in Chapter 2, if managers or other decision makers fail to pay attention to employees' needs, it will likely result in reduced motivation and poor morale—which is a direct cause of subpar performance and attrition.

In today's workforce, employees have specific wants and standards based on their needs, and if they don't get them met in one environment, they are all too ready to take advantage of other opportunities that will meet their needs better. So if we want to retain our quality employees, we must learn about need satisfaction; an absolute requirement for retention.

Power at Its Finest

When Lynn Fairwood worked as a salesperson for Administrative Systems, LLC, she had it all: a solid paycheck, a team that she got along with, customers that she bonded with, and a position she thrived in. For Lynn, her high power needs translated into not only wanting to be a top performer but also a standard that she wanted to live up to. She wanted to earn a certain amount of money so she could throw lavish parties, finance a new Range Rover, and rent a three-story condo in a prime location. In other words, Lynn met her specifics for feeling accomplished and important through her paycheck, as well as by being number one in her division.

Additionally, she satisfied her love and belonging needs through good relationships with her coworkers and customers whom she genuinely liked; and her fun and learning specifics were met through the vibrant company culture. While she was meeting her needs, life was good and she was producing like no other.

Administrative Systems is the place where small businesses go to outsource everything from payroll and tax preparation to administering retirement plans and worker's compensation. With Administrative Systems, businesses can focus on their core competencies, while outsourcing the time-consuming, yet critical aspects of a growing business, like accounting and HR responsibilities.

Lynn was an ace, outselling everybody in her company, as well as the competition in her local market. For her contribution, she got a base salary and a split of the revenues she brought in—a generous percentage that Lynn enjoyed.

But when Administrative Systems made changes to Lynn's compensation plan, they unwittingly made changes in her motivation levels as well. The changes implemented were not in favor of the employees, but rather in the best interest of the company's bottom line—all the while, assuming that the Lynns in the company would continue to generate top-line revenue. Lynn's response to the changes? She quit.

As soon as Lynn learned that the percentage she was used to earning had gone down, she was taking a hit to her power needs and the standard of living she wanted. The CAP puzzle was coming apart, too—more cost than payoff. She thought about how tough the marketplace was and how much harder she was going to have to work to earn the same amount of money, and it just didn't seem possible to hit those kinds of numbers. Yet, at the same time, she didn't want to have to cut back on her spending habits. She had specifics around what percentage she wanted and if she couldn't find it at Administrative Systems, then she would look elsewhere.

And with Lynn's track record, it didn't take long for her to land a new job. Though she found a company that doesn't offer payroll services, it still sells insurance services to a slew of the same buyers. So she was able to keep her customer base, she already knew a couple of her new coworkers, she still had the same flexibility afforded to all salespeople and, most important, she was offered a bigger cut of the pie. The new company got her closer to what she wanted, so she made the change.

The Lesson

If companies toy with people's specifics about what they want, then employees will seek out a different environment where they can get what they want. The wants are not only specific, but they are also very powerful because they are tied to the needs.

People's power and survival needs, and thus their paycheck, however, don't always supersede all else. For example, an employee may be drawn to her company not only to pay her bills, but also because of a loving environment. She has a sense of family in the people she works with and her core relationships are grounded in the company. This individual wouldn't jump ship if her compensation were substandard because she doesn't believe she can get her love and belonging needs met this well elsewhere. In this case, changing the compensation slightly wouldn't be cause for resignation.

Another instance would be if an employee had a stock option plan—equity in the company. This individual may be willing to forgo compensation in light of a future payout once the company is thriving.

The key is to know where people stand with their need profiles and the specific preferences that are tied to that profile before making an offer. If we're too far off, then we're at risk when it comes to retention.

Not Feeling the Love

At the staffing firm the Merick Group, Barbara Larson was feeling pressured from all sides. As the marketplace was evaporating beneath the company, Barbara found the climate for recruiting clients to be very competitive. Not only that, as competition grew fierce externally, tensions continued to worsen internally. Her boss didn't hold back either, criticizing her for almost everything she did. "Why can't you land this client yet?" or "Where are you going with this, it makes no sense?" were some of the comments she found herself fending off. She felt like a failure all around and her morale was at an all time low.

No matter where she was—on the field or back in the fold—she wasn't feeling the love. Her boss was constantly yelling at her and pushing her in different directions. Motivation, performance, and results fell. The cost of staying on was greater than the payoff, so she left.

The Lesson

When criticisms are too much to bear or praise and kudos fall by the wayside, people may leave. Based on these powerful love and belonging needs, they want to be recognized and appreciated; add to that their needs for power, and they can only take the ridicule for so long. Don't forget what the Gallup Poll discovered: The number one reason people leave a company is a bad relationship, or no relationship, with the boss. So this is one lesson that shouldn't be underestimated. "The beatings will continue until morale improves . . ." doesn't work. The beatings only continue when there's someone still there to beat and if people have choices, beating-free environments win.

It's a Buyer's Market

Important relationships don't stop with our colleagues; they extend outside the office doors as well. And Regalo Golf, in its attempt to move one of Scott's coworkers, Michael Follier, to another division, found this out the hard way. Many times when a customer buys products from a certain company, he's buying from that company because of a relationship he has with the salesperson—relationship, relationship, relationship. Salespeople have told me over and over that sales are 80 or 90 percent relationship. Of course, if the product doesn't deliver as expected, the buyer will still move to a competitor. Sales is partly about the customer's power needs—their desire to achieve some purpose with our product—but the differentiator in buying decisions is more focused on the quality of the relationship than on the features of the product. As long as the product is up to par, the buyer continues to use the company thanks to his buddy that sells him the product.

At least that was the case for Michael and his big account with several golf courses. One of his customers, Luke, bought all the supplies for this golf course and he and Michael had a solid relationship. Michael knew everything there was to know about the golf course. Even when Luke didn't order a certain product, Michael knew the golf course's operations so well that he would recommend a product that Luke hadn't even thought about.

So Luke turned to Regalo Golf because Michael satisfied his belonging needs as much as his power needs; and since Regalo Golf had a strong product, he was also meeting his power needs by accomplishing his goal of getting superior golf supplies. While Luke preferred shopping with Regalo Golf because he liked Michael better than the competitor's salesperson, it wasn't that he totally disliked the other salesperson. After all, he did receive a call from the competitor's salesperson every six months, saw him at various trade shows, and had lively conversations with him whenever they spoke. But Michael and Luke's relationship was simply too strong to break, so Luke never wavered when approached by competing companies, regardless of all the promises of discounts and other incentives. Vested interest relationships trump bribes every time.

That is until Regalo Golf moved Michael to a different division in the company and replaced him with Charlie Withers. Now Charlie was a nice enough guy, had been in sales for over 12 years, and could handle Michael's accounts. What he didn't have any control over, however, was the relationships he hadn't formed with customers yet. Meanwhile, Luke figured if he couldn't work with Michael, then he would give the competitor's salesperson a call. He thought it would be a good time to give this other guy a chance, considering he had been calling and slowly building a relationship with him.

The Lesson

We all need to meet our love and belonging needs, whether at work or at home. And even buyers have specifics around who they want to have their buying relationships with. Relationships are a powerful force in sales and when companies take that away from customers, key accounts are often taken away from companies.

Had any one of these three managers understood how potent people's needs were, they may have never had to lose star employees or long-time customers. Once managers understand the Intrinsic Motivation Points in the human decision-making and performance process—once they learn about the incredible power of the needs, for example—these management foibles can be dramatically reduced way before they spiral out of control.

A colleague of mine, Maria Rodriguez, who has been coaching and consulting businesses since 1983, saved one toxic manager from sending her subordinates packing and the owners of the company from a financial hit. And she did it all using one tool: The A-HA! Performance Map of Intrinsic Motivation Points.

When Maria met with the senior team at that company, she quickly learned that one manager in particular, Lucy Webber, was managing by intimidation. Lucy's bullying ways were putting her employees into adversarial mode and the tension was starting to impact her peers and senior leadership as well. Maria realized, "Here was someone in a very powerful position who had a leadership style that was not only ineffective, but was counterproductive; clearly lowering morale everywhere."

So Maria spent four months with Lucy and her colleagues helping them understand how people perceive, think, decide, and act—

why we do the things we do—using the A-HA! Performance Map as an illustration.

She didn't necessarily follow the exact steps of any one of my A-HA! Performance applications, but simply pointed out that in order for Lucy to get what she wanted from her employees, she needn't try to control their behavior, but understand their needs and the CAP buy-in puzzle. "After she realized that she was browbeating to no avail (what she was doing wasn't working), she wanted to know how she should change in order to effect the changes she wanted," Maria explains. "She learned about how to use clarity, attainability, and payoff that is greater than or equal to the cost—from the employee's perspective." That was a key a-ha for her.

> Getting it and getting good at it are two different stories, but getting it is the start.

The outcome to this point? Maria says that Lucy's style, while still brusque, has become much more effective and employees are noticing a difference.

As for the others who were feeling the repercussions of Lucy's temper, learning the A-HA! Performance Map has had a different set of benefits. "The rest of the team now takes things a bit less personally, as they have a clearer understanding of why we, as humans (and that does include Lucy), act the way we do," says Maria. "The end result of my work with them is an increase in both morale and productivity."

Summation

A major benefit to having self-motivated employees is a workforce that is proactive. And with the Address and Improve application, we can address employees who are already performing well and encourage them to perform even better. But not only that, through the A-HA! Performance paradigm we know about the critical importance of need satisfaction and why employees would seek different work environments if their needs are not being met in our workplace. Understanding the importance of needs, we can work with them to address and improve performance in ways that build retention as well as increase our bottom line. Whether we're using bits and pieces of the model, or the A-HA! Performance application in its entirety, understanding the motivation root of behavior not only gives us the tools to effect change positively, but also gives us the A-HA! Performance Edge. It allows us to manage motivation rather than skills, tasks, or processes. When we do that well enough, skills, tasks, and processes follow naturally.

Rapid Conflict Resolution and Rapid Team Tune-Up: Dealing with Conflicted Employees or Building Teams

Conflicts in the workplace are costly. They can result in lost productivity, key talent attrition, and the chronic dysfunction or complete failure of a team.

Conflicts are common. Look at the numbers. One San Diego company had its human resources (HR) department track which problems brought employees to their offices. Here is what they found:

- 61 percent: Conflict issues
- 20 percent: Performance/attendance issues
- 12 percent: Harassment complaints
- 2 percent: Code of conduct
- 5 percent: Complaints about terms and conditions of employment

Conflict can be defined in a variety of ways but basically conflict is:

- Two or more people going in opposite directions
- Energy/resources expended
- Little or no progress made

Some of the problems Rapid Conflict Resolution (RCR), based on the rapid relationship counseling work of William Glasser, MD, can be used to address include:

- Acrimony:
  —Issues between team members that adversely impact quality/efficiency
- Dysfunction:
  —Other employees resist using a particular group or team
- Communication issues:
  —Lack of clarity/completeness
  —Tone
  —Frequency

Problematic conflicts include:

- Ownership of responsibility and authority
- Disagreement with direction or strategy
- Communications—frequency, clarity, or tone
- Personality conflict
- Quality of work or performance
- Work procedure issues

Temptations for dealing with conflict that we'd do well to resist include:

- Telling combatants to shape up or knock it off
- Getting into the rescuer, persecutor, victim loop
- Wishing and hoping
- Giving advice

Managers should get involved:

- When it comes to our desk; when we're made aware of it by someone
- If a conflict adversely impacts any of the links in the service profit chain:
  —Revenue
  —Customer satisfaction
  —Quality of product or service
  —Employee gruntledness
- When wishing and hoping don't work

We should bring in outside facilitators:

- When the internal person is uncomfortable
- When internal person "knows" the solution
- When internal person has a favorite in the conflict
- When the people involved have senior positions to an internal person and the internal person is intimidated
- When the cost of doing nothing is more than the cost of the intervention

Wouldn't it be beneficial if managers had skills to handle 80 percent of these issues before they got to HR and before an external facilitator is required?

Whether the conflict is two employees who refuse to speak to one another or many employees who are at odds, conflicts waste people's time and cost companies a lot of money. Worse yet, if tensions are ignored, they grow, fester, and perpetuate problems that can permeate an entire organization.

That's why I've included both Rapid Conflict Resolution and Rapid Team Tune-Up™ in this book. Both consist of two-session, eight-question, facilitated interventions by a manager or neutral third party. You may think that the Nike approach should work here—that telling employees to stop bickering, to just knock it off would be sufficient—but that would require a certain amount of maturity on the part of the conflicted employees. If they were that mature, then they would've solved the issue on their own or not gotten into the conflict to begin with. It's unlikely that telling them to cut it out is going to resolve the conflict. It may quiet it down, and send it underground for a bit, but resolve it? Not likely. There's a difference between an uneasy absence of war and the productive presence of peace. And the presence of peace is not the absence of tension. It's the harmonizing of tension. Rapid Conflict Resolution doesn't just seek an absence of war although a reduction in acrimony is one of the outcomes. The goal of this intervention is a harmonizing of tension.

The two interventions shared in this chapter are basically the same one with minor modifications allowing it to be utilized in two different situations. When applied to a conflict that's become a problem, it's called Rapid Conflict Resolution. When applied to making good teams even better, it's called Rapid Team Tune-Up. That's the added beauty of this intervention—there doesn't have to be a problem in order to utilize and benefit from it (Table 12.1).

Regardless of which intervention we're referring to, the premise is the same: Don't blame anybody or judge anybody, just focus on working with all parties toward finding a solution. According to Marshall Thurber, "When it comes to solving problems, we can play below the line or above the line. Below the line, people blame, shame, and justify. Above the line, we take personal responsibility. Playing below the line always fails; the only real chance we have for solving

TABLE 12.1   Rapid Conflict Resolution and Rapid Team Tune-Up

Rapid Conflict Resolution	Rapid Team Tune-Up
Day One	
Do you want things to be better in this situation? (or would you be against things being better around here?)	As good as things are, would you like it if things were even better? (or would you be against things being better around here?)
Whose behavior do you control?	Whose behavior do you control?
What's working in this situation now?	What's working well in this situation now?
What needs to be fixed (improved)?	What could be improved further?
What's one thing you would be willing to do differently every day for a week that you think would improve one thing on your list?	What's one thing you would be willing to do differently every day for a week that you think would improve one thing on your list?
Criteria for a good plan: –Clear –Attainable –Payoff ≥ Cost (makes things better, not worse) –Measurable –Do plan, not don't do plan –Dependent on doer only –Immediately implementable –Repeatable	Criteria for a good plan: –Clear –Attainable –Payoff ≥ Cost (makes things better, not worse) –Measurable –Do plan, not don't do plan –Dependent on doer only –Immediately implementable –Repeatable
Day Two	
Did you do what you said you'd do?	Did you do what you said you'd do?
If not, what did you do instead?	If not, what did you do instead?
How did it work?	How did it work?
What now?	What now?

problems is playing above the line. Taking personal responsibility, we can solve almost anything." Rapid Conflict Resolution is a focused set of questions leading relentlessly to personal responsibility.

Because serious conflicts in the workplace are more frustrating, and the need to deal with them more pressing than simply revitalizing lackluster teams, I'll cover RCR in detail first, but keep in mind that the same tools can be used for Rapid Team Tune-Up with very little modification. You'll notice a slight tweak in only three of the questions. While the largest group I've used this with was just under 30 people, this explanation will assume we're facilitating RCR with just two people.

The set up, when we sit down with the two people, is something close to this: "Let me tell you how this works because it may be different than you're expecting. We're going to spend two sessions together—that's it. This isn't court; it's not an ongoing coaching or therapy session. We'll meet today and one week from now. I'll ask you a total of eight questions—five this first day and three when we meet again a week from now. If each of you gets the answer right, then we move on to the next question and we'll have a strong chance of solving this issue; if you don't get the answers right, then I can't help you."

The purpose of this set-up is to:

- Put pressure on the participants to solve the conflict.
- Acknowledge the fact that we can't solve it for them.

We're not the ones responsible for the solution. Who does that introduction take the pressure off of and on whom does it place responsibility? One of the issues with mediators who come in to settle disputes is that the people in conflict think it's the mediator's job to determine the solution. People come prepared to make their case to the judge, so their focus is one-sided; on a win for themselves. We need to be clear that it's not our responsibility to come up with the solution. "If *they* get each answer right . . ." *they*, not us.

> Managers who understand the A-HA! Performance Model know we can't control other people into a solution they don't buy into and that we probably couldn't come up with the best solution for them anyway.

We don't have the personality of either of the two people nor the background, nor the depth of resources, thoughts, behaviors, or ideas that they have in their automatic, back-up, and creative options zones. They have access to viable options for themselves.

Maria Rodriguez, who has used the RCR questions in her coaching practice, says, "It's the questions that allow people to come up with their own plan for their life; it's not me telling them what will work." The series of questions for Rapid Conflict Resolution (and Rapid Team Tune-Up) are discussed next.

Day One—Rapid Conflict Resolution

1. Do you want things to be better in this situation?
   - What is better to you (clear)?
   - Do you believe it is fixable (attainable)?
   - What's the payoff for you to make this better (payoff)?

Another way to ask this question is: Would you be against things being better around here? I use "would you be against . . ." frequently. It allows negative people to use their favorite word, no, but in this case it means yes. So they get to use the word they like and I get the answer I want. A win/win. I also use it because it's very hard for people to say, "Yes, I'm against it being better . . ." The goal here is to get some version of, "Yes, I want things to be better," or "No, I'm not against them being better." This creates one prong on the hook we can loop back to if they resist coming up with solutions when we get to the solution stage. We can say, "But you told me in question one that you wanted things to be better around here."

Rapid Team Tune-Up Version: As good as things are, would you like it if things were even better? Or, would you be against things being even better than they already are around here?

2. Whose behavior do you control?

This sounds simple and straightforward enough, but we may want to spend a little time on this one to be sure it soaks in. If we are going to solve this issue, we have to go where the controls are. Conflict is about counterproductive or adversarial behavior between people. Control of the behavior of the adversaries is in the room. "Who controls your behavior?" This creates the other prong of the hook we're preparing in case people balk at the solution stage: "But you told me in question one that you wanted things to be better around here . . . and in question two that it's your behavior you control." It also helps us avoid the, "well if she will . . . then I will." The only acceptable answer to this question from each person is, "I control my own behavior." But be sure they understand what that means . . . that regardless of what the other person does, each person in this room is responsible for his own behavior.

3. What's working in this situation now?

Rapid Team Tune-Up Version: What's working well in this situation now?

This question is designed to change the momentum from a focus on the problem to a realization that not everything is wrong. If done well, it closes the gap a bit, it comforts the afflicted. Sometimes people will be slow to come up with things, but trust that there are some things in this category and stay on the question until we get at least one answer. . . . If we get one or two, ask, "What else?" That's a great question to get the brain to go deeper, beyond its automatic zone of answers. What else is working well?

4. What needs to be fixed (improved)?

Rapid Team Tune-Up Version: What could be improved further?

Cautions

- Just list and move on, don't comment or ask for much detail.
- Avoid getting drawn into issues.
- Don't judge.

Before we move on from this question, ask, "Do we have the main thing on the list?" If not, we don't have a chance of resolving it.

5. What's one thing you would be willing to do differently everyday for a week that you think would improve one of the things
   on your list?

Both partners in this conflict have to agree that if the other
does it, it will make things better, and the facilitator has to agree that
if each does it, it might make things better, too. I added that one because a participant in one of these sessions said, "If he'll make those
changes he just offered to make, I'll work on my anger."

"That's a no go," I said. "You're already good enough at it
. . . you don't need to work on it. Besides, angering is a behavior, not
a condition. You've been angering to get his attention and to make an
impression that he was in a kind of danger if he didn't go along with
what you wanted. He's going along with making some changes. Now,
if you'll make some changes, too, you'll both improve a lot of things
and you'll switch from angering to joying with no effort at all."

Here is more detail about each question:

1. Do you want things to be better?

It may seem rhetorical, but the fact is, if one or more of the parties doesn't want to fix the problem, then we won't get a resolution.
So we ask this question up front because it can save a lot of time later.

If they get the answer wrong, we can't help them. When I was
facilitating this with a married couple, I asked this question and the
husband said, "Yes." But the wife was silent. We glanced over at her,
she thought for a moment and said, "I want a better marriage. If he's
willing to make some changes, he can be in it." I asked the husband if
that was enough of an answer for him and he said, "I'll take it."

I have never had anybody say to me that they didn't want to
fix the situation. As I've already mentioned, we can make it pretty
difficult for them to say they're not interested in fixing the problem by asking them, "Would you be against things being better
around here?"

Not many people would say, "I'm against making it better." It's
hard to say that. Again, the reason we ask this question up front is
because it sets the hook. Later on in the process, if people are

stalling, we can remind them, "Wait a minute; you said you wanted to make things better."

2. Whose behavior do you control?

When conflicts arise, many people not only blame the other(s) involved, but they also want the other person to change—without changing themselves—in order to solve the problem. We ask this question so people stop trying to control other people's behavior and focus where the control is; on their own. If individuals want to make it better, the only way they're going to have a chance is by going where the control is. The boss can't solve it. HR can't solve it. Even legal, if the organization has attorneys, can't solve it. Who are the only ones in a position to make things better? The parties who are in conflict. So, "Whose behavior do you control?" Another straightforward question. Participants always answer, "Mine." As much as we'd like to control the behaviors of others and, to some extent, that's what all conflicts are about, the only person's behavior we actually can control, is our own.

But even when people admit they only control their own behavior, sometimes I push a bit further to make sure they grasp this point by asking them to finish this sentence in their own head . . . don't say it out loud: "Life would be great around here if only . . ." Once they both have something in their minds, I say, "Let me guess what you didn't say."

"I'm guessing neither one of you said, 'Life would be great around here if only they gave me a stiff margarita when I walked in the door and I could work half drunk all day;' or, 'Life would be great around here if only the computers didn't go down;' I'm guessing neither of you said, 'Life would be great around here if only I wasn't such a jerk.'" Sometimes, I get a laugh or two, sometimes not, but they get the point. Most people answer that question by saying, "Life would be great around here if only he . . . or if only she . . . But who's behavior do you control?"

What this question begins to teach is:

> Our power in getting others to change is our own willingness to change ourselves.

This is where we have to focus if we're serious about solving conflict—If we want things to be better, we can change our own behavior. While deceptively simple, this question is critical and profound.

3. What's working in this situation now?

Most people come to these sessions focused on what they've got that isn't even close to what they want, which often leads to the faulty belief that nothing is close to what they want. If what we've got is nothing like what we want, our gap is huge. We're likely to be overwhelmed and believe that the situation is hopeless. Since we don't know what to do to close that gap, we'll probably be emoting a bit and focused on negative combative thoughts.

But if we can get people focused on the fact that in spite of the conflict, there are still some things that are good for them, they're still getting some of what they want, it will close the gap a little. We'll be comforting the afflicted and narrowing that gap to the point where they're more likely to be whelmed just right for a productive solution. When gaps close, even a little, then thoughts, emotions, and physiology settle down . . . their brain and blood chemistry changes for the better. When one of the components of chosen behavior changes, they all change. Change an awareness about what is, and the gap will narrow, reducing the energy that's driving the options zone and settling down emotings. If the emotions change for the better, then thoughts and actions for dealing with the other person will improve, too.

This question reminds employees that their current environment isn't a complete disaster. There's been some good at this job. Sometimes the bright side is easy to find and people acknowledge the good fairly quickly. There could actually be much that they like about each other and about their work environment, but there are maybe just these two issues, significant ones for sure, that right now are overshadowing everything.

Other times it's not as easy to find what's working. I was once facilitating an RCR with a small team of people. One of the women accused one of the men of crossing a personal line. She was feeling pursued by him and was scared; therefore, she did not want him in her cubicle, didn't want him e-mailing her, and didn't want him calling her on the phone. On a small team, everyone must be willing to interact. Two people could not be permitted to sever communication completely; they had to collaborate on some level in order to get their jobs done. That's why their manager asked me to help. As some background, the evidence as to whether or not the man had really crossed a line was less than compelling. Had it been compelling, the issue would have gone right to HR, not to me. Still, things had degenerated to an intolerable state as far as their manager was concerned so we were into the process. I asked this third question, but the only answer they could muster was that they both still had their jobs. There wasn't much else.

Whether it's only their jobs and paychecks or any number of other things people identify as still working, at least they are reminded that there is something worth saving, maybe worth building on. Again, this shifts the thinking from problem issues to more positive realizations, which relaxes the brain and opens it up for the more difficult questions to come.

4. What needs to be fixed?

Notice that this question does not try to get at who did what to whom. This shouldn't create an opportunity to blame or point out who is at fault. The question isn't: what's wrong? Or what's not working? Those are questions that focus us in the past and on what's broken. Reinforcing that the situation is bad doesn't energize us for making it better. "What needs to be fixed," focuses the discussion on acting in the present to make something better in the future. If we allow ourselves to get stuck on how bad the past has been, even if it was just 10 minutes ago, we'll be demoralized and bogged down because fixing the past is not attainable. We want to use questions that help us get clarity around attainable issues that will payoff for all of us. What needs to be better? Read these next three questions and see if you can feel a difference in the energy they evoke in you:

1. "What's our problem?"
2. "Why have we got this problem?"
3. "How do we fix this problem?"

> Focusing on a fix is more energizing for most of us than focusing on a problem.

We encourage each person to share whatever it is that needs to be improved between the parties involved so that tomorrow is a better day. And whatever the issues end up being, we want to ensure they are clear. If, for example, one employee says that Bob could be nicer, what does she mean by "nice?" Should he say "hello" every morning, invite her to lunch, or just use a softer tone with her?

The purpose of question 4 is to identify the main issues that need to be fixed. Most times they surface quickly, but sometimes people are slow to put their primary ones out there. I facilitated one of these sessions with a group of more than 20 people and the main point of contention never did surface . . . too much fear I suppose. They just brought up polite little issues that, if fixed, would make things better, but not enough to overcome the pain of the main issue. Getting the key issues identified is critical here or everyone is wasting time; spend as long as the participants need to get to the key issues on the list.

We as facilitators may not always realize whether or not the primary issues have been shared, so, after a while, once people seem to have exhausted their list, we can ask, "Do we have the main things on the list?" If not, then we need to bring them out now and add them to the list. This isn't an exercise in avoiding the main things; it's a tool for dealing with them.

5. What's one thing you would be willing to do differently every day for a week that you think would improve one of the things on your list?

At this stage, I remind the conflicted parties of their answers to all four questions so far: "You said you wanted this issue to be better, that you wanted things fixed; you said it's your behavior that you control; you also said that there are some things that are working well, but that there definitely are some issues that need to be improved." Then we move right on into question five. "What's one thing—not a bunch of things—that you can do differently every day for the next business week that you think will fix one or more of the things on your list?" Participants then tap into their behavior options to come up with one thing that might help the situation. But here's the catch: All parties have to agree that, "If you do what you're offering to do, it will have a good chance to fix one of those things on our list." So if Bob says, "I'll change the tone of my voice from a condescending one to a friendly one," his partner has to believe that the change will impact positively one of the things on their list. And the facilitator, too, has to agree that the change will have a chance of fixing things.

Once the answers to question 5 are on the table, once people come up with a plan to make things better, it's probably a good idea to ensure that it's a good plan. The criteria for a good plan in RCR are the same as that of Address and Improve, in that the plan to do something better should meet most of the following eight criteria. A good plan is:

1. Clear
2. Attainable
3. Payoff $\geq$ Cost (makes things better, not worse)
4. Measurable
5. A do plan, not a don't plan
6. Dependent on the doer only
7. Immediately implementable
8. Repeatable

Those are the criteria I look at when determining whether the proposed plan is a good one. If the new plan passes the criteria, then I believe they have a chance at making the situation better. At the end of the session, we tell the employees that they are done for the day and that we'll reconvene in a week, at which point we'll ask them three more questions. But for now, all employees have something that they said they would do differently everyday. Changes start, now.

Day Two—Rapid Conflict Resolution/
Rapid Team Tune-Up

Here are the three questions that you ask during the second session:

6. Did you do what you said you'd do? If not, what did you do instead?

7. How did it work?

8. What now?

Here is more detail about each question:

6. Did you do what you said you'd do? If not, what did you do instead?

Again, if they answer the question with a "yes," then we can move on to the next question. If not, then we might ask, "What did you do instead?" It's possible that they left and thought about something better, I'm not against that.

7. How did it work?

Sometimes I begin the second day with this question: "How did it go?" I did that one time with two people who answered by saying, "Well, we don't think this is going to work."

"Oh?" I said. "What happened?"

"Well, actually, it did work pretty well the first three days and we were pretty excited, but on the fourth and fifth day, we were right back to the problems we had when we came in."

"So did you do what you said you'd do?" I was puzzled, but stuck with the questions.

"We did for the first three days," they said, "but something came up and we weren't able to keep it up for days four and five."

"Oh," I said, "well, you're disappointed but I couldn't be happier. The whole purpose of this exercise is to teach you that your current behaviors are the reason for your problems. If you don't like what you've got, you can change what you're doing. You made the changes you agreed to on the first three days and got something better . . . life was pretty good. You went back to your old practices on day four and life got bad again. The lesson has played out perfectly. The question is, 'Did you learn it?' Which led me to the last question."

8. What now? Where do we go from here?

"Do you want to go back to the misery you came in with, or would you rather have more days like the first three of last week?" Sometimes people feel pretty good about the gains they've made, but reasonably insecure about their ability to keep it up. Sometimes they want to continue to meet for a while to lock in the new behaviors and maybe see if they can't fix a few more things on their list. Where we go from this start depends on us and the people we're working with.

> The lesson we're trying to share with people is that if they'll change what they're doing, they'll change what they're getting.

If they can register that, then they won't need us anymore. When we make it to this last step, we ask if the employees want to stay with the new behaviors that have cranked the situation up a notch, or if they want to go back to the old habits that had them in conflict. The hope is that they want to maintain the progress they've started. Sometimes people get it right away and really don't need to meet anymore. Other times they may need us to stick with them and help them with their changes for a little longer.

I facilitated RCR in a small organization one time where the people had formed themselves into three different camps. Each group kept to itself and didn't set foot in the other camps' areas for almost three years. They simply refused to talk to each other. They talked about each other plenty, but not to each other. As is the case with most conflicts, the tensions only worsened with time and one day it came to a tumultuous boil.

Two people, in particular, harbored such animosity that during a meeting with a large number of key customers, they blew up at each other. That's when the board decided that this situation had to stop and they brought me in.

With a group of this size, as well as this much resentment, I suggest that you meet with people individually before bringing them together. You may want to share the questions you'll be asking so they don't worry about being embarrassed, put on the spot, ambushed, or in any other way, surprised. We don't want people to be afraid of this session or for their fight or flight response to kick in, so we need them to trust us and know that we're not there to judge or criticize them. Brief them on your approach. Tell them this is not an old-fashioned "honesty" group where people unload their frustrations all over each other. No one is going to be blamed or singled out. The focus will be on the here and now, and on the immediate future. Prefacing the meeting in such a way will hopefully relax the participants a bit before everyone sits down together.

In meeting with those 11 people, I received the right responses to questions 1 and 2—everyone agreed that things could be better and they all agreed they control their own behavior. And I received a lot of positive feedback to question 3: What's working now? One said it's a joy to serve our customers, another said that coming to a place where people are being helped is extremely rewarding and still others said that the organization had a great reputation in the community (with the possible exception of some minor fall out from the recent blow out).

What needed to be fixed? "Communication" almost always comes up in these meetings. I've learned to divide communication issues into three major ones: frequency of communication, clarity and completeness of communication, and tone of communication. They needed to communicate more (increase the frequency); the tone of communication needed to be improved; the criticisms and attacks had to stop; and many more little details needed to be ironed out.

What's one thing they could do differently? Here was a warring organization that had been in combat for years, but when we got to question five, the response was incredible. One person said that there was a person around this table who he hadn't talked to in two years and he needed to seek her out and apologize. He also committed to going to that other person's office every day . . . just for that week . . . to greet her and say good morning. Another person said that he hadn't visited one group's area for a year and a half and that maybe he could peak his head in every morning to say "hello"—just get out of his space and step into their space to greet them everyday. Participants continued to go around the room and volunteer to make one positive change that they could do every day for that next week. There was almost a reverent tone at that table. It's quite dramatic, noble even, what people will come up with when they are allowed to solve their own issues.

I returned the next week to see if everyone had done what they said they would do. And everyone had. In fact, the director said, "This is the best week we've had in two years." Little changes, big results.

A two-person RCR that I facilitated not too long ago combined belittlement, bossiness, and bad-communication—all great fodder for a workplace conflict. John LeRoule and Kerry Mannis had been working together at a warehousing and shipping firm for over five years. They both started out in the administrative department and soon climbed their way up to managers of different regions. But it wasn't until late in their tenure at the company that Kerry got promoted over John and became the district manager of John and his peers.

Tensions between Kerry Mannis and John LeRoule soon started to develop—perhaps John harbored resentment for Kerry's success or Kerry thought her position as district manager meant that now it was her job to control everyone below her. Regardless of where the issues stemmed from, it was poisoning the environment.

Similar to Samantha Flemmings' refusal to report to Catherine Hopkins, John too didn't keep Kerry in the loop. It wasn't that Kerry micromanaged him, it was that she was bossy in her delivery and insensitive to his needs. Whenever she asked John to do something, he felt she was belittling him and that he wasn't good enough. So he clammed up and decided to ignore her altogether. He was still efficient and hardworking, Kerry just wasn't aware of it.

Although as soon as I stepped in, I didn't care about what John didn't do or what Kerry did do, only about what could be done to fix the unhealthy atmosphere. Here's how John and Kerry's RCR played out:

DOUG: I'm here because you two have some issues. Let me tell you how I'd like to work with you. This won't be an ongoing session. I'll meet with you twice. I'll meet with you today and in a week. My plan is to ask you a total of eight questions—five today, three next week. Assuming you get each answer right, we move on to the next question. If you don't, there's really not much I can do. Sound good?

I get a nod of heads.

DOUG: I realize there is something wrong, you're clearly saying there is something wrong, do you want it to be better? Do you want to get this situation fixed?

KERRY: Yes.

DOUG: You do? How about you John, would you like to get it fixed?

JOHN: Well, I'd like to get it fixed but she needs to understand that the problem is that she's too bossy.

DOUG: Let's just stick to one question at a time. We'll deal with your specific frustrations in another question. But right now, whatever the issue is . . .

JOHN: Yes, I'd like to get it fixed.

DOUG: Okay, question number two. And this sounds like a trick question, but it's pretty straightforward and it's key in our ability to fix this. Whose behavior do you control? 100 percent control. Not whose behavior would you like to control, and not whose behavior would you influence if you were skillful at influencing, but whose do you control beyond a shadow of a doubt?

KERRY: My own.

JOHN: I control mine.

DOUG: I know we would all like to control somebody else's behavior but you answered right. You control your own behavior. So what's working between the two of you now?

JOHN: Well, the job always gets done.

DOUG: Okay, you complete the work. What else?

Silence.

DOUG: I'll be glad to repeat the question, that's not a problem. The question is, what's working between the two of you now? Let me tell you my assumption: If nothing was working, you'd be gone. You're both still employed here; neither one of you has quit nor have you been fired. There must be some reason you're still here. If you were in a situation where everything was total misery and nothing was going right, how long would you stay in the situation? Are you still getting a paycheck? Maybe that's working. Something is working. So what's working in terms of your work situation now? It doesn't have to be much.

KERRY: The job is getting done.

DOUG: Okay, anything else?

KERRY: Isn't that enough?

DOUG: It may be, but I'm giving you an opportunity to lay everything on the table. I don't know unless I ask. John, is there anything else you can think of? So far, you both came up with the same thing, that the work is getting done.

JOHN: I can't think of anything else.

DOUG: I understand. It's a little hard to think when you're both upset. Ask yourself question four: If you had to make a list of things that needed to be fixed—you said you wanted to make it better—what needs to be changed or fixed in order for it to be better? At this point, we're making a list, not of who did what and when, but of what needs to be better.

KERRY: I need to be updated on what John is doing.

DOUG: Okay, communication could improve. There are at least three levels of communication that I can think of. One is frequency of communication—are we getting together enough? Another is tone of communication. Is the tone condescending, angry or belittling? The third is completeness of communication—do we communicate what we really mean? What exactly do you mean by communication?

KERRY: For me, it's frequency of communication and completeness of communication.

DOUG: And who do you have in mind to initiate the communication, to schedule it, or plan it?

KERRY: John needs to come find me.

DOUG: In what sense? Does John need to come find you, hold you down, and stop you to communicate?

Right now, I'm trying to get some clarity around what it is about communication that needs to be fixed.

KERRY: No, e-mail is fine.

DOUG: So somehow you need to get the message and e-mail is fine.

KERRY: Yep.

DOUG: John, from your perspective, what would you add to this list of things that can be changed to make this not only an okay place to be but why not ratchet it up 10 percent and make it a great place to be?

JOHN: Well, I'd really like to be treated like a human being. I'd like to be asked to do things in a pleasant manner, instead of ordered around.

DOUG: It seems that you're referring to the tone of communication?

JOHN: Yeah. And if she has specific items that she wants me to complete or report on, then maybe she can create that specific list so I could satisfy the list. I know she wants results but she never really specifies. She just orders me to get this all done, but does she want me to report on all of it or just the big picture items?

DOUG: Okay, so not only tone of communication, but clarity and completeness of communication is on your list of things that could be better, too?

JOHN: Yep.

DOUG: What else? Anything is fair to put on the list.

JOHN: We could have a meeting every once in a while instead of just sending e-mails. Maybe meeting once every couple months just to see how things are going and that we're both happy with the results.

DOUG: Anything else?

Silence.

DOUG: It's mainly communication that is the issue?

Nods.

DOUG: Question five—What's one thing that you could do differently every day for the next business week that you think could positively impact one or more things on the list? And you need to come up with something that the other person would agree to; that if you made this change, it really would make a positive impact in terms of the list. I also have to agree.

JOHN: I could communicate the results of the projects she requests if she'll specify exactly what she needs to know.

DOUG: Do you have an idea of what she might want to know? In other words, I'd like to get you to come up with something that doesn't have the "if she" piece to it. Just what you're willing to do, whether she participates or not.

I'm trying to make sure his new behavior is dependent on the doer only.

JOHN: I'm willing to communicate with her on a daily basis—keeping her up to date on my progress.

DOUG: When you say communicate, do you mean by phone or e-mail?

JOHN: I'll communicate via e-mail on a daily basis. If she wants to ratchet it up, we can do that, too.

DOUG: So you're open to more, but you'll commit to this—that's what you're saying?

JOHN: Yep, that's what I'm saying.

DOUG: Kerry, does that work for you?

KERRY: Sure does.

DOUG: Great. What's one thing you could do differently that will fix one of the things on your list?

KERRY: I can say please and thank you.

DOUG: Okay, now there are lots of tones for saying please and thank you. Guys can say to each other, "Hey, you SOB, how are you doing?" If the tone is lighthearted, then the guy being greeted that way will smile and say, "Good." Women, on the other hand, rarely say, "Hey, you fat cow, how are you doing?" Women and men communicate differently. Please and thank you will go a long way but is there anything else you could add to how you do it or how you deliver your communication?

Again, I'm trying to draw specifics around what Kerry is saying she will do.

KERRY: Yeah, I'll say please and thank you in a polite, patient, and friendly tone. And I'll show my appreciation in front of others as well.

DOUG: John, is what she's saying good?

JOHN: Yeah, it's great.

DOUG: Okay. That's the plan then. Let's give it a try for a week. We'll meet after a week goes by and the first question I'm going to ask you is, "Did you do what you said you'd do?" Okay?

Both parties nod.

DOUG: Do you want to start today?

KERRY: Sure.

JOHN: Why not.

Day Two—One Week Later

DOUG: Did you do what you said you'd do?

KERRY: Yep.

John nods in agreement.

DOUG: How did it work?

KERRY: It worked well, I feel so much better about knowing what John is doing. Just being kept in the loop allows me to focus on other things, and not waste my energy worrying about it.

JOHN: And I have to be honest—I don't mind e-mailing Kerry everyday and letting her know what I'm doing. It makes such a difference when I'm not annoyed with her for treating me like a child.

DOUG: So what now? Do you want to keep up the positive changes or revert back to the way it used to be?

KERRY: I'm happy to keep it up. It's obviously better not only for the company, but for our sanity around here.

JOHN: Yeah, I'd have to agree with that. I'd much rather have a normal environment, like it used to be.

DOUG: Well, just commit to doing what you've been doing every day and you should see the same results.

Just like that, RCR created a process where the two people were able to change a painful and uncomfortable work situation into a jovial and productive one. The key to achieving the same results is staying focused on the questions. It's so easy to veer off track—digging up old wounds or getting lost on tangents—but the power of Rapid Conflict Resolution and Rapid Team Tune-Up is in the eight questions.

> Not only are the questions designed to get people doing and thinking positively, but they work in getting people thinking about personal responsibility solutions, rather than blaming, shaming, and justifying.

The advantage of a neutral third party is that this individual has no history with the conflicted employees; she doesn't have an agenda and isn't biased. But if that's not an option, then, as the manager who is witnessing the quarrel, we can try to detach ourselves from the situation and be as neutral as possible. We'll want to forewarn our employees that our approach may seem detached, and not to interpret it as our being cold.

In the last chapter, I discuss how to get more comfortable using the A-HA! Performance model and these applications. When you use this tool for as long as I have, you get to be almost unconsciously competent with it. The A-HA! Performance Model and applications are so embedded in my mind that I use them automatically with almost no thought at all. Conversely, when you initially sit down with employees after being introduced to this model, you'll likely be in an early stage of learning, where you may need the questions in front of you and your effort will feel a little more scripted. As you practice the A-HA! methodologies and applications, however, you'll get more and more comfortable with the language and the focus on drivers and options, as opposed to advice. Soon, it will be an unconscious effort for you as well. And that's the beauty of A-HA! Performance—it's simple enough to learn in a few hours, yet its substance is profound enough to keep us engaged in probing its intricacies, mining its insights, and mastering its applications over a lifetime.

Summation

Keeping employees self-motivated toward organizational goals sometimes requires a Rapid Conflict Resolution to clear-up unnecessary conflict and focus them back on collaborating; synergy making conversations. It is a curative piece, but it can also be used as Rapid Team Tune-Up, a preventive and energizing team experience.

Making the Shift

My intention in introducing the A-HA! Performance Model and Map is to fundamentally change the way managers understand and approach performance in the workplace. For many, this will be a change in understanding—a paradigm shift from an unconscious belief in an external control set of assumptions regarding employees to a conscious belief in an internal control series of Intrinsic Motivation Points (IMPs). This shift in understanding impacts not just the way we manage our subordinates, but the way we manage peers, bosses, customers, and ourselves. Many people find that in order to manage the performance of others through Intrinsic Motivation Points, it's helpful to understand and manage ourselves through this model first.

Today's competitive organization can no longer afford to rely on external controls for motivating its people. Retention, morale, and performance from the progressively decreasing labor supply are at stake. Managers can't afford to employ antiquated management methods either because employees are less accepting of working conditions that lack a need satisfying environment; top performers want an environment amply filled with belonging, power, fun, and freedom. In other words, carrots and sticks won't convince top people to work for us. Top performers work for companies and managers who satisfy their vested interest; their needs.

Managing a self-motivated workforce is an inside out job—one that starts with a manager understanding what really drives her own behavior and how she has choices about how to act. And because she has choices as to what she's going to do, she's responsible for what she does. So are our employees. This adjustment can be a big one because most of us have grown up using external controls such as incentives (what I call bribes and managers call carrots) or sanctions (what I call threats and managers call sticks). Without knowing about or understanding the potency of the Intrinsic Motivation Points, we'll continue to fall back on the carrot and stick approaches we do know in our attempts to manage and motivate others. Typically, it is neither natural nor effortless for us to operate with complete faith in internal controls. Yet once we make that shift to the A-HA! Performance Edge, operating any other way will be unfathomable.

Showing up at the workplace with a belief that people are internally controlled can actually be quite a leap, but quite a relief, too. Relief, because now we don't have to control our employees . . . all we have to do is see if we can kick-start their internal motivators toward achieving the goals we want and guide their choices as to what they do when so motivated. That's a very different outlook from the one that says somehow it's my job to make people do what the company wants them to do. It is quite a leap, both in understanding and in behavior, but making it and maintaining it will have tremendous payoff, for managers and managed alike. Helping people understand these ideas and experience the edge these ideas give us when managing others is the goal of this book.

Internalizing these concepts, moving them into our automatic zone is the only way to make them ours, ready to use successfully in all situations.

> Making this shift, and maintaining this shift, gives us a powerfully unique edge that could otherwise take a lifetime of experience to grasp.

Acquiring the A-HA! Performance Edge requires a rewiring process of sorts. Letting go of the old ideas tied to external control is not as easy as simply letting go. Our current beliefs and practices are in our automatic zone; they are habits. Our brains get wired, over years, to relate to people, challenges, and reality (our perceived got) in certain ways. Learning the Intrinsic Motivation Points and practicing leveraging them in solving our management challenges may clash somewhat as they mix with older beliefs (even though those older beliefs about external controls ultimately don't serve us well). "Success" from employing the old ways too often comes at a cost that companies and managers are becoming unwilling to pay, particularly if we want higher sustained performance and retention of good talent. Expect somewhat of a fight from old patterns because they're easy, they are firmly in the habit zone, but don't give up.

So much of what I'm suggesting is geared toward a new mindset, a new understanding of the Intrinsic Motivation Points that are active between a manager's input and an employee's output. As we develop the mindset of internal controls—self-motivation—our ability to manage with a focus on the other person's vested interest strengthens. It's a gradual and progressive process. Don't give up before the a-ha happens. The suggestions for daily use in this chapter will help the integration happen sooner. So would taking one or more of the live training sessions we offer in the model. So, how will we get ourselves to buy in and then put forth the effort to develop the A-HA! Performance habits?

First, CAP it. The concepts we are teaching in this book are simple to talk about; at first tougher to do, but they are clear, attainable, and payoff in incredible ways.

Clear. We can explain the concepts.

People have needs. Based on needs we form wants. When we are aware that what we've got is different from what we want, when there's a gap between the two, we are energized by a GapZap to act. We have choices about what to do, how to act. Our choice will be some combination of doing, thinking, emoting, and physiology, generated in an effort to close the gap between got and want. Simpler yet: Needs—CAP—Gap (Want—Got) Choose—Behave, or Drivers—Options—Output. If in managing you, I can get you to want what I want you to want because it pays off for you in need satisfaction, and you believe the gap between that want and where we are is closeable, you'll figure out something to do to close it.

So how do we internalize these ideas?

Review the model, the map, and the applications. We know what goes on between our input and our employee's output (see Figures 13.1 through 13.8).

A-HA! Performance provides us with a graphic illustration of the model—which puts it in a tangible form so we can assess where we are in the performance management process anywhere from our

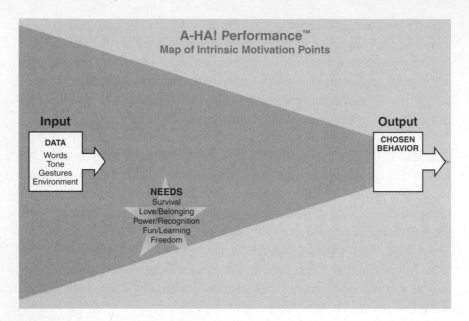

FIGURE 13.1 Intrinsic Motivation Point 1—Needs: The Hidden Drivers of All Motivation, Morale, and Behavior

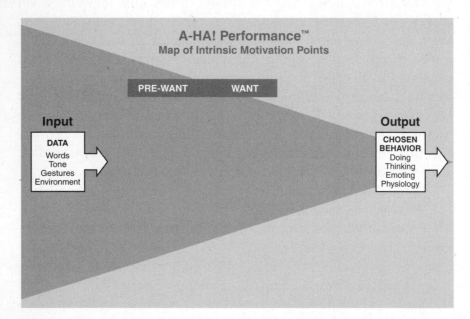

FIGURE 13.2 Intrinsic Motivation Point 2—Wants: The Not-At-All Hidden Drivers of All Motivation, Morale, and Behavior

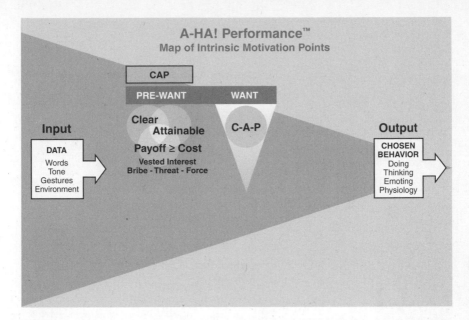

FIGURE 13.3 Intrinsic Motivation Point 3—CAP: The Fundamentals of Buy-In

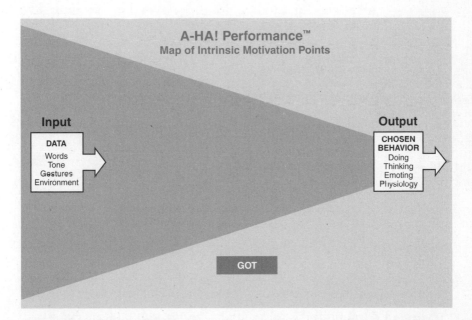

FIGURE 13.4 Intrinsic Motivation Point 4—Got: Perceived Reality

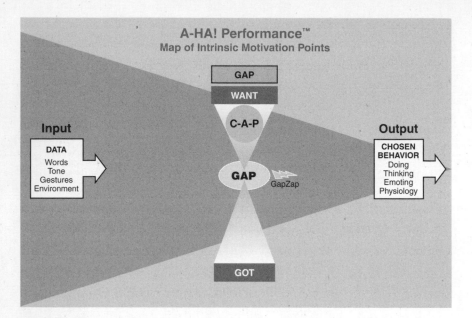

FIGURE 13.5 Intrinsic Motivation Point 5—Gap and GapZap: The Immediate Precursor to Action—Provides Energy and Impetus to Do Something—The Gap Is the Difference between Want and Got

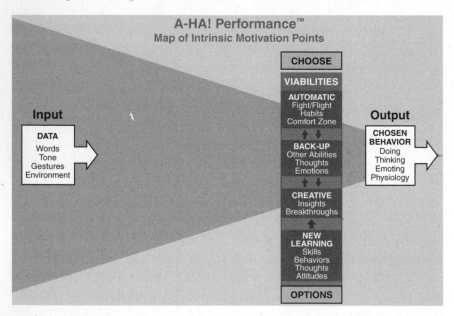

FIGURE 13.6 Intrinsic Motivation Point 6—Viable Options: The Range of a Person's Behavior Choices

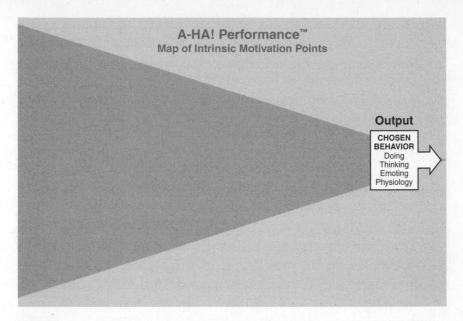

FIGURE 13.7 Intrinsic Motivation Point 7—Chosen Behavior Output: The Four Components of Behavior—Doing, Thinking, Emoting, and Physiology

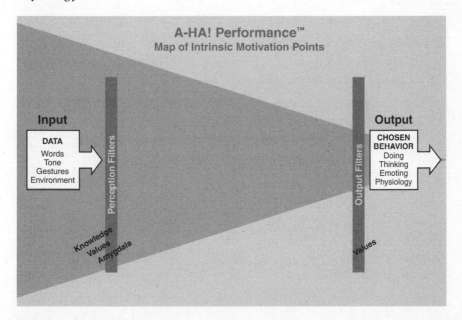

FIGURE 13.8 Intrinsic Motivation Point 8—Filters; Where Meaning and Value Is Placed on Input and Need Satisfying Limits Are Placed on Output

input to our own and our employees' output. It's designed so we can use it as a guide, a compass, an assessment tool, and a template for managing conversations and aligning efforts for greater organizational success. Whether we reference it before meetings, communications, or one-on-one interactions, we are reminded of these Intrinsic Motivation Points and their interconnectivity. We quickly see our employee's decision making process and the motivation points that must be addressed in getting his buy-in to want what we want him to want, and to act on that want. The map was designed to help us stay on the vested interest motivation track. Whether we put it on our desk, hang it on the wall nearby or have it on our computer, the map is a reference guide for daily Intrinsic Motivation Point management.

> The A-HA! Performance Map is our edge, graphically.

The full version of the A-HA! Performance Map (Figure 13.9) is also included at the end of this book. Whenever we need a detailed re-

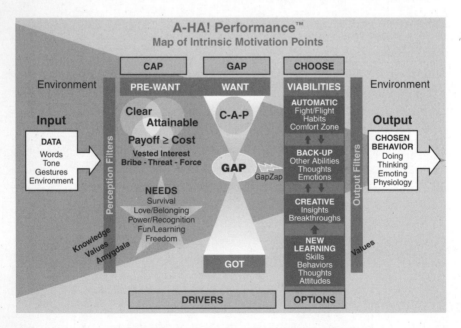

FIGURE 13.9 A-HA! Performance Map

fresher, we have the Intrinsic Motivation Points explained, each in a separate chapter.

To take full advantage of this A-HA! Performance paradigm and map, I've included Table 13.1, the A-HA! Performance Applications: Address and Improve, Rapid Conflict Resolution, and Rapid Team Tune-Up. The applications help us wrap dialogue around the Intrinsic Motivation Points, and allow us to put the paradigm into action.

Learning and utilizing A-HA! Performance is attainable. Think back to attainability's 10 Es. Are we missing any Es? We may be. Experience with the model, for example, or Education in it. That's available through A-HA! Performance training, but it's also available in this book and through our trying out and playing with the ideas. We have everything at our fingertips in this book. With the map in mind—specifically the vested interest (need satisfaction) approach to motivation—we can utilize the steps of Address and Improve the next time we have a performance correcting conversation with an employee. We will start seeing positive changes almost immediately. Over time, with practice and repetition, we will relate to the workplace differently—with the eight Intrinsic Motivation Points as a foundational framework for our interactions. Making the shift to the world of intrinsic motivation is doable, satisfying, and fun (see Figure 13.10 on page 246).

It pays off. The rewards for intrinsically motivating employees are powerful. It doesn't take much to convince anyone of the value of a self-motivated workforce. When goals are achieved with less management effort, there is an abundance of need satisfaction for all and an overall higher capacity, and propensity, for enjoying the actual process of work. In self-motivated environments, managers and employees take more responsibility for their behaviors—less blame is placed on others or "the system" when things go wrong. Roles of self-righteousness and victimization are rendered pointless.

> The A-HA! Performance manager is able to see what other managers don't see.

They see what goes on between input and output. A-HA! Performance managers truly have the edge as they approach their work

TABLE 13.1 A-HA! Applications Performance .

Address and Improve	Rapid Conflict Resolution	Rapid Team Tune-Up
Day One		

Assess strength of relationship:
  –Care
  –Credibility
	Do you want things to be better in this situation? (or would you be against things being better around here?)	As good as things are, would you like it if things were even better? (or would you be against things being better around here?)

Identify the gap	Whose behavior do you control?	Whose behavior do you control?
CAP the want	What's working in this situation now?	What's working well in this situation now?
Examine current total behavior	What needs to be fixed (improved)?	What could be improved further?
Evaluate how well it's working	What's one thing you would be willing to do differently every day for a week that you think would improve one thing on your list?	What's one thing you would be willing to do differently every day for a week that you think would improve one thing on your list?

Plan to do something that will work better	Criteria for a good plan:
	  –Clear
	  –Attainable
	  –Payoff ≥ Cost (makes things better, not worse)
	  –Measurable
	  –Do plan, not don't do plan
	  –Dependent on doer only
	  –Immediately implementable
	  –Repeatable
		Criteria for a good plan:
		  –Clear
		  –Attainable
		  –Payoff ≥ Cost (makes things better, not worse)
		  –Measurable
		  –Do plan, not don't do plan
		  –Dependent on doer only
		  –Immediately implementable
		  –Repeatable

TABLE 13.1   *(Continued)*

Address and Improve	Rapid Conflict Resolution	Rapid Team Tune-Up
Criteria for a good plan:		
–Clear		
–Attainable		
–Payoff ≥ Cost (makes things better, not worse)		
–Measurable		
–Do plan, not don't do plan		
–Dependent on doer only		
–Immediately implementable		
–Repeatable		
Get/make commitment:		
–Review consequences of success/failure		
–No excuses		
–Never give up		
–Give up (confer/refer)		
Day Two		
	Did you do what you said you'd do?	Did you do what you said you'd do?
	If not, what did you do instead?	If not, what did you do instead?
	How did it work?	How did it work?
	What now?	What now?

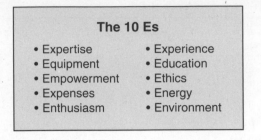

FIGURE 13.10   The 10 Es of Attainability

with greater insight and increased confidence, based on their focused Intrinsic Motivation Points management approach.

From New Learning to Automatic

While we have everything we need to start today, the objective is to practice A-HA! principles in our daily managing so we get to the point where our utilization of these principles is automatic. For some people, the A-HA! Performance Map, and the principles it illustrates, just confirm what they already know and do. Those people tell me that these ideas give words to their practice and clarity to the framework that helps them shortcut their approach in solving problems and improving performance.

For others, A-HA! Performance comes as a dramatic new learning, a completely different way of approaching motivation and management. First, a giant a-ha! This might work! Then, through consciously incorporating the A-HA! approach in their daily managing conversations, they eventually move A-HA! Performance managing from new learning, to their automatic or habitual behaviors. The way they get there is through practice and repetition. That's the way we all learn. Hear, see . . . do! The "hear and see" portion is reading this book or taking an A-HA! Performance workshop, while the "do" portion is using the methodologies in conversations and teaching the model to others (see Figure 13.11).

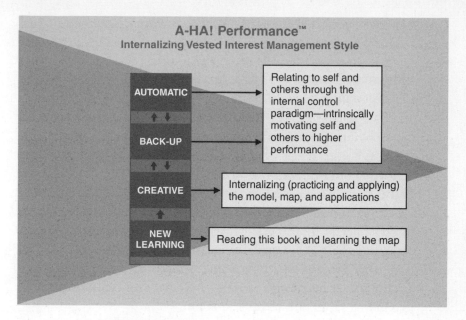

FIGURE 13.11 A-HA! Learning Process

Securing the Shift—Suggestions for Daily Use

Internalizing the model can either be a quick or slow process, depending on how much effort we choose to put into it. The suggestions that follow provide easy, everyday ways to become acquainted and comfortable with the A-HA! Performance paradigm of internal control and the eight Intrinsic Motivation Points it identifies.

A good place to start, as we internalize this way of understanding workplace motivation and behavior, is Intrinsic Motivation Point 1: Needs. I strongly encourage you to question everything in terms of how your and others' needs are being satisfied, protected, or frustrated. Observe behavior, your own as well as others, and then identify which needs that person is trying to meet. Trying to figure out our own needs profile or watching other people over time and trying to figure out their needs is a good way to learn about the needs in action, too.

We might also try the following:

- *Teach the A-HA! Performance Model to others.* Whether with a friend, a spouse, coworkers, or employees . . . even your kids at home . . . walk them through the A-HA! Performance Map from input to output. The more we teach it, the easier it will be to understand and use it.

- *Start an A-HA! journal.* At the end of the day, write down the most obvious bribes and threats you used that day—whether at work, at home, or with friends. Then, for each one, write down how you could've used one or more of the Intrinsic Motivation Points to try to accomplish the respective goal. What could you have said in place of the bribe or threat? Which of their vested interest needs might you have tied your request to? Which pieces of the CAP puzzle were in place; which were not? At first, this process will take some effort and a little discipline. Over time, it becomes effortless because eventually we will be journaling from our automatic zone.

Consider reading Glasser's books, *Choice Theory* (New York: HarperCollins, 1999) and *Reality Therapy* (New York: HarperCollins, 2000), and Powers' book, *Behavior: The Control of Perception* (New Canaan, CT: Benchmark Publications, 2005). These authors are the pioneers of this work and their explanations of the material might add to your understanding of Intrinsic Motivation Points, these potent internal controls, as they relate to your particular performance challenges.

Breaking it down even further, let's explore how we can practice each of the drivers.

Needs (More Specifically)

Needs are present in people everywhere—at the grocery store, on television, at restaurants, and in the workplace. So start taking notice. Here are some circumstances to be aware of:

- When we're watching commercials, try to identify which needs the company is appealing to. Or when listening to songs, or looking at photography and paintings, what needs are being addressed or expressed?

- At the workplace, when morale and motivation are low, which needs are being frustrated? When morale and motivation are high, what needs are being satisfied?

- Consider conventional values that we live by—like all of the "thou shall nots"—how do they relate to our needs being protected or satisfied? Corporate values, too. How do they relate to our needs for fun, freedom, survival, belonging, and power?

- Assess people's needs through observation and conversations. See if we can figure out what their need profile is? Which seems to be the strongest for each person? Love/Belonging? Power/Recognition? Fun/Learning? Freedom? Survival?

Want—Got—Gap

- Do we have a gap right now between what we want some of our employees to be doing and what they're actually doing? If we can think of one gap with one employee, how would we go about getting that gap whelmed just right in our employee's mind? Think through the needs and the CAP puzzle with respect to each employee's gap. Pay special attention to whether you believe your employee's behavior, or lack thereof, is related to an overwhelmed or underwhelmed gap. The idea here is to get sensitive to whether gaps are overwhelmed or underwhelmed so we can have conversations aimed at whelming that gap just right to generate an optimum GapZap.

- Likewise, analyze good performance seeking to understand how the gaps were in place before that good behavior and how they were whelmed just right. Reflect on good performance and times when we achieved significant buy-in from others. How was the gap managed then? Which needs were satisfied and how was the want CAPped?

- Begin to detect whether our employee's gaps are overwhelming or underwhelming. Doing so is part of a proactive vested interest management process. When we proactively monitor, or detect, overwhelming and underwhelming gaps, we keep ourselves in a better position to anticipate, understand and intrinsically motivate self and others through performance challenging situations. We'll find opportunities to comfort the afflicted . . . and to afflict the comfortable.

CAP—CAPping the Want

- Think about one task that you meant to get done yesterday but didn't get done. What's one call, email or conversation that you meant to engage in but didn't? Write down how you would CAP the unfinished task to get it done today. CAP your own wants/goals.
- Is there something someone asked you to do where you declined? What piece of the CAP puzzle was missing? Is there a C, A, or P that that person could have covered that would have changed your mind, whereby you would be engaged in that activity, or would have bought-in to their request?

Clear

- How are the goals we are moving forward on clear?
- How could the ones we're procrastinating on be made clearer?
- If we keep telling ourselves to be better about something—time-management, organization, communication issues—how could we increase clarity as to what "better" means?

Attainable

- The big goal that we think about from time to time, but have not yet started on . . . do we believe it's possible? Why? Why not?

- Which of the 10 Es are in place?
- Which of the 10 Es need to be added?

Payoff

- Think of wow moments. Think of times where we'd say, "Life just doesn't get any better than this!" Times (okay, for some of us maybe just brief moments) where life was filled with excitement, exhilaration, gratification, success, and happiness. How did these meet our needs and which ones did they meet?

- Conversely, think of ow moments in your life and analyze which of your needs were frustrated. This exercise will sensitize us further into thinking about the importance of need satisfaction at work. Do we want a wow workplace? If we've been in an ow workplace, which needs were frustrated for us?

- Sometimes when we want to change a behavior, like eating late or eating too much, thinking of the cost helps clarify what the payoff isn't. Is there a habit that you've been meaning to change lately but haven't gotten around to? Perhaps it's the same New Year's resolution that we vow to change every year but don't. Well, if clarity and attainability are locked-in, yet the payoff for changing isn't obvious enough, then think of the cost. If we convince ourselves that the cost of sustaining that habit is greater than the payoff, we'll pull the CAP puzzle apart by removing that payoff piece and stop wanting . . . therefore stop doing that habit. We'll have to CAP the new habit we want to replace it with, though, so don't forget that part.

- What's the cost of continuing the bad habit? If we want to eat healthier, but the late night visits to the fast-food joint aren't subsiding, maybe we should remind ourselves of the cost? Of course, the cost is that our health is at risk, and the payoff, therefore, is staying healthy . . . feeling better. So what's the cost to the habit that we've wanted to change?

Summation

We all spend years making assumptions about why people behave the way they do.

> The irony, or paradox, relative to the A-HA! Performance Model, is that the external controls many of us learned in our journey to managerial positions are exactly what we need to avoid doing now.

This model in many ways is counterintuitive. It's like that children's party favor the Chinese finger trap—a woven straw tube we put opposing index fingers in and then try to pull out. When we do the intuitive thing—pull—the trap tightens, and rather than the release we want, we find ourselves stuck more. The counterintuitive solution is . . . push. A-HA! Performance, in many ways is a counterintuitive model. It says we should replace sticks and carrots with vested interest conversations and give up giving advice in favor of CAPping our requests and exploring viable options for that person. Its counterintuitive quality may pose the greatest challenge to internalizing a true internal control or vested interest management style. But like pushing our fingers together to escape the finger trap instead of pulling them apart . . . the A-HA! Performance approach works better. In fact, the number one comment we get from students of this model? "It works!" And right after that, "Why didn't someone teach me this in high school?"

In this book, you'll find some new ideas for effectively managing yourselves and others in a way that everyone's best interests, or needs, are met in maximizing performance. What these pages offer is a process—one that works through helping others want what we want them to want . . . because it satisfies them in some way. As student after student exclaims, "This model is (life) transformational." And as one put it, "Once you learn it, you can't not use it." We have yet to learn of one reason why any manager would not want to learn, internalize and realize the A-HA! Performance Edge. It certainly doesn't lead us to do things that would be harmful or make us less effective. In fact, once we learn it, we won't have to expend as much energy in getting others to change, and we'll usually get buy-in and willingness to change quicker—plus, if we do it really well, they may even thank us for it!

A by-product of learning the A-HA! Performance principles and cementing them into our automatic zones is that it applies to other relationships in all areas of our lives, not just in the workplace. A-HA! Performance gives us the edge in all relationships: parent/child, husband/wife (well, actually still working on that one . . . if you try this at home and it doesn't work, go back to "yes dear" as quickly as possible), friendships, customers, teams, seniors, peers, and so on. It's just a more powerful and meaningful way to relate and manage because it helps us meet our needs in these relationships by focusing on meeting theirs.

Epilogue

Susan Moore and Richard Harper's ill-fated confrontation was actually the impetus for me to create A-HA! Performance for managers, which is built on the great ideas I'd learned in working with Glasser. Their story was about missed opportunity and botched conversation between two good people, but it served as a last straw for me—a final gap opener between the skills I knew managers could have and the ones I kept seeing them use. There are so many technical managers, like Richard, who are good at what they do, whether sales, science, engineering, accounting, or manufacturing, and then someone makes them a people manager without giving them the tools they need—human performance management tools—so that they can be successful at that, too. For all of us who manage, an understanding of the Intrinsic Motivation Points in the human thought process is priceless. It's such a powerful alternative to sticks and carrots.

Although I had been toying with the idea of creating the A-HA! Performance Model for managers for some time, until that incident, my GapZap hadn't been strong enough, I had not been whelmed just right to actually do it. After that incident, though, and the waste in resources, time, energy, emotions, and dollars . . . for the company, Richard, and Susan, I knew I had to get started. After all, the powerful psychological insights and practices Glasser had simplified for frontline people in the field of psychology—counselors, corrections officers, educators, clergy, therapists—combined with William Powers' breakthrough explanations of the mental process that leads to behavior could be tailored for managers, too. By adding a few of what I believe are crucial components like the pre-want CAP piece, and the Amygdala, for example, and simplifying some of the other components, such as the filtering system, I've made the ideas even more attractive and useful for managers like Richard.

But are they useful? Do they work? What better way to find out than to test them in the exact same challenge that Richard Harper faced? I didn't realize it, but I needed a grumpy receptionist to prove the power of the A-HA! Performance approach. So it was all too serendipitous when, shortly after developing A-HA! Performance, and fully six years after the original incident with Richard and Susan, I was asked to coach a curt receptionist who exhibited many of the same characteristics as Susan. This time, however, both the approach and the outcome were profoundly different.

When I first sat down with Sheryl Mathers, I asked her if she knew why I was there, why I had been hired. She shrugged her shoulders, nodded her head a little, and said she did. She had been told that if she didn't change how she answered the phone, she'd be fired.

As an A-HA! Performance Coach and Manager, I know certain things before I ever start to talk with an employee or a client. For example, I know that people will not change unless they want to change and that they won't want to change unless all pieces of the CAP puzzle are in place.

I knew the owner of the company wanted a change in the receptionist style at the front desk and that his want passed the **CAP** test. It was **C**lear to him what cheerful should sound like, **A**ttainable for him in that if this woman wouldn't change, he'd exchange her for a new receptionist, and the **P**ayoff for having a cheerful receptionist answering phones, if you're a boss who is concerned about the customer experience, is huge. I knew he wanted a cheerful receptionist and was willing to do whatever was needed to get one.

What I didn't know yet, was did she want to be that receptionist . . . was it Clear to her, did she believe it was Attainable and was the Payoff greater for her than the cost, both in ego and effort? So with that CAP puzzle very much in mind, I told her that my understanding was the same as hers. They had asked me to work with her around changing her style as a receptionist, so it sounded like we both knew why I was there.

"So you've been told that if you don't change how you answer the phone, you'll be fired," I said. "Do you want to change?" I asked her this because I knew if she didn't want to change, she wouldn't. Knowing that upfront could save me a lot of wasted time and the company wasted money on my fee.

"Do I want to change?" Sheryl asked. "Sure."

"Can I test that a bit?" People often claim they want to do things, but then don't do them. Why? That CAP puzzle, that's usually why. . . . Most people say they want things when really they're just wishing for those things to magically happen. To want something enough to energize actions requires that the CAP puzzle be in place. If all three pieces are not locked in, the person is unlikely to be internally motivated enough to do the hard work required to achieve the change. I asked if I could test her claim to want to change. "You say you want to make those changes, but can I ask you a few questions about that?"

"Sure."

"Do you know what your boss is asking you to change?" I asked.

"That's the problem," Sheryl said, "he wants me to answer the phones more professionally, but I am answering them professionally. I think he wants me to answer like I'm some sort of cheerleader."

"Well if you do agree, and try, do you think he'll actually let you change in a way that he'll notice so you can keep your job?" I wanted to know if Sheryl thought that the boss had already decided that no matter what she did, he was going to fire her anyway. If she didn't think all this was attainable, she'd be unlikely to have the motivation to change.

"No," she said. "I don't really think this is possible, and I think he's already made up his mind, so no matter what I do, he'll find something wrong and fire me. And besides, you can't change my personality. How I answer the phone is just who I am."

She had said she wanted to go through this coaching and make those changes, but is it sounding that way to you? It wasn't to me. Still, I asked that third category question around Payoff versus Cost. "So why would you want to do all that work and go through all that effort to make these changes if you can't win anyway? You said you want to go through this coaching and make the changes he wants, but it doesn't sound like that to me."

"You're right." She said with a little "okay, you've got me" grin. "Actually, I've already got my resume out there in the job market."

Now that made sense. Of course she had her resume out there and a job search started. The CAP puzzle had not come together enough for her to work much at making the changes needed to keep her job. In the first place, she wasn't clear on what those changes needed to be. Second, she didn't really think there was a chance in the world they were going to let her be successful, and a personality change was probably needed and that was impossible, too. And third, too much work for little or no payoff. The CAP puzzle had not come together in Sheryl's mind.

So I decided to loop back through the CAP pieces, but to see if I could frame them differently. "What if you were to tell your boss that you want to make the changes he wants, in ways that he'll notice, but you'd like to be sure you've got it right? So you'd like to ask him not just to describe how you should answer the phone, but also to demonstrate it, to role-play it for you. Then he can let you role-play it back to be sure you've got it. Would that at least help you know what he wants?" (Clarity is critical if she's to have a chance at making the changes he wants.)

"That would be good," she said. "At least I'd be sure I knew what he wanted."

"You might even ask for some reassurance that if you make the changes he wants, in ways that he notices, then you will get to keep your job," I continued.

"Yes, I can do that," Sheryl said, "but you still can't change my personality. I'm not going to be all Suzie Q. Cheerleader. That's just not me."

"I don't want to change your personality, just your behavior," I explained. "Do you ever smile on the phone, like when your kids or friends call?"

"Sure," she said with a little grin as she thought about her kids and friends.

"That's all we're talking about—just doing what you already do. Smiling on the phone is a behavior, not a personality trait. And it's a behavior that you already have. Just do what you're already good at, but do it in this setting. It's not a personality change; it's not even a behavior change, really, because you already do it . . . it's just adding another situation to those where you already do this behavior. So what do you think?" I asked. "Does that make it seem possible?"

Her face began to light up. "I see what you mean. I guess if you put it that way. Somehow now it doesn't seem like that big of a deal, but I don't know . . ."

I kept going with the CAP puzzle, now addressing payoff. "And let's talk about whether doing this is a win or a lose. Do you really want to be out there looking for another job or are there some good reasons to keep this one?"

"Well, I do have some good friends here," she said, "And I basically like my job. I like my immediate boss, too, she's been real supportive . . . sticking up for me to the owner . . . the big boss."

"And what about your kids? You're a single mom, right? Would it be nice to set the example of facing a challenge and overcoming it, as opposed to walking away from it? Wouldn't you rather say to them, 'I had a major challenge at work, but I didn't back down. I faced it, addressed it, and overcame it.'"

Sheryl thought for a moment and said, "You know, you're right. Now I really do want to do what I have to do to keep this job. Do you think she'll role-play for me what she wants me to do?"

"I do," I said, "but let's check to be sure." We checked with Sheryl's immediate boss, who was more than willing to role-play and Sheryl actually started to get excited about making the changes.

That's how it works. If we can cover the three pieces of the want puzzle—Clear, Attainable, Payoff ≥ Cost—then we'll always get buy-in.

In light of how unpleasant an ending Richard Harper had had with Susan Moore, I was elated to hear from Sheryl that within the first week, customers and colleagues already noticed the changes. In fact, one customer who had been calling throughout one day was so impressed by her attitude on the phone that when he placed his last call at 4:45 P.M., he asked, "How are you still as cheerful at the end of the day as you were this morning?"

And the following day, a colleague walked by Sheryl's desk in the morning and said, "What's going on these days? You can feel the love in the lobby."

When she told me about these comments, I told her to be sure to share those with her boss. When people make changes for others, they have to be sure those others notice. Change in the workplace is about two things: Making the change and managing the perceptions of others to be sure they notice.

A-HA! Performance principles are effective because they focus on the Intrinsic Motivation Points that are active any time a person enthusiastically engages in an activity. Once we as managers are aware of these points, as illustrated on the A-HA! Performance Map, we can focus our conversations to get the buy-in we want without blowing up relationships.

Sheryl's boss called and said she was doing great. They took her off probation and her job became secure.

So now we've come full circle. We started with an example of the costly missed opportunities that happen daily in the workplace. We've learned a new set of eight Intrinsic Motivation Points that can be strung together to help us be more effective with those we manage, coach, teach, or parent. And we've seen that when they are applied—particularly compared to situations without them—they produce a very different and mutually beneficial outcome.

As good as it is for improving below the line performance, companies are also using A-HA! Performance practices to enhance performance that is already strong.

Through one success application after another, the A-HA! Performance Intrinsic Motivation Points can be used in turning around negative situations as well as progressively building on positive ones, and enhancing professional and organizational success through leading and managing self-motivated human capital.

Appendix

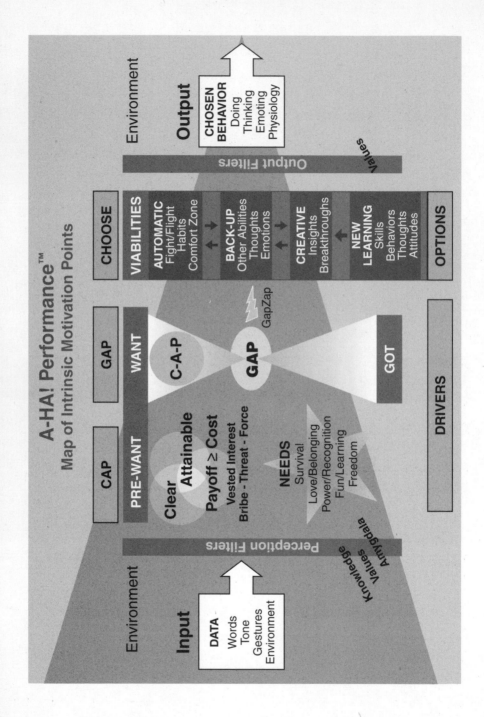

A-HA! Performance™
Map of Intrinsic Motivation Points

Performance Changing A-HA! Applications

Address and Improve	Rapid Conflict Resolution	Rapid Team Tune-Up
Day One		
Assess strength of relationship	Do you want things to be better in this situation? (or would you be against things being better around here?)	As good as things are, would you like it if things were even better? (or would you be against things being better round here?)
–Care		
–Credibility	Whose behavior do you control?	Whose behavior do you control?
Identify the gap	What's working in this situation now?	What's working well in this situation now?
CAP the want	What needs to be fixed (improved)?	What could be improved further?
Examine current total behavior	What's one thing you would be willing to do differently every day for a week that you think would improve one thing on your list?	What's one thing you would be willing to do differently every day for a week that you think would improve one thing on your list?
Evaluate how well it's working		
Plan to do something that will work better		
Criteria for a good plan:	Criteria for a good plan:	Criteria for a good plan:
–Clear	–Clear	–Clear
–Attainable	–Attainable	–Attainable
–Payoff ≥ Cost (makes things better, not worse)	–Payoff ≥ Cost (makes things better, not worse)	–Payoff ≥ Cost (makes things better, not worse)
–Measurable	–Measurable	–Measurable
–Do plan, not don't do plan	–Do plan, not don't do plan	–Do plan, not don't do plan
–Dependent on doer only	–Dependent on doer only	–Dependent on doer only
–Immediately implementable	–Immediately implementable	–Immediately implementable
–Repeatable	–Repeatable	–Repeatable
Get/make commitment:		
–No excuses		
–Never give up		
–Give up (confer/refer)		
–Review consequences of success/failure		
Day Two		
Did you do what you said you'd do?	Did you do what you said you'd do?	Did you do what you said you'd do?
If not, what did you do instead?	If not, what did you do instead?	If not, what did you do instead?
How did it work?	How did it work?	How did it work?
What now?	What now?	What now?

A-HA! Performance Essentials for Success

For Individuals

Drivers
Options
Output
Environment

For Organizations

Motivation/morale
Skill sets/resources
Process
Marketplace

Because an organization is made up of individuals, the psychology of an organization is the same as the psychology of people. Factors for success of one are the same as factors for success of the other.

	Motivation Morale	Skills Resources	Process	Environment Marketplace	Success Level
CAP					
Current					
Plan 1					
Plan 2					

Glossary

Address and Improve   An A-HA! Performance-based intervention that gives managers the tools to either improve the performance of one or more of their employees or to develop promising talent into leadership positions.

A-HA! Performance Managers   Those managers with the A-HA! Performance Edge.

A-HA! Performance Manager's Edge   The competitive advantage one manager has over another due to an understanding of the A-HA! Performance map and internal control performance paradigm it illustrates.

A-HA! Performance Map   A graphic illustration of the 8 Intrinsic Motivation Points that make up the A-HA! Performance Model and shows the sequence of events inside the mind that explain the intrinsic motivation process.

A-HA! Performance Model   The foundational framework for understanding why people behave and how to intrinsically motivate self and others to perform.

Amygdala   A tiny gland in the back of the brain that detects threat and, when activated, puts people into a "fight and flight" mode.

Attainability   The belief that a certain task is achievable, doable or possible.

Attainability, The 10 Es   Expertise, Experience, Equipment, Education, Empowerment, Ethics, Expenses, Energy, Enthusiasm, Environment.

Automatic Behaviors   Our habits or comfortable way of doing things.

Back-Up Zone/Repertoire   The things we know but may not be comfortable with or accomplished in. See **Options.**

Behavior   All of what we do, think, and emote, as well as the physiology we generate in order to close a gap between something we want and whatever it is that we've currently got.

Belonging   See **Needs.**

Bribe   Utilized in an attempt to extrinsically satisfy the needs; also called incentives or carrots and used to sweeten buy-in to doing a task that may not be seen as pleasant or intrinsically rewarding.

Buy-In Puzzle   The synergistic relationship between Clarity, Attainability and Payoff. Must come together before desired behavior occurs.

CAP   Clear, Attainable, Payoff $\geq$ Cost

CAP Puzzle   Clear, Attainable, Payoff $\geq$ Cost; all three pieces must come together before desired behavior occurs.

Care and Credibility   The two tenets of a successful relationship, whether between salesperson and customer, coworkers or employee and manager.

Choose   See **Options.**

Chosen Behavior   Comprised of doing, thinking, emoting, and the physiology that supports them, it is the behavior combination our brains' choose to get what we want from the world around us. See **Output.**

Clarity   When the who, what, when, and where is covered and understood.

Control   See **External Control** and **Internal Control.**

Creative Zone   Our ability to come up with something new from knowledge, thoughts, skills, and behaviors we have already used.

Drivers   The Needs, CAPed (clear, attainable, payoff), Want, Got, and Gap/GapZap are the five Intrinsic Motivation Points that trigger behavior.

8 Intrinsic Motivation Points   The eight factors in the human mind that drive all behavior. The eight leverage points within the employee that managers can use to motivate high performance behavior.

Environment   or Marketplace. The world within which we operate in order to meet our needs.

Essentials for Success   CAP, Motivation/Morale, Skills/Resources, Process, Environment.

External Control   The belief that forces outside of us control us.

Extrinsically Motivated   The belief that forces outside of us motivate us to do things. True for tables and chairs; not true for human beings.

Fight or Flight   A psychological term to explain our seemingly automatic actions in a situation that is threatening our needs, where we either quickly get away from the situation or attack it in an effort to protect our needs. See **Amygdala.**

Filters   How we calibrate all the information coming in and how we limit what behaviors go out. Input filters include: a knowledge filter, a valuing filter and the amygdala. output filters include a valuing or values filter.

Force   External physical power or energy applied to limit, compel, or control the behavior of others. Frustrates and threatens all of our needs.

Freedom   See **Needs.**

Fun   See **Needs.**

Gaps   The difference between a want and a got; provides the energy to drive behavior.

GapZap   That perceived energy, often felt as degrees of urgency to do something. When we have a gap, we experience a zap—the GapZap—that gets our attention focused on finding a chosen behavior that can close the gap and turn off the GapZap.

Got   Our current filtered perception of reality; our belief about what the facts are.

IMPs   See **8 Intrinsic Motivation Points.**

Input   Words, tones, gestures, and environment.

Input Perception Filters   See **Filters.**

Internal Control   The belief that control of behavior is inside us, not outside us, and because our brains choose our behavior at all times, we are always responsible for our own behavior.

Intrinsic Motivation Points   The internal controls that determine all behavior. See **8 Intrinsic Motivation Points.**

Knowledge Filter   Recognizes things we've seen before so when we see them again, we know what they are and have a belief about what they do.

Learning   See **Fun.**

Lessergy   When one and one come together frivolously, carelessly, or acrimoniously and produce less than two.

Love   See **Belonging.**

Motivation   See **Drivers.**

Needs   The hidden fundamentals of motivation:

> *Basic:* Five powerful forces within that must be tended to, protected, and satisfied or else life itself is at risk.
>
> *Survival:* The physiological needs for air, food, water, shelter, and safety.
>
> *Love/Belonging:* The need to have companionship, love, and feel connected to others.
>
> *Power/Recognition:* The need to achieve purpose; to be recognized and appreciated for one's efforts and achievements.
>
> *Fun/Learning:* The need to have a good time and grow in knowledge, experience, and skill.
>
> *Freedom:* The need to be free physically, intellectually, and creatively.

New Learning   The ability to learn a new behavior from outside of ourselves.

Options   The viable behavior choices available to us for utilization in our attempts to do something that will close a gap and turn off a GapZap. Our options exist in four places, or zones:

> *Automatic:* See **Automatic Behaviors.**
>
> *Back-up:* See **Back-Up Zone/Repertoire.**
>
> *Creative:* See **Creative Zone.**
>
> *New Learning:* See **New Learning.**

Output   Comprised of actions, thoughts, emotions, and the physiology that supports them, it is the behavior we choose to get what we want from the world around us.

Output Filters   Values that limit the behavior we're willing to engage in.

Payoff   When the reward or satisfaction for doing something is greater than or equal to the cost.

Perception Filters   Help us know what we've got and how it will impact our needs. See **Knowledge Filter, Valuing Filter,** and **Amygdala.**

Photo Album   Where we store all of our quality world reference pictures or specific wants.

Power   See **Needs.**

Pre-Want   Before someone wants something, before the CAP puzzle is locked in place, there may be a vague awareness of or interest in something, but until it becomes a want with the CAP puzzle locked together, it will not produce behavior.

Problem   The difference or gap between a want and a got.

Puzzle   See **Buy-In Puzzle** and **CAP Puzzle.**

Quality   Another way of saying the ideal want.

R2E2   Research, Reason, Experts, and Experience. Can be used to determine the accuracy or validity of the got and maybe the worthiness of a want.

Rapid Conflict Resolution   A two-session, eight-question, facilitated A-HA! Performance-based intervention that resolves a costly or problematic conflict between two or more employees.

Rapid Team Tune-Up   A two-session, eight-question, facilitated A-HA! Performance-based intervention that makes the rapport between two or more employees even better.

Recognition   See **Power.**

Samergy   When two people come together and each does his or her own thing, producing the equivalent of the sum of its parts.

Silhouette   The stage when a want isn't clear yet; a need hasn't been translated into a clear picture or want.

Survival   See **Needs.**

Synergy   When two people come together and support each other in collaborative and complementary ways, producing more than the sum of their individual contributions.

Threat   Utilized in an attempt to extrinsically frustrate the needs; also called a stick or coercion and used to suggest that failure to buy-in to doing a task will result in some sort of negative (need frustrating) consequences. Performance Improvement Plans are an example.

Valuing Filter   Lets us know the value of what we're perceiving relative to our needs.

Values Output Filter   The ability to determine whether or not the behavior we've just thought of will meet or protect our needs in both the short- and long-term.

Vested Interest   Authentic and direct need satisfaction. Tying the desired task directly to need satisfaction. Also referred to as Intrinsic Motivation.

Viabilities   The area of the brain we access to figure out what's uniquely realistic for each person to do in an attempt to close a gap; to get from got to want. See **Options.**

Wants   Specific preferences that are tied to and developed based on our needs. See **Pre-Want.**

Zones   See **Options.**

Index

Address and improve, 161–205
  CAP criteria, 166–169, 172–173
  evaluating Chosen Behavior, 169–171, 173–174
  examining Chosen Behavior, 169, 173
  getting/making commitment, 177–179
  identifying gap, 165, 171–172
  inadequate performance behavior, 161–185
  overview of phases, 162–163, 185
  planning for change, 174–177
  relationship reflection, 164–165
  retention mishaps to avoid, 198–204
  sales goal example, 189–198
  sample conversation, 180–184
Advice, 124–125, 128, 130–131, 144, 174
Afflicting the comfortable, 101–102, 168–169
Amygdala, 12–13, 151–152, 153–154, 191
Angelou, Maya, 32
Anger, 136–138, 141–142, 165, 216
Animals, fun/learning needs of, 31
Ask-a-Person Test, 79
Assessment tools, 78–79
Attainability. *See also* CAP criteria

address and improve, 166–167, 190–195
awareness of, 250–251
described, 58–60
landing man on the moon, 58
light bulb invention, 58
map, 53
in romantic movies, 45, 46
sales goal example, 190–195
singing example, 52
10 Es of, 60, 167, 246
TWA on-time arrival, 58–59
Automakers, disgruntled employees of, 83
Automatic zone. *See also* Zones
  address and improve, 175
  options, 110–113, 118–119, 246, 247
  road rage, 140–141
Autopilot, brain as, 92

Back-up zone, 113–115, 117, 129, 154, 214, 247. *See also* Zones
Balanced score card, 82–84
Behavior. *See also* Chosen Behavior; Drivers of behavior
  bad/good/great, 75
  to close gaps, 135
  components of, 140–145
  defined, 135

Behavior *(continued)*
  immediately implementable,
    176–177
  repeatable, 177
Behavior (Powers), 90–92, 248
Belonging needs. *See*
    Love/belonging needs
Best practices, myth of, 35,
    127–128, 174
Blink (Gladwell), 151
Blower, Craig, 69
Brain, as control system, 91–92
Bribes, 23–24, 66–68, 69, 70, 235,
    248

CAP criteria, 51–71. *See also*
    Attainability; Clarity; Payoff
  address and improve, 166–169,
    172–173, 190–195
  awareness of, 250–251
  depressed client example, 144
  getting buy-in from others, 54–56
  leadership positions, 46
  managing sideways, 55
  managing up, 56
  maps, 52, 53, 54, 71, 239
  marketing, 46
  overview, 45–47
  receptionist example, 256–260
  recruiting employees, 47
  romantic movies, 45–46
  sales goal example, 190–195
  singing example, 51–54
  to stop behavior, 56
  and wants, 45–47
Care and credibility, 11–12, 28–29,
    164–165
Carlin, George, 30
Carrot approach. *See* Bribes
Chambers, John, 34–35
Changes:
  evaluation of, 222–223
  willingness to make, 216, 220–222

Choices. *See* Options
Chosen behavior, 135–146
  automatic zone, 140–141
  behavior components, 140–145
  driving car example, 135
  emotions as choices, 136–138
  Essentials for Success, 194
  evaluating, 169–171, 173–174
  examining, 169, 173
  hit on head example, 136–138
  map, 142, 146, 241
  output as, 124
  road rage, 139–141
Cisco Systems, 34–35
Clarity. *See also* CAP criteria
  address and improve, 166
  awareness of, 250
  described, 57–58
  map, 52
  in romantic movies, 45
  scary face painting example, 57
  singing example, 51–52
Clear, being. *See* Clarity
Comforting the afflicted, 100–101,
    169
Commitment, 177–179
Communication, 209, 210,
    224–231
Community, 156–157
Confer/refer, 179
Conflict, 209–210, 210, 231–232.
    See also Rapid Conflict
    Resolution
Congenital insensitivity to pain
    with anhidrosis (CIPA),
    76–77
Connectors, 196–197
Consequences of success/failure,
    178–179
Control:
  conflict resolution, 214–215,
    217–218
  external, 121–124, 235

internal, 121–123, 130, 235–236, 247, 252, 277
over behavior, 214–215, 217–218
over other people, 6, 135–136
Control system, brain as, 91–92
Creative zone, 110, 115–117, 125, 154, 214, 247. *See also* Zones
Credibility. *See* Care and credibility
Criticism, 29–30
Customers:
fixation on, 156
lifetime value of, 77–78
love/belonging needs, 201–203
satisfaction and quality, 82–84

Death of loved one, 40, 96
Depression, 141–142, 143–145
Desire to improve situation, 214, 216–217
Disaster training, 113
Disgruntled employees, 82–84
Diversity training, 153
Doing:
as behavior component, 140–145
levels of, 18
Do plans, 176
Drivers of behavior. *See also* CAP criteria; Gaps; Got; Needs; Wants
and control, 122–123
described, 109
Essentials for Success, 194
map, 105, 126, 146

Eating in moderation, 154
Edison, Thomas, 58
Education, 60, 167
8 Intrinsic Motivation Points. *See* Intrinsic Motivation Points maps
Einstein, Albert, 115, 117

Ellis, Albert, 136
Emoting:
automatic zone, 112–113
as behavior component, 140–145
as choice, 118, 136–139, 137
depressed client example, 144–145
Employees:
assessing satisfaction, 78
incentive/recognition programs, 23–24
options, 124–131
recruiting, 47
Empowerment, 60, 167
Energy, 60, 167
Enthusiasm, 60, 167
Entitlement, sense of, 161
Environment, 60, 65, 80, 146, 167, 193–195
Equipment, 60, 167
Es of attainability, 60, 167, 246
Essentials for Success, 193–195, 264
Ethics, 60, 167
Excellence, 156, 189–198
Excuses, 179
Expenses, 60, 167
Experience, 60, 167
Expertise, 60, 167
External control, 121–124, 235

Failure, consequences of, 178–179
Fear, 137–138
Feel, felt, found tool, 99–102
Fifth Discipline, The (Senge), 32
Fight or flight:
and amygdala, 12–13, 151–152, 153–154
automatic zone, 112
as reaction to threat, 10, 12–13, 22
Filters, 149–158
amygdala, 151–152, 153–154
got, 80–81

Filters *(continued)*
  input perception, 149–154,
    157–158
  knowledge, 149–150, 151
  map, 149, 153, 155, 241
  output, 154–157, 158
  values, input, 150–151, 152–153
  values, output, 154–157, 158
Food, as need, 20
Force, 25, 61–63, 69
Freedom needs:
  address and improve, 168
  as basic need, 21
  bath example, 70
  described, 32
  and wants, 43
  Yahoo! core values, 156
Fun/learning needs:
  address and improve, 168
  as basic need, 21
  bath example, 70
  described, 31–32
  and wants, 43
  Yahoo! core values, 157

Gallup organization, 28, 80, 201
Gaps, 89–105. *See also* GapZap;
    Wants
  address and improve, 165,
    171–172
  awareness of, 249–250
  and behavior, 135
  brain as control system, 91–92
  change in, 93–94
  college degree example, 98,
    100–101
  death of loved one, 96
  defined, 89
  feel, felt, found tool, 99–102
  garage cleaning example, 92–93
  identifying, 165, 171–172
  map, 89, 91, 96, 240
  and options, 119–120, 130–131

problems as, 7–9
  reducing, 100–101, 169
  and resetting wants, 95
  retirement example, 101–102
  size of, 90, 92–93, 98, 103
  technology implementation
    example, 94–95
  widening, 101–102, 168–169
GapZap. *See also* Gaps
  address and improve, 168–169
  defined, 89
  map, 91, 240
  and options, 127
  size of, 90, 92–93, 104–105
  technology implementation
    example, 94–95
  as tool, 104–105
Generation X, 161
Giving up, 179
Gladwell, Malcolm, 151, 196
Glasser, William:
  address and improve, 162
  A-HA! Performance, 80, 255
  books, 248
  bribes, 67
  conflict resolution, 209
  needs, 21, 24, 31
  persistence, 179
  wants and quality, 44
Goals, 95, 97–98
Gordon, Thomas, 67
Got, 75–85
  accepting, 96–97, 103–104
  assessment tools, 78–79
  balanced score card, 82–84
  customer satisfaction and
    quality, 82–84
  customer value, 77–78
  filters, 80–81
  identifying gap, 165
  importance of, 76–78
  map, 77, 85, 96, 104, 239
  R2E2 criteria, 79–80

starting with, 165
testing accuracy of belief, 79–80
Grief, 40, 96

Hawes, Dick, 79
Henry, Patrick, 32
Hierarchy of needs, 21, 27
Hiring assessment tools, 78
Human beings, basic nature of, 75

IMP maps. *See* Intrinsic
  Motivation Points maps
Incentives. *See* Bribes
Individuals, Success Essentials for,
  194
Innovation, 156
Input perception filters, 149–154,
  157–158. *See also* Filters
Internal control, 121–123, 130,
  235–236, 247, 252, 277
Intimidation, managing by,
  203–204
Intrinsic Motivation Points maps,
  242, 262. *See also* CAP; Gaps;
  Got; Needs; Options; Wants
  attainability, 53
  between input and output, 17
  bribe, 66
  CAP criteria, 52, 53, 54, 71, 239
  clarity, 52
  drivers of behavior, 105, 126,
    146
  Essentials for Success, 194
  filters, 149, 153, 155, 241
  force, 62
  gaps, 89, 91, 96, 240
  GapZap, 91, 240
  got, 77, 85, 96, 104, 239
  needs, 21, 33, 238
  options, 109, 126, 146, 240
  output, 142, 146, 241
  payoff, 25, 54, 62, 64, 66, 68
  threat, 64

vested interest, 68
wants, 19, 39, 238
Irwin, Steve ("Crocodile Hunter"),
  152

Job loss, 40–41
Johnson, Cotton, 79
Journal, keeping, 248

Kennedy, John F., 58
King, Martin Luther, Jr., 24
Knowledge filters, 149–150, 151.
  See also Filters

Learning. *See* Fun/learning needs;
  New learning
Lessergy, 5, 31, 182. *See also*
  Synergy
Lexus cars, 43–44
Light bulb invention, 58
Los Angeles Job Corps, 115–117
Love/belonging needs:
  address and improve, 168
  as basic need, 21
  bath example, 69–70
  case study, 22
  customers, 201–203
  described, 27–29
  retention mishaps to avoid,
    201–204
  and wants, 43, 44
  woman who drowned her
    children, 25–26
  at work, 28–29
  Yahoo! core values, 156–157

Management by Walking Around
  (MBWA), 34–35
Managers, in Rapid Conflict
  Resolution, 210, 232
Managing:
  bad/good/great, 75–76
  by intimidation, 203–204

Maps. *See* Intrinsic Motivation Points maps
Marketing, 26, 46
Marketplace, 194, 195
Maslow, Abraham, 21, 24, 27
Measuring improvement, 176
Menninger, Karl, 29–30
Microsoft, 26
Milestones, 95, 97–98
Moon, landing on, 58
Morale, 34–36, 194, 195
Motivation. *See also* Drivers of behavior; Intrinsic Motivation Points maps
  Essentials for Success, 194, 195
  internal versus external, 18–19, 93
  needs as, 20–21
  wants as, 41–43
Myers Briggs assessment, 118–119

Needs, 17–36. *See also specific needs*
  awareness of, 248–249
  hierarchy of, 21, 27
  map, 21, 25, 33, 238
  as motivators, 20–21
  overview, 21
  profile of, 33–36
  satisfying through wants, 39–40, 41–42
Nervousness, 143
New learning, 118, 125, 175, 179, 246–247

Options, 109–132
  automatic zone, 110–113, 118–119, 246, 247
  back-up zone, 113–115, 117, 129, 154, 214, 247
  behavior sources, 109–110
  and control, 122–123
  creative zone, 110, 115–117, 125, 154, 214, 247
  employee, 124–131

Essentials for Success, 194
  and gaps, 119–120, 130–131
  and GapZap, 127
  internal versus external control, 121–123, 130
  map, 109, 126, 146, 240
  new learning, 118, 125, 175, 179, 246–247
  and payoff, 120
  and vested interest, 120
Organizations, Success Essentials for, 194, 195
Output. *See* Chosen Behavior
Output values filters, 154–157, 158. *See also* Filters
Outside facilitators, 210, 231–232
Ow moments, 27, 251
Oxymorons, 30

Payoff. *See also* CAP criteria
  address and improve, 167–168
  awareness of, 251
  bath example, 61, 63, 66–67, 69–70
  and bribes, 66–67
  versus cost, 22
  described, 60–70
  and force, 61–63
  map, 25, 54, 62, 64, 66, 68
  and need profile, 34, 36
  as need satisfaction, 61
  and options, 120
  in romantic movies, 45, 46
  singing example, 52–54
  and threats, 63–66
  and vested interest, 68–70
People, basic nature of, 75
Perception filters, 149–154, 157–158. *See also* Filters
Perceptyx, 78
Performance improvement plans, 23, 64–65

Performance Success Essentials, 193–195, 264
Persistence, 179
Photo album analogy, 44, 46, 47
Physiology, as behavior component, 140–145
Planning criteria, 174–177, 221
Postal service shootings, 26
Power/recognition needs:
  address and improve, 168
  as basic need, 21
  bath example, 70
  described, 29–31
  retention mishaps to avoid, 198–200
  of top performers, 24
  and wants, 43
  Yahoo! core values, 156
Powers, William, 18, 80, 90–92, 248, 255
Pre-want. *See* Wants
Problems, 7–9, 89, 90, 103, 130, 220
Process, in Essentials for Success, 194, 195
Psychological testing, 79
Purchases, as need satisfaction, 26
Puzzle. *See* CAP criteria

Quality, 43–44, 47, 82–84

R2E2 criteria, 79–80, 158
Rapid Conflict Resolution:
  action to improve situation, 216, 220–222
  communication issues, 209, 210, 224–231
  conflict types, 209–210
  control over behavior, 214–215, 217–218
  day 1, 214–222
  day 2, 222–223
  desire to improve situation, 214, 216–217

evaluation of changes, 222–223
future actions, 222–223
improvement suggestions, 215, 219–220
overview, 211–214, 244–245, 263
progress report, 222
responsibility for solution, 213–214
sample sessions, 226–231
working elements, 215, 218–219
Rapid Team Tune-Up:
  action to improve situation, 216, 220–222
  control over behavior, 214–215, 217–218
  day 1, 214–222
  day 2, 222–223
  desire to improve situation, 214, 216–217
  evaluation of changes, 222–223
  future actions, 222–223
  improvement suggestions, 215, 219–220
  overview, 211–214, 244–245, 263
  progress report, 222
  working elements, 215, 218–219
Rattlesnakes, 151–152
Recognition needs. *See* Power/recognition needs
Recruiting employees, 47
Reductions in workforce, 84
Relationships:
  address and improve, 164–165
  as key to managing others, 4, 11–12
  in sales, 201–203
Repertoire, 109, 114
Responsibility for solution, 213–214
Retention, 198–204
Road rage, 139–141

Rodriguez, Maria, 203–204, 214
Romantic movies, 45–46

Sales, 189–198, 201–203
Samergy, 5, 31. *See also* Synergy
Sanctions. *See* Threats
Selfishness, 30
Senge, Peter, 30, 32, 80
Service profit chain, 82–84
Silhouettes, 44, 46
Silva, Bill, 5
Skill sets/resources, 194, 195
Snakes, 151–152
Solution, responsibility for,
    213–214
Solzhenitsyn, Alexander, 32
Stick approach. *See* Threats
Success, consequences of, 178
Success Essentials, 193–195, 264
Survival needs, 21, 27, 69, 168
Synergy, 4–5, 30–31, 182, 232

Tall poppy syndrome, 30
Teamwork, 156. *See also* Rapid
    Team Tune-Up
Tegel, Dan, 58–59
10 Es of attainability, 60, 167, 246
Thermostat, brain as, 91
Thinking, as behavior component,
    140–145
Threats:
    address and improve, 178
    avoiding pain of, 63–66
    map, 64
    overview, 9–10
    performance improvement plans
        as, 23, 64–65
    reaction to, 10, 12–13, 22
    and resistance, 26
360 assessment tools, 78
Thurber, Marshall, 211–212
Time-out, 114

Tipping Point, The (Gladwell), 196
Trump, Donald, 24
Turnover, cost of, 10
TWA, 58–59

Untrustworthiness, 154

Values filters. *See also* Filters
    input, 150–151, 152–153
    output, 154–157, 158
Vested interest, 68–70, 120, 168,
    178–179

Wants, 39–48
    and CAP criteria, 45–47
    and grief, 40
    and identifying gap, 165
    and job loss, 40–41
    leadership development versus
        gliding through work,
        41–43
    map, 19, 39, 238
    as motivators, 41–43
    for need satisfaction, 39–40,
        41–42
    and quality, 43–44
    resetting to close gap, 95
Welch, Jefferson, 30
What's-In-It-For-Me (WIIFM).
    See Payoff
Whiting, Bryce, 122
Windows 95 packaging, 26
Wow moments, 26, 61, 251

Yahoo!, 154–157

Zones. *See also* Automatic zone
    back-up, 113–115, 117, 129, 154,
        214, 247
    creative, 110, 115–117, 125, 154,
        214, 247